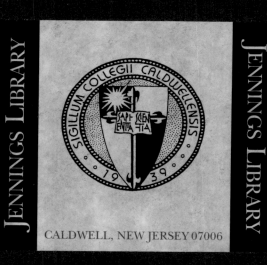

From Other
Worlds

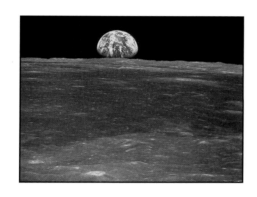

A READER'S DIGEST BOOK

Produced by Carlton Books Limited
Text and Design copyright © 1998 Carlton Books Limited

Library of Congress Cataloging-in-Publication Data

Evans, Hilary, 1929–
    From other worlds : aliens, abductions, and UFOs / Hilary Evans.
       p. cm.
    Includes index
    ISBN 0–7621–0107–5 (hardcover). – – ISBN 0–7621–0108–3 (pbk.)
    1. Human–alien encounters. 2. Alien abduction. 3. Unidentified
flying objects. I. Title.
    BF2050.E93 1998
    001.942– –dc21   98–26766
                               CIP

Printed and bound in Dubai

From Other Worlds

ALIENS, ABDUCTIONS AND UFOS

HILARY EVANS

Reader's Digest

Contents

Foreword

It would have been more convenient if each visitor to Earth had been made to sign a visitors' book, giving a name and address and indicating the purpose of the visit. Unfortunately, the absence of any customs control means that we have no certain information about who has visited our planet; we have only the reports of those of us who claim to have met them, once they have arrived. Some of these visits seem intended not to be noticed. For example, spirits of the dead insist on rigorous conditions when they revisit the world of the living, and play hard to get if skeptics are present. And extraterrestrials tend to land their spacecraft in remote parts of the country where often there are only one or two present to witness the event.

Some of these visitors are perhaps illegal immigrants, coming to our planet for reasons that we would not approve if we knew them. It is said that the devil has his own sinister agenda to seduce us away from our allegiance to God. The motivation of many aliens, too, is definitely suspect, judging by the way it is claimed they abduct us against our will into their space ships, where they subject us to humiliating physical examinations and involuntary impregnation.

Indeed, there have been so many of these hostile or malicious visitors that it is tempting to conclude we would be better off without any visitors at all. Even in the case of those who come with the very finest intentions—the great spiritual teachers who brought us the world's dominant religions—it is arguable that they have done more harm than good, if we judge by the riots, wars and fanatical terrorism caused by intolerant adherents of various belief systems. However, this book does not set out to pass judgment, either as to whether these visits actually took place, or whether it would have been better if they hadn't. Many of these otherworldly visits have given rise to widespread beliefs, ranging from spiritualism to flying saucer cults, which have attracted hundreds, thousands, even millions of people. That makes them a social phenomenon, if nothing else.

Is it important to decide whether the people who claim to have these experiences are telling the truth? This is a question we shall return to in the final chapter: For the moment, let us try to perceive these claims of visitation from other worlds as though they really happened. Though I have never had such an experience myself, I have met people who have—people who have seen ghosts or met aliens and been taken aboard their spacecraft. To none of these people did I express my doubts as to whether what seemed to them to be happening was what was really happening. This is partly because they never asked me, but also because I believe their experiences may have had value for them which I had no right to undermine. On some level, if not the here and now level of everyday reality, these things happened.

That everyday reality provides the basis for the way we perceive the universe. Our existence is bound by space and time. The notion that time could go on—and on—and on, never ceasing; that the universe could stretch forever, never reaching a final frontier—these are concepts that our minds are incapable of grasping. Eternity and infinity are the most frightening things we can think of.

Compared with the notion of visitors from other parts of the universe—or from other dimensions of time—is relatively comfortable. We can imagine the entities themselves; we can draw imaginary pictures of the worlds they might come from. Yet we cannot do more than speculate how they could get here from wherever it is they come from—the vast distances of the universe present a challenge to which only the fantasies of science fiction can respond. If that is true of extraterrestrial entities, what can we say about beings who are supposed to visit our planet from other levels of reality? We may have abandoned the idea of a heaven "up there" and a hell "down there," but most of us retain a belief in angels, demons and spirits, concluding that if they come here they must come from somewhere.

If the spirits of the surviving dead exist in space, it would seem to be a different kind of space than ours on Earth, another level of reality. But what about time? Are those who have reached the end of their Earthly life span still bound by the chronological time that controlled them when alive? Or have they moved to another level of reality in which space and time have ceased to have the meaning they have for us?

These are abstract questions, but we shall see that they have a very real application when we come to consider these visitors from other worlds. For there are problems to be faced. How does a spirit of the dead, whose body has been turned to ashes in a crematorium, return to the séance room in his/her true likeness? How does an alien from a distant part of the universe, who must have escaped time to reach us, snap back into time, our Earth time, for the duration of his visit? Do all our otherworldly visitors come from places we could find on a map of the Universe, or do some of them come from other dimensions?

If you and I are to appreciate the problems involved in these visits from other worlds, we must be prepared to let our notions of what constitutes reality hang loose.

Imagining Other Worlds

And the Lord said unto Moses, "Lo, I come unto thee in a thick cloud, that the people may hear when I speak with thee, and believe thee for ever." And Moses brought forth the people to meet with God; and Mount Sinai was altogether on a smoke, because the Lord descended upon it in fire, and the whole mount quaked greatly. And when Moses spake, God answered him by a voice … And all the people saw the thunderings, and the lightnings, and the mountain smoking; and they said unto Moses, "Let not God speak with us, lest we die."
… Then went up Moses, and seventy of the elders; and they saw the God of Israel; and there was under his feet as it were a paved work of sapphire stone. Upon the nobles of the children of Israel he laid not his hand; also they saw God … and he gave unto Moses two tables of stone, written with the finger of God … .

Earth's first visitors from other worlds were gods. This was when mankind was still a new idea: Those who had created us wanted to know how we were getting on and make sure we were behaving ourselves. So they came to see us with their own eyes.

The most famous of all meetings between Man and his creator is the encounter of Moses with the God of Israel on Mount Sinai, described in Exodus, in which God gives Moses instructions as to what the people of Israel should and should not do, promising them rewards if they do as he tells them, punishments if they don't. He is an all-powerful god, yet he takes note of what his creatures say and, unlike most absolute rulers, his mind can be swayed. Angry when the people of Israel go whoring after strange gods, he tells Moses, "I have seen this people, and behold, it is a stiff-necked people; now therefore leave me alone, that my wrath may wax hot against them, and that I may consume them." But he listens when Moses speaks up in their defense: "and

LEFT: *An illuminated manuscript (circa 840) depicting God giving Moses the Tables of the Law on Mount Sinai.*

the Lord repented of the evil which he thought to do unto his people."

So Moses makes a covenant with God, and God presents him with a set of the Ten Commandments: "And the tables were the work of God, and the writing was the writing of God, graven upon the tables."

Although Moses, along with his senior colleagues, is described as seeing God, he has not really seen him face-to-face. When he asks, "I beseech thee, show me thy glory," God answers, "Thou canst not see my face; for there shall no man see me, and live." But God considerately adds, "Behold, I will put thee in a clift of the rock, and will cover thee with my hand while I pass by; and I will take away mine hand, and thou shalt see my back parts; but my face shall not be seen."

We cannot know when, how, or why man raised his head from the concerns of everyday life to contemplate higher levels of reality. But it seems there was never a time when man did not feel that otherworldly realms existed. Our earliest records show an awareness of superior, superhuman beings, who from time to time made their presence known to the inhabitants of Earth.

Why should our ancient ancestors—who we would expect to be preoccupied with surviving the risks of life on Earth and dealing with their fellow humans—bother with the Heavens, which would seem to have been remote and irrelevant to their existence? Some philosophers hold that a propensity for religious belief is inherent in the human state, that it is one of the things that makes us human. Perhaps even the caveman, along with the instinct for survival he shared with the bears and tigers, had something more, this sense of the numinous. Alternatively, the search for an all-powerful god could have simply been a more highly developed version of the hierarchical order that exists among animals. Or maybe it was the first stirrings of scientific curiosity that drove people to speculate about such things as the origin of thunder and lightning and to consider where they themselves came from, leading them to the reasonable conclusion that there must be gods.

But it is possible that the ancient chronicles record fact, not fable? Did our earliest ancestors believe in gods because they actually met them face-to-face? There can be no doubt that, so far as the author of the book of Exodus was

Ramses IV with the god Horus: The Egyptians depicted their rulers meeting with divine beings.

otherworldly beings described in this book? If not, where do we propose drawing the line?

These questions will confront us throughout this survey. Whether we are concerned with gods or demons, spirits of the dead or extraterrestrial aliens, we shall find ourselves in the same dilemma: Are these stories of visits and encounters with otherworldly beings based on real experiences, or are they no more than wishful or fearful thinking? Do the beings themselves physically exist, or are they simply fanciful inventions, saviors or bogeymen created by people as outward embodiments of their hopes, fears and expectations?

Even if we conclude that the stories the Greeks told about Zeus and Athena —or that the Egyptians told about Horus, or the Norse about Thor—are no more than legends, we may still ask if the remote origins of those legends were rooted in fact. Did real beings do real things that were magnified into tales of superhuman gods? It is not always easy to believe that encounters with beings from other worlds have taken place. However, its is also hard to dismiss stories so widespread and persistent as out-and-out fantasy.

In our modern age, we see that man has lost none of his ability to create elaborate myths out of simple happenings. Phone calls from the dead, aliens who beam us up through the air to their hovering spacecraft— man's ability to believe in wonders never ceases. Should we see this mythmaking skill as a childish thing, or as one of the most enduring, and endearing, of man's attributes?

It is easy for educated citizens of advanced cultures to relegate such stories as God's meeting with Moses to the category of myth and legend. But a blanket dismissal of this kind hides the fact that what we see as myth was, for millions of people—many of them thoughtful and intelligent—a powerful reality. The Crusaders who went to war in the name of the Christian god and the Saracens who resisted them in the name of Allah were not all cynics and pious frauds. Many, perhaps most, devoutly believed they were carrying out their god's will. Nor is it only the Supreme Deity who commands genuine belief. A

concerned, Moses had been privileged to have a physical encounter with the God of Israel. This is no metaphor, no pious abstraction: God spoke. He wrote. He became angry. He changed His mind. And Moses had seen His back parts, at least, and if God had not allowed him to see His face, it was for his own good, for God knew that no one could do so and live to tell the tale.

Not all who read this book will be prepared to say that, yes, they believe that Moses did actually meet God, or that the Greek warriors who besieged Troy enjoyed the daily interaction with their gods and goddesses that Homer describes. But are we prepared to assert that these things are total fabrication? If so, will we be equally skeptical of all the other claims of encounter with few years ago, I attended a prestigious conference at which an Austrian professor presented a paper on diabolical possession, which we will examine in Chapter Six. I took it for granted that, as a highly educated person, he would regard the phenomenon as, at best, a psychological delusion. To my astonishment, I learned that the professor firmly believed his subject had been possessed by an evil spirit as actual and material as any described in medieval legend.

OTHER LEVELS OF REALITY

Many of the stories of visits from other worlds defy our sense of what is "real." The Virgin Mary visits Bernadette Soubirous at Lourdes, where she is seen by Bernadette, but not by those standing right beside her. Joseph Smith is visited by an angel, who reveals to him the Book of Mormon, but no one else sees the angel or the golden pages. Linda Napolitano is visited by aliens who carry her through the Manhattan sky to a hovering spacecraft. Why is it that the stories told by those who claim to have witnessed the event are said to make it more incredible, rather than more believable?

Even if we accept that these events do occur, we need to consider the possibility that they happen in some other sense than, say, our own astronauts' landing on the Moon. But, if that is the case, what does that imply? Are there dimensions of space and time that parallel our own and intermittently interact with it, so that visitors shift from their reality into ours like someone stepping off an escalator onto solid ground? The moment we abandon our literal "here and now" reality— which serves us so well in our everyday lives—we enter uncharted realms of metaphysical and spiritual possibility, where anything that the human mind can conceive becomes possible.

Nevertheless, as we confront the stories told in this book, we must keep such possibilities in mind. For whether or not we decide that the events really happened to Bernadette, Smith and

Napolitano as they claim, there is no question that *something* happened to them. There is more to these stories than fireside tales, wishful thinking, and private fantasy. Today's physics requires us to accept the paradoxical nature of reality, while notions of "virtual reality" show that although something is outside of common experience, it may still possess an objective validity of its own. Placed on a level different than our everyday lives, it cannot be judged by the same rules.

Can spirits of the dead return to Earth from wherever it is we go when we die? Many would say that the question is meaningless, because we aren't going anywhere, and that the notion of survival

after death is a biological absurdity. Even those who are willing to accept the idea of life after death often dispute whether it is possible to return, even to make a brief ghostly appearance or to materialize at a spirit séance. Are extraterrestrials able to cross the awesome distances of space to visit us? Scientists tell us it is so impractical as to be scarcely worth considering, except as an academic exercise. Nevertheless, when we are confronted with these and the other "impossible" stories that witnesses share with us, we must consider the possibility that they seem impossible only because they are taking place in some other dimension that we do not know.

As depicted in this artwork, San Gennaro fails to protect the people from the 1872 eruption of Vesuvius in spite of their prayers, causing them to attack his statue.

The apparition of Thérèse of Lisieux is shown during World War One guiding French stretcher bearers to where a soldier lies wounded.

DIVINITIES AND DEMONS

For us today, contemplating the reality of otherworldly visits is an intellectual process; we assess the claims in the light of scientific principles. But for our ancestors, it seems to have been a matter of simple, unquestioning belief. But how *literally* did our ancestors believe in divine beings? Thunder and lightning are real enough—but were the deities that personified them anything more than convenient abstractions? There seems little doubt that most people believed then, as many do now, in the material existence of these beings. They also believed that divine beings actively participated in human affairs.

Even now, when the volcano Etna threatens to erupt, Sicilian peasants pray to Sant' Egidius to save their villages from destruction, while those who live near Vesuvius trust in their local saint, San Gennario. However, in 1872, when San Gennario failed to answer the people's prayers and an eruption resulted in the death of three, the people reproached him and attacked his statue. Evidently, for these unquestioning believers, the power they are invoking is not some theological abstraction, but a powerful individual who they are convinced has the power to save them. Their attitude to San Gennario is much like that of peasants in feudal times towards the local lord of the manor.

The ancient cultures best known to us—Egypt, China, Mexico and Peru, classical Greece and Rome—possessed elaborate hierarchies of deities of greater or lesser importance. Each has his or her own attributes—kindly or menacing, helpful or vengeful. Each has a role to play on the cosmic stage. Some deities are vast in scope, creating worlds and ordering the galaxies. Others are more earthy. The Celtic goddess Brigid helps women bear the pains of childbirth; the Chinese goddess Tse-Kou-Chen, a pious lady who was ignominiously murdered by a jealous rival while on the toilet, is consecrated Goddess of the Privy and much honoured by her devotées for undertaking this humble but important position.

This tradition was carried over into more sophisticated religions. In the Roman Catholic version of Christianity, it is believed that particular religious figures may be called upon to deal with particular problems. Saint Antony of Padua will help you find lost objects, while if your cause seems hopeless, you should call on Saint Jude. Many trades and professions honor patron saints who, it is supposed, will manifest on Earth and give protection—thus, French bakers invoke Saint Honoré and English shoemakers honour Saint Crispin.

During World War One, many such beings—saints, angels, Jesus and his mother, Mary—made appearances to encourage and comfort the warring soldiers. Nor was their support confined to mere appearance. Some, like the gods in Homer's *Iliad*, played an active part. Thérèse of Lisieux, ten years before she was canonized, appeared on the Western Front and guided stretcher bearers to where a French soldier was lying wounded.

For the Greeks and Romans, the pantheon of divinities was not very different from an Earthly royal court. The gods described by Homer indulge in power struggles and love affairs, jealousies, rivalries and warring ambitions, like any other ruling class. The gods and goddesses may possess superhuman powers, but their emotions and motivations are no more highly developed than ours. The Egyptian gods are pictured with the heads of dogs, birds or hippopotami, but for all that, they are as human in their behavior as any dweller on Earth.

As religions grow more

Tse-Kou-Chen, a concubine, murdered in the privy by her master's jealous legitimate wife, is rewarded by being appointed Goddess of the Privy.

sophisticated, their divinities become less human, more remote. The gods become metaphysical abstractions who are not perceived in human terms at all.

Yet the tendency to anthropomorphize them persists. Throughout religious teachings, we persistently come across such phrases as "It is God's will that ... ," though in fact no one has the least idea of God's wishes or sentiments. The Christian belief system cleverly manages to have it both ways. After his summit meeting with Moses, God remains in Heaven, but He sends an aspect of Himself, His "Son," to be born as a human being.

But where do these visitors—Jesus, Sainte Thérèse and the rest—actually come *from*? Where do the gods dwell? Is there a Heaven, located somewhere in the Universe?

HOMES OF THE GODS

The Gods of Homer's world don't live very far away. They can watch the progress of the Trojan War, and if they feel disposed to intervene, they simply pop down from the clouds. Just as these gods are not far removed from the human in appearance, so the places where they live are not very remote from our Earth.

Though from the start it was recognized that the gods could transcend the limitations of our earthly life, it was impossible to conceive of them existing outside space and time: they must live *somewhere*.

Early myths provided them with homes of their own here on Earth—in

paradisal gardens, mountaintop citadels, island sanctuaries, underground caverns. If you sail sufficiently far into the Atlantic Ocean, you may reach the Island of the Blest. If you climb Japan's Mount Fujiyama, you may find yourself at the gateway to the next world. We have seen Moses ascend a mountain to receive the Ten Commandments. Sinai was the highest peak in the area, and by climbing it, Moses was meeting God halfway, as it were. The body of King Arthur is carried in a boat to the enchanted isle of Avalon, whose inhabitants know all the magic of the world. When the Frankish King Dagobert dies in the year 634, he is seized by demons who plan to take him to Hell, the entrance to which is via a volcano, specifically Mount Etna on the island of Sicily. Fortunately, a posse of saints in shining white vestments repulse

Heaven was not a distant place for the early Christians. Here, a medieval missionary finds a place where Heaven touches Earth.

the demons as they sail across the Mediterranean, saving Dagobert for an afterlife that is presumably more comfortable.

More generally, though, the homes of the gods are out of this world. Traditions worldwide presume the existence of a Heaven of some kind, and the more naive religions suppose that it has an actual location in space, meaning that if we set off into the cosmos in the right direction, we could get there. What we would find there would not be so very different from what we are used to on Earth. Early Christian depictions of Heaven often showed it as a garden. In later, less pastoral times, it was compared to a celestial city, the New Jerusalem. Subsequently, the image of Heaven has not changed greatly. The concept of "Summerland"—where the spirits of the dead assured Nineteenth-Century spiritualist séance-goers that they were enjoying a blissful afterlife—is a lakeside park. The glimpses of gardens and cities of light described by those who undergo Near-Death

When King Arthur is fatally wounded in battle, he is taken to the Island of Avalon, where he dies.

Airborne saints rescue Frankish king Dagobert from demons trying to carry him to Hell.

Experiences are usually of indescribable beauty. The distant planets to which people describe being taken by the occupants of friendly spaceships are peaceful and well-ordered. All of these planets, rather than rivaling the fantasies of science fiction artists, tend to resemble the nicer bits of the planet we know and love.

Wherever they are located, one attribute of the otherworlds remains constant: The *good* places, Heaven and its equivalents, are always perceived as *up there*, while the *bad* places, Hell and the like, are *down below*. When Jesus dies, he ascends to Heaven, where a seat is reserved for him at the right hand of his father; when the rebel angels are routed by Saint Michael and the faithful angels, they are sent plunging down to an underworld which seems to have been prepared with their reception in mind. Christians believe that when they die they will go "up" to Heaven if they have been good; "down" to Hell if they have been bad. If they are Roman Catholics, they have a third alternative, Purgatory, where they can be cleansed of their wickedness and qualify for Heaven.

Whether rewarded with Heaven or punished with Hell, the presumption is that the dead individual survives in some form. How much of us survives and how much we continue to be ourselves remain much-discussed questions, but allied with the notion that there are places designated Heaven and Hell is the notion that traveling to and from them is possible. As we shall see later, return visits from the surviving dead, though under restricted conditions, form a significant category of otherworldly visits.

Are the places where the gods reside, and the places where the spirits of the dead survive, one and the same? The experiences of some UFO contactees seem to confirm that this is the case. For example, on October 7, 1975, French motor-racing journalist Jean-Claude Vorilhon (aka "Raël") said he was taken by friendly extraterrestrials to their planet, which he described as "relatively close to Earth." His host, Iahve, President of the Council, told him that there were 8400 Earthpeople now living on the planet. Vorilhon described a party at which he was entertained by naked female robot dancers, with various deities in attendance.

As culture progresses and religions develop, the homes of the gods are more remote. God—who had visited Earth when Adam and Eve were its only inhabitants and personally

delivered the Ten Commandments to
Moses—becomes a voice from the
heavens, an abstract entity whose
existence is a matter of faith rather
than observation. However, although
we no longer expect God himself to
come visiting, many Christians have no
difficulty believing that Jesus, who
once walked among us in the flesh,
pays periodic return visits to some
individuals. We come across instances
of this in many different contexts. The
case of Julie makes a good example.

JULIE

Julie is a Star Person—that is, an
Earthperson who has come to realize
that she is, in fact, an extraterrestrial.
She had always realized that she was
"destined for some kind of special task."
However, she had no idea just what this
meant until one night, while her
husband was away on business, when
she experienced the first of a sequence
of visits from otherworldly beings.

The first visit was from an entity
named Ashtar, an extraterrestrial ship
commander well known to New Age
channelers and UFO contactees. Ashtar
remained in her home for *two years*,
standing always in the same place.
Nobody else was able to see him. Two
days later, Julie had a second visitor—
this time, it was Jesus, no less. She says
Jesus started projecting light beams on
her, giving her an incredible feeling of
total love. She describes her encounter
in much the same terms as religious
visionaries describe theirs. She lost
consciousness, and when she woke,
Jesus had gone, leaving a golden light
which has remained with her ever since.

Jesus, though, is a rather unique
visitor; the frequency of his visits world-
wide no doubt reflects the fact that he
came from Heaven, took on human
form and lived on Earth as a human.
In most of the world's major religions,
no travel takes place between here and
there, or it is a one-way journey. The
leading figure, whether it is Buddha,
Mohammed or Zoroaster, is
transformed from a mortal into an
immortal. The place of residence is

LEFT: *The Hindu deity Vishnu takes a variety of forms ("avatars") for his periodic visits to Earth. Eighteenth Century image from Jaipur, Rajasthan.*

VISITS FROM THE GODS

reality, whose nature is beyond our conception. Any visits paid to Earth are occasional and brief. For the most part, heavenly beings stay in their heavens.

Even if such concepts are not taken literally by the more sophisticated belief systems, the human mind does have difficulty conceiving of any form of existence that is not subject to space or time. How can it be "existence" if it doesn't happen somewhere, sometime? So throughout human history, and for most people today, divine beings are not abstractions on some other level of reality. Even if we no longer picture God—except in caricature, as a white-bearded old grandfather enthroned among the clouds—divinities still tend to be perceived as sufficiently like us that we could, given the appropriate circumstances, speak with them, interact with them, see them—even if it is only their back parts.

If gods exist, it is only natural that they would wish to inspect their property, much as a landowner goes round his estates. This is especially understandable if they were also the creators of the Earth, particularly if it was their one and only creation. The Christian Bible shows us a God very much concerned with His Earth and its inhabitants. There is no suggestion that He has created other races on other planets with whom He is equally concerned, and Jesus makes no mention of other species existing elsewhere in the universe.

So long as this has been the case, visits from the gods have been expected, and early legends contain many accounts of such visits. Thus, Vishnu, the supreme deity of the Hindus, is believed to have appeared on Earth in nine avatars, or incarnations, to help out when mankind has been threatened with some catastrophe engineered by malevolent forces.

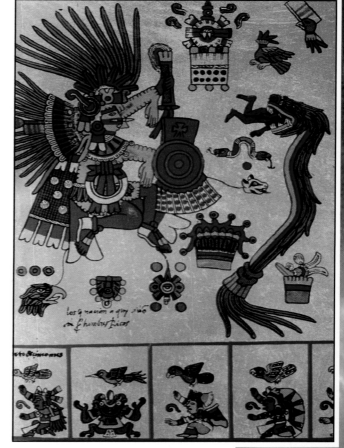

For the gods were real beings who would come to Earth to reward the good and punish the wicked.

The Aztecs of Mexico had a similar belief, but with rather more fatal consequences. They held a tradition that Quetzalcoatl, the god who had brought them knowledge of the arts and civilization, had landed at Vera Cruz and departed from there on a magic raft when his time with them was over. His return was much hoped for, and when Hernando Cortes and his conquistadors landed there in 1519—coming from the same direction in their magnificent ships —the Aztecs were eager to hail him as their hero-god. Cortes did not disabuse them, and their hesitation to see him as a dangerous enemy made his initial successes possible.

Hernando de Soto, in Peru, was able to benefit from a comparable tradition. The creator-god of the native Peruvians, Viracocha, had walked among them incognito, disguised as a beggar, performing miracles and instructing the people. He left Peru when the Spanish conquistadors crossed the Atlantic, walking away to the west on the waves of the Pacific, promising to return. A

Despite his alarming appearance, Quetzalcoatl was a benevolent deity who brought learning and culture to the Aztec people.

Astronomer-priests of Ancient Egypt (circa 2880 B.C) are shown using the Great Pyramid of Khufu as an observatory.

prophecy stated that during the reign of the thirteenth Inca, "white men of surpassing strength and valor would come from their father the Sun, and subject the Peruvians to their rule." De Soto was content to be seen as their leader.

For most of us today, the gods no longer exist in their ancient form, if they exist at all. We do not expect them to visit us or revisit us. Still, all our lengthy traditions of belief in otherworldly deities, of Heavens and Hells, have left their impression.

However skeptical we may be, at the back of all our minds is the vague notion that other worlds may exist, populated by other beings. Visionary encounters with divine beings are reported as frequently as ever, and while most of us no longer look for the gods or the saints to intervene in human affairs, the "Second Coming" of Jesus is an article of faith for many Christians. Stories of angels have found a renewed popularity as the Twentieth Century closes and, like devils and demons, they have been among the most persistent of all our alleged visitors.

THE ONLY CREATION?

Faith is all very well, but it's always reassuring to have it reinforced by fact. As long as people believed that the homes of the gods and the demons were physical places, the problem of locating Heaven and Hell was a practical one that the scientists of the day could reasonably be called upon to solve. The belief that the stars and planets play a significant part in human affairs was a central one in many early religions.

The Priests of Chaldea and Egypt became astronomers, as well, and science served religion by observing the Heavens. Hell interested the Priest-astronomers less, as it was buried beneath the ground, approachable only via volcanoes and offering few attractions as a tourist destination. The gods, if they lived anywhere, lived among the stars.

By far the most prominent of the celestial bodies—the only ones that appeared to the eye to have any bulk—were the Sun and Moon. As a result, it is not surprising that Sun Gods and Lunar Deities have been among the most honored of divinities, and that both have been the subject of widespread worship in every part of the world. The Sun god Re was one of the most powerful of Egyptian deities. For the Bacongo people of Zaire, the solar deity Nzambi was judge, protector, sustainer of the universe. For the Greeks, Apollo personified this dynamic life force.

As theology grew more sophisticated, "Heaven" came to be perceived as not so much a place as a state of grace in which we mortals, freed from our physical bodies and transfigured into some superior form, are absorbed into a divine super-being. When God became a spiritual abstraction, no longer likely to visit Earth in person, there was no longer any need to imagine him actually living anywhere. The idea of Heaven and Hell as places that could be physically located on a map of the universe no longer seemed appropriate. But the visible celestial bodies—the Sun and, more probably, the Moon—remained possibly inhabited by other kinds of beings. Old mythologies had referred to beings who were neither gods nor humans—Titans, giants, sphinxes, genies and other monsters of land, sea and air. In the minds of those who made imaginary journeys to the Moon, one must be prepared to meet creatures very unlike themselves. Mankind was learning to stretch its imagination.

The earliest accounts of imaginary journeys into space were not intended to be taken literally—if they were to be considered seriously, it was as moral documents rather than travel accounts. Writing in the second century A.D., Loukianos of Samosata told, in his "True History"—a satire on travelers' tales—how his ship was caught up by a whirlwind which swept their vessel up "some three thousand furlongs" (about 375 miles) into the air, where all were able to observe the Moon and its inhabitants. The description is pure fancy. There are no women, for the young are born from the thighs of their fathers. They drink air, and remove their eyes as if they were eyeglasses. In short, this is fantasy rather than scientific conjecture.

A quite different account is given by Loukianos's near-contemporary, Plutarch, whose imaginary description is a mixture of intelligent speculation and utter credulity. What is interesting is that Plutarch is convinced the Moon *is* inhabited. As evidence, he cites the fall of the Lion of Nemea, which plunged from the Moon into the Greek Peloponnese. Other accounts enliven the theological writings of the day. The Christian theologian Origen wonders what Saint Matthew meant when he wrote:

> … his angels shall gather his elect from the four winds, from one end of heaven to the other …

Origen concludes that this points to a literal Heaven where the dead come to reside, retaining physical dimensions. The Jewish religious book, the *Zohar*, refers to "the God of all worlds known and unknown." Some take this as evidence for the multiplicity of inhabited worlds. A Sixth-Century legend tells of three monks who travel in search of Paradise, stray beyond the edge of the world and eventually find it. The Italian poet Dante, on Good Friday 1300, is led by the spirit of the Roman writer Virgil into the Inferno—where the damned are tortured everlastingly—and is given a glimpse of Paradise by his beloved Beatrice. Ariosto and Rabelais are two more of the eminent writers who incorporate space voyages into their writings.

None of these, however fine as literature, can be considered in any way a serious scientific document, and their authors are careful to present their ideas as fantasies, moral fables or satires on Earthly lifestyles. The penalties for not doing so tended to be serious. The Italian philosopher Giordano Bruno was burned to death in 1600 for spreading the heresy that Earth is not the center of the cosmos, but just one small world in an infinitely large universe.

Hundreds of these scattered hints tell us that people everywhere have cast thoughtful eyes to the heavens, and that often the consequence was another

The Lion of Nemea, according to ancient Greek legends, fell to the Peloponnese from the Moon. From Flammarion's Histoire du Ciel *(Story of the Sky).*

fantastic tale added to our literature. None of these writers added to our stock of scientific knowledge. In addition, and none hinted that, just as we have thought about visiting other worlds, so people of other worlds might be thinking of visiting Earth.

MORE WORLDS THAN ONE

In the year 1609, mankind's view of the universe changed dramatically. The Italian astronomer Galileo, recognizing the potential of the recently-invented telescope, adapted it for observation of the heavens—the first effective use of the device for astronomical purposes. Though only a handful of scholars were aware of the discovery, let alone able to grasp its implications, this was a turning point in man's conception of the cosmos. Nothing would ever be the same again. For what Galileo saw through his crude instrument confirmed that the theological view of creation —in which our Earth is the center of the universe and mankind is God's special creation— was no longer tenable. The sky could be seen to be filled with other worlds—worlds that may be like our own, even inhabited by people like ourselves.

The Italian poet Dante Alighieri enjoys an otherworld journey when his beloved Beatrice gives him a vision of Paradise.

The discovery sparked off a new era of excited speculation. Scientists and philosophers alike felt free to consider the possibility of other inhabited worlds, and book after book came off the press debating the matter. Some authors, such as Pierre Borel, physician to the French court—whose 1647 book was entitled *A New Discourse Proving The Plurality Of Worlds, That The Stars Are Inhabited Worlds, And That The Earth Is A Star, Etc.*—gave the question serious consideration. Borel's reasoning was based on the new discoveries:

> But Galileo who, within our own lifetime, has seen clearly into the Moon, has observed that it could well be inhabited, seeing that there are mountains and plains there.

Other writers were more fanciful. Among Borel's contemporaries was the satirist Cyrano de Bergerac who, in his 1649 book, *Histoire Comique des Etat et Empire de la Lune*, told of placing flasks of dew around his waist at night. When the sun rose, it caused the dew to rise, enabling him to be lifted through the skies to the Moon.

The English writer Francis Godwin published his *Man in the Moon* in 1638, using as his main character and pen name Domingo Gonsales. The story told of training wild swans to tow weighted objects through the air. Like the Montgolfier brothers in the following century—and the Russian space program two centuries after that—Gonsales experimented first with animals. He describes his trained swans making an aerial voyage drawing a lamb "whose happiness I much envied, that he should be the first living creature to take possession of such a device." Needless to say, one thing led to another, and soon Gonsales had occasion to make use of his device, at which point his ship was wrecked and he escaped, thanks to his birds.

An even stranger adventure awaited him. Earlier, Gonsales had wondered why this species of birds disappeared for a part of the year; now he learned that it was because of hibernation. The birds spent part of every year in the Moon. When the time came to hibernate, they set off for the Moon,

Science and poetry meet: The Italian astronomer Galileo, under house arrest in Florence, is visited by the English poet John Milton, in 1638–39.

carrying Gonsales with them. As the air grew thinner, the Earth's pull diminished, so the birds had no trouble carrying Gonsales such a distance. On the Moon, he discovered giant Lunarians, whose society and lifestyle were vastly superior to those on Earth.

Such fantasies may not add much to scientific knowledge, but they fanned popular interest. When in 1686 Bernard Le Bovier de Fontenelle published his *Conversations on the Plurality of Worlds*, he imagined himself walking in a park after supper with an intelligent noblewoman. The Marquise questioned him about what they were seeing in the sky above their heads, and he was delighted to have a willing audience for his explanations. The author did not think that other worlds contained people like ourselves, but that each would be inhabited by beings suited to the prevailing conditions. Though, as he was first to say, all he can do is speculate, this was not satire or science fiction. Rather, it was true speculation as to life on other worlds—what kind of life, and how it would cope with the problems of existence elsewhere. For example:

What do we know but that the inhabitants of the Moon, incommoded by the perpetual heat of the Sun, do not hide in deep wells, perhaps building their cities there. The entire race lives there, moving from one well to another by subterranean passages.

As technology improves, so Man's knowledge of the universe increases and the possibility of other life forms becomes a stronger possibility. But at that time, the question was merely an academic one—a game of the imagination, with no practical application. In his 1647 book, Borelhad wrote:

Some have thought that just as man has imitated the fish by swimming, so he can equally learn to fly, and by this means resolve the question [whether there are other inhabited worlds]. History reports many examples of men who have flown. But even if man should learn to fly, it will do him little service for, apart from the fact that, due to his weight, man will not be able to rise high, nor will he be able to stop to study the other worlds, but all his spirit will be directed on controlling his machine.

But the rapid advance of technology was to prove Borel unnecessarily pessimistic. We have risen high indeed, and have studied other worlds.

Galileo's telescope and other instruments, preserved in the Museo delle Scienze, Florence.

MAN LEAVES HIS PLANET

The first aerial voyage—a brief flight over Paris on November 21, 1783 by Pilâtre de Rozier and the Maréchal d'Arlandes in a Montgolfier hot air balloon—marked a dramatic development. Though the journey was a very brief one, and Earth was never more than a few hundred feet below, the achievement was of overwhelming significance. For the first time, man was able to look down on his planet and see it as a visitor from other worlds might.

Now, for the first time, travel beyond Earth could be considered not just as a fantasy, but as a serious possibility. Through the century that followed, thousands of inventors all over the world developed the concept of flight in many forms—many of them foolish and fruitless, but some containing the seeds of future developments. Running ahead of the inventors were the authors of science fiction, which became less fantasy and satire, and more a projection of what are now seen as scientific realities.

Jules Verne's 1865 publication, *Autour de la Lune, (Round the Moon),* and its 1870 sequel, *De la Terre à la Lune (From the Earth to the Moon),* were landmark works. For the first time, serious consideration was given to the "space ship," though Verne's picture of a projectile with its padded walls and Victorian furnishings is somewhat less than scientific. However, the existence of the padded walls showed that Verne had given serious thought to the problems of weightlessness. On the other hand Verne's proposed solution for allowing the projectile to escape the pull of Earth's gravity—a huge cannon buried in the ground, from which the space ship is fired like a military shell—was naive, to put it kindly. Congreve's rockets, demonstrated in 1827, offered a far more realistic solution.

Verne's books were aimed at a popular audience, and what was significant was the fact that space travel had now become an idea that everyone could toy with, not simply an academic game for sophisticated writers. Though the notion of space travel was evidently an idea whose time had come, much of the credit for turning it from academic game-playing to a popular notion must be is due to Camille Flammarion, a French astronomer of repute. In his *Les Mondes Imaginaires* of 1866, Flammarion surveyed the history of man's developing notions of extraterrestrial worlds. Through the remainder of the Nineteenth Century, he followed it with a series of books and articles in which he championed the idea that ours is not the only inhabited world in the universe. Translated into many languages, Flammarion's well-informed opinions carried great weight, and were an inspiration to many writers who pioneered the genre which would later be labeled "science fiction."

LETTERS FROM THE PLANETS

Cassell's Family Magazine was a sober and respectable publication intended to entertain and instruct the middle class households of England. Its pages were filled with domestic advice, nature studies and moral stories about good girls who triumphed over difficulties to win the men of their hearts. How astonished its readers must have been when they opened the issue for February 1887, to find the first of a series of papers entitled "Letters from the Planets." If we today are bewildered to find accounts of extraterrestrial abduction appearing beside recipes and marital counsel in weekly magazines, imagine how much more amazing it must have seemed to a family in Victorian England.

The letters were purported to be written not by the author, an English country gentleman, but by an extraterrestrial friend of his named Aleriel, who supposed—reasonably enough—that an account of his travels would interest an Earthperson. Aleriel told of visiting the Moon, where he found traces of former life, but where

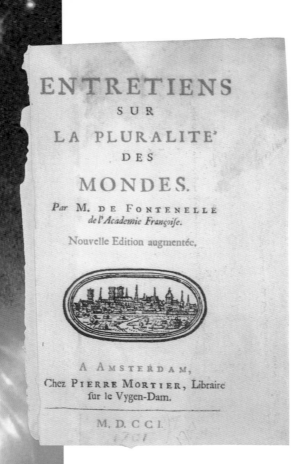

In Fontenelle's 1686 book Entretiens Sur La Pluralié des Mondes, *he discusses with a Marquise the probability of extraterrestrial life.*

RIGHT: *On November 21, 1783, Pilâtre de Rozier and the Marquis d'Arlandes made the first successful manned flight in a hot air balloon.*

COLECCION·MOLINO

N.° 18

DE LA
TIERRA
A LA
LUNA

JULIO VERNE

E. Freixes

only ruins remained. On the other hand, when he visited Mars, he found it teeming with life and bustling with activity. The Martian cities were built on islands which floated on the surface of the canals. Aleriel told of being excited by:

> … this huge masterpiece of the marvelous skill and power of the Martians—an achievement as far superior to any man has yet achieved in this age of steam and iron, as the works of human skill in the Nineteenth Century are superior to the works of man in the Stone Age.

In supposing that life on Mars was more advanced than on Earth, the author was voicing the general opinion. H. G. Wells pointed out that Mars is considerably older than Earth, and because it was smaller, would have cooled more rapidly. As a result, conditions that were capable of supporting life would have appeared there while our own planet was still a mass of molten rock. With such a start, it was only to be expected that Martian civilization would be superior to ours.

Besides, there are the famous canals as evidence. In his brilliant fantasy, *To Mars Via the Moon*, Mark Wicks depicted the canals as being made by Martians as a way of linking towns similar to our highways. Not everyone

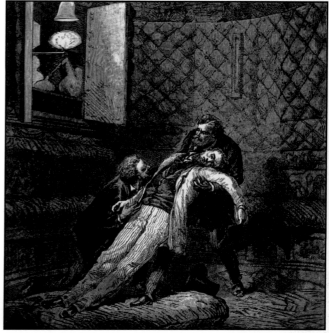

In Jules Verne's 1870 sequel, Round the Moon, *travelers recover from the blast-off.*

agreed with the American astronomer Percival Lowell that the canals were artificial constructions. But whatever they were, they were the most prominent physical feature on the planet, and they encouraged the hope that life might exist there.

"The hope?" While the idea that there might be life elsewhere in the universe is exciting, it is by no means sure that those who share the cosmos with us will be friendly. It might be prudent to be on one's guard ….

One day in the 1890s, H.G. Wells was walking with his brother, Frank, when their conversation turned to the people of Tasmania, and how astonished they must have been by the arrival of the first Europeans. "Imagine," observed Frank, "how we would react if beings from another planet were to drop from the sky and install themselves here."

That remark provided the starting point for what is possibly the finest science fiction story ever written: *The War of the Worlds.* The story opens with these splendidly ominous words which, in themselves, show how much more sophisticated man's ideas about his place in the cosmos had become:

> No one would have believed, in the last years of the Nineteenth Century, that human affairs were being watched keenly

This imaginary scene of a distant planet, an illustration from Camille Flammarion's best-selling Astronomie populaire, *encouraged people in the 1880s to take seriously the idea of traveling to other worlds.*

and closely by intelligences greater than man's and yet as mortal as his own; that as men busied themselves about their affairs they were scrutinized and studied, perhaps almost as narrowly as a man with a microscope might scrutinize the transient creatures that swarm and multiply in a drop of water ... No one gave a thought to the older worlds of space as sources of human danger ... At most, terrestrial men fancied there might be other men upon Mars, perhaps inferior to themselves and ready to welcome a missionary enterprise. Yet, across the gulf of space, minds that are to our minds as ours are to those of the beasts, intellects vast and cool and unsympathetic, regarded this earth with envious eyes,

and slowly and surely drew their plans against us ...

As Wells tells his story, mankind quickly learns that the Martians are distinctly unfriendly. But they were also—and this was a turning point in the development of the Martian myth— distinctly *non-human*. Previous writers had conceived of extraterrestrials as being more or less variations on humankind. After all, the Bible tells us that man was created in the image of God, and it must be supposed that other races would enjoy the same privilege. Yet, though the artists who illustrated Wells' book and the film makers who created screen versions of it differ

RIGHT: *David Hardy's painting reflects the technological superiority of Wells' Martians.*

widely in their interpretation of Martians, all agreed on one thing— Wells' Martians are not a bit like us.

Is Wells right? During the early years, at least, authors and artists were not so sure that the Martians would be monsters. Later, we will look more closely at changing fashions in extraterrestrial style. For the moment, though, let us simply note that while Wells undoubtedly set a fashion with *The War of the Worlds*, not every author felt bound to assume that visiting aliens would be unfriendly.

Readers of Cassell's Family Magazine *in March, 1889, must have been astonished by this illustration showing a Venusian spacecraft flying over Mars at night.*

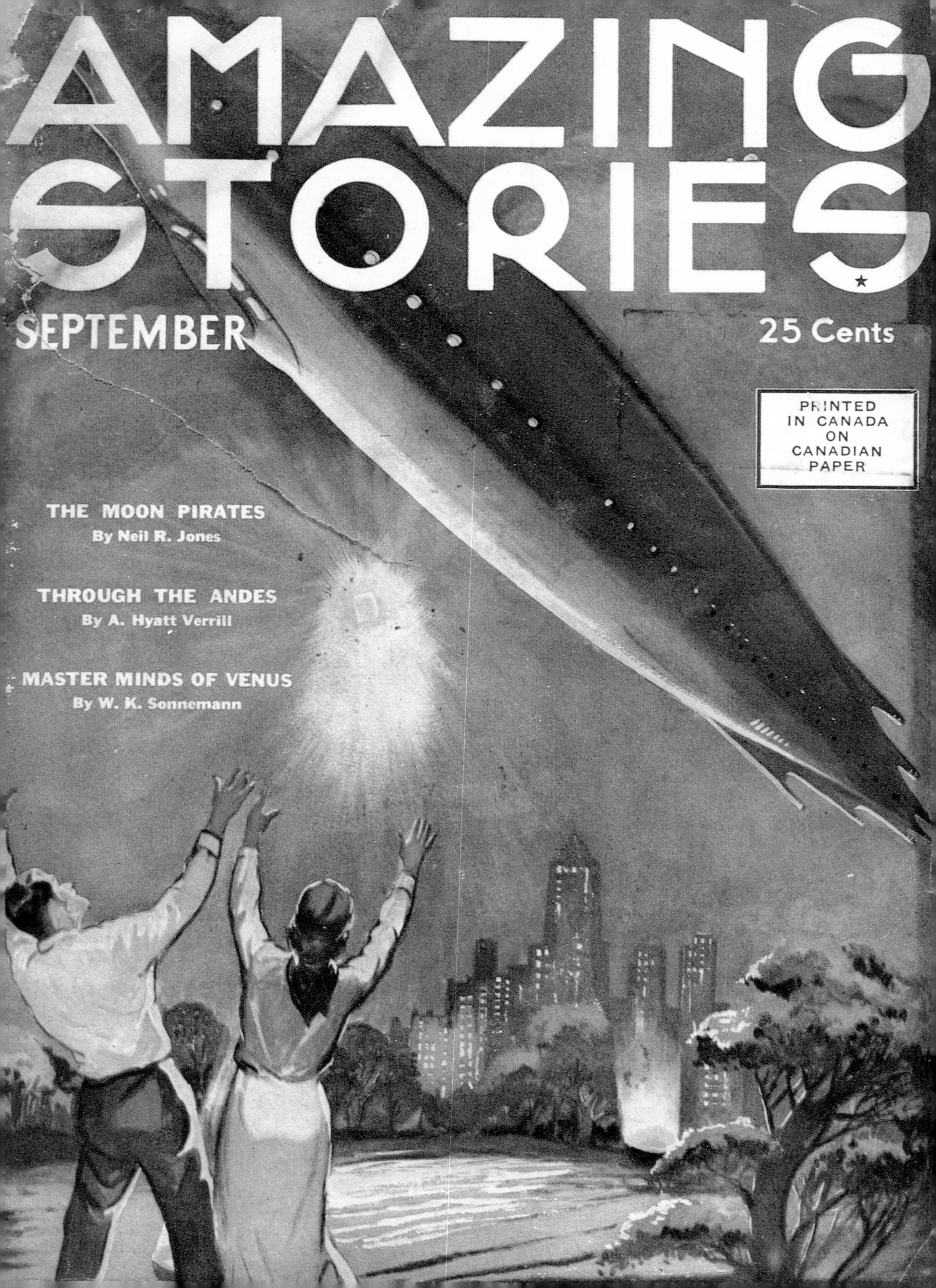

AMAZING
STORIES
SEPTEMBER
25 Cents
PRINTED IN CANADA ON CANADIAN PAPER
THE MOON PIRATES
By Neil R. Jones
THROUGH THE ANDES
By A. Hyatt Verrill
MASTER MINDS OF VENUS
By W. K. Sonnemann

LEFT: *The aliens aren't always hostile: The friendly "Master Minds of Venus" in W. K. Sommermann's 1934 story come to Earth's assistance.*

Then as now, some feared the worst from encounters with other worlds, and some hoped for the best.

AMAZING STORIES

Hugo Gernsback (1884–1967) was born in Luxembourg, and emigrated to the U.S. at the age of twenty. As early as 1916, Gernsback was writing articles with such titles as "Thought Transmission on Mars." In 1926, he launched the magazine *Amazing Stories*, the first of a number of periodicals which have been variously termed "comics" and "pulps," but which deserve a more respectful label. Later came *Air Wonder Stories, Science Wonder Stories* and others, all featuring what Gernsback called "scientifiction." The slogan printed on every title page of *Amazing Stories*, "Extravagant Fiction Today— Cold Fact Tomorrow," neatly expressed Gernsback's belief that what his authors drew from their imaginations, later generations would put into practice. In a 1927 editorial, he wrote:

> The editors of AMAZING STORIES are trying their best to keep from this magazine stories that belong rather in the domain of fairy tales than of scientifiction. The editorial board makes this fine distinction: a story, to be true scientifiction, should have a scientific basis of plausibility, so that while it may not seem possible to perform the miracle this year or next, it may conceivably come about 500, 5000 or 500,000 years hence.

Because they paid poorly, the pulps did not attract the best writers in the genre, but the sheer bulk of their output ensured that a great many variations on the basic themes were produced, often with remarkable ingenuity. What distinguishes these stories is not the quality of their prose, but the inventiveness of their ideas. Between them, these hundreds of authors, most of whose names are now forgotten

Illustrating one of Gernsback's own stories, this spacecraft of 1929 anticipates later "flying saucers."

except by connoisseurs of the genre, anticipated almost every idea that was later to appear in the flying saucer myth. This included not only alien spacecraft of every conceivable shape and size, but also their occupants, no less diverse, along with abduction by aliens, immobilisation by rayguns, physical examination of victims strapped on operating tables, cloning and brainwashing.

The possibility of visits to Earth by extraterrestrials was covered from almost every angle. There was speculation that our planet had something that other worlds lack. In Eando Binder's *The Thieves From Isot* (1934), invaders from Pluto come to mine the Earth for malachite, a substance they need for their technology. Really, it's our entire planet they are after. The title of Isaac Nathanson's *The Conquest of the Earth* (1930) announces its theme. Huge reptilian creatures from Andromeda seize control of the planet but are ultimately defeated. In Don Stuart's *The Invaders* (1935), the

Tharoos, a race of big-headed humanoids of superior intelligence, colonize Earth, treating humanity as farm animals.

In John W. Campbell's *When The Atoms Failed* (1930), a massive landing of Martians seems certain until an Earth scientist develops a ray that blasts their spaceships out of the sky. In P. Schuyler Miller's *Tetrahedra of Space* (1931), crystalline beings from Mercury land in South America. Fortunately, the extraterrestrials are allergic to water, and when Earth people explain how much of Earth's surface is covered with the deadly liquid, they depart to try their luck elsewhere.

Sometimes the extraterrestrial visits are motivated by simple curiosity. For example, the 40-mile long spacecraft that lands in the Russian steppes in 1995 in Stanton A. Coblentz's *The Golden Planetoid* (1935) shows no sign of aggression, and stays on Earth as long as it does only because it is damaged when landing and needs to be repaired. But even a non-aggressive

Alien invaders: in John W. Campbell's 1930 story, the Martians are once again Earth's natural enemy.

"WHAT TIME WILL IT BE THE END OF THE WORLD?"

It is significant that the golden age of science fiction should culminate in an incident in which fantasy impinged on real life so forcefully that it was actually perceived as reality. The Columbia Broadcasting System's radio production of H. G. Wells' *War of the Worlds* on the evening of October 30, 1938, was a remarkable demonstration of what can happen when the edge between fact and fiction becomes blurs.

The radio show was only one hour long, and contained incidents which would have required, at the very least, several hours to occur. However, so besotted were the listeners with the *idea* of what they were hearing that they abandoned even the most fundamental notions of reality. The following morning, under the headline "RADIO LISTENERS IN PANIC, TAKING WAR DRAMA AS FACT," the *New York Times* reported:

> The radio listeners, apparently, missed or did not listen to the introduction, which was "The Columbia Broadcasting System and its affiliated stations present Orson Welles and the Mercury Theatre on the Air in 'The War of the Worlds' by H. G. Wells."
>
> They also failed to associate the program with the newspaper listing of the program. They ignored three additional announcements made during the broadcast emphasizing its fictional nature.

At least 6 million listeners heard the broadcast, and subsequent research established that over a million of them had been frightened or disturbed. For many, it was more than that. Thousands of those listening became firmly convinced that Martians had actually landed in New Jersey, and that they represented a dire and immediate threat to humanity. The *New York Times* gave many specific instances of the panic:

mission can be misinterpreted. Eando Binder's *The Robot Aliens* (1935) tells the sad story of robots sent from Mars who are instantly perceived as enemies by Earth authorities, though they use no weapons and cause no damage. Several people are killed as the result of their visit, but only through panic or in the course of aggression by Earth's security forces. One robot survives long enough to explain matters to an Earthman who befriends and hides it, but in the end both the Earthman and the robot are killed by villagers who suspect another Frankenstein is creating a monster like they've seen in the movies.

Binder's moral intention in that story is evident, and several science fiction stories try to counter the image created by Wells, in which the aliens are inevitably hostile. In W. K. Sonnerman's *Master Minds of Venus* (1934), the visiting Venerians [sic] come to Earth specifically to help us. Their intentions are misunderstood, and the conflict is between Earthpeople who want to destroy the aliens and those who recognize their goodwill.

W. P. Cockcroft, in *The Alien Room* (1934), goes one step further. When climbers on Mount Everest find an abandoned alien spacecraft containing the skeleton of its occupant, they enter it, toy with the controls, and are sent hurtling back to the alien world leaving only their companion—who hadn't entered with them—to tell their story.

A wave of mass hysteria seized thousands of radio listeners throughout the nation between 8:15 and 9:30 last night when a broadcast of a dramatization of H. G. Wells' fantasy, "The War of the Worlds," led thousands to believe that an interplanetary conflict had started with invading Martians spreading death and destruction in New Jersey and New York ....

In Newark, in a single block, more than twenty families rushed out of their houses with wet handkerchiefs and towels over their heads to protect them from what they believed was to be a gas raid. Throughout New York, families left their homes, some to flee to nearby parks. Thousands of persons called the police, newspapers and radio stations, seeking advice on protective measures against the raids.

Large numbers asked how they could follow the broadcast's advice and flee from the city, whether they would be safer from the "gas raid" in the cellar or on the roof, how they could safeguard their children.

One man who called from Dayton, Ohio, asked, "What time will it be the end of the world?" and a lady who called the bus company explained to the operator that "the world is coming to an end and I have a lot to do."

A notable feature of the event was the way in which rumors, totally divorced from the radio play, sprang up. A man rushed into a New York police station shouting that "enemy planes" were crossing the Hudson River and asking what he should do. Many persons stood on street corners hoping for a sight of the "battle in the skies," while elsewhere one fugitive found "hundreds of people milling about in panic." A phone call to a police station asked "if the wave of poison gas will reach as far as Queens." In college dormitories, students waited in line to "take their turn at the telephone to make long distance calls to their parents, saying goodbye for what they thought might be the last time."

A Newark hospital treated fifteen men and women for shock and hysteria. At nearby Caldwell N.J., an excited parishioner ran into the First Baptist Church during evening service and shouted that a meteor had fallen, showering death and destruction. One caller went onto his roof to check the story that "they're bombing New Jersey" and claimed, "I could see the smoke from the bombs, drifting over toward New York." Another said, "I stuck my head out of the window and thought I could smell the gas. And it felt as though it was getting hot, like fire was coming." Yet another said, "I looked out of my window and saw a greenish, eerie light, which I was sure came from a monster. Later on, it proved to be the lights in the maid's car."

The interweaving of fiction and reality is explicit in this witness statement:

> At first, I was very interested in the fall of the meteor. But when it started to unscrew and monsters came out, I said to myself, "They've taken one of those *Amazing Stories* and are acting it out." It just couldn't be real. It was just like some of the stories I read in *Amazing Stories*, but it was even more exciting.

"MASS HYSTERIA?"

This remarkable episode inspired widespread comment from observers of social behavior, professional and amateur. "Mass hysteria" provided a convenient label, but it was only a label, not an explanation. Journalist Dorothy Thompson, writing in the *New York Herald Tribune* on November 2, wrote that "nothing whatever about the dramatization was in the least credible" and blamed the panic on the "incredible

The first Martian emerges—one of Alvin Correa's classic illustrations in H.G. Wells' War of the Worlds.

William Dock, 76, stands ready with loaded shotgun to repel the Martian invaders of New Jersey.

coming after the recent war scare in Europe and a period in which the radio frequently has interrupted regularly scheduled programs to report developments in the Czechoslovak situation, caused fright and panic throughout the area of the broadcast.

The Nazi invasion of Czechoslovakia had precipitated an international crisis, and though temporarily defused, the threat of World War Two was hanging over the world. It must surely have been at the back of the minds of many of those listening to the broadcast, and some people articulated it.

One panicking listener reported, "I knew it was some Germans trying to gas all of us. When the announcer kept calling them people from Mars, I just thought he was ignorant and didn't know yet that Hitler had sent them all." Another said:

> The announcer said a meteor had fallen from Mars, and I was sure he thought that, but in back of my head I had the idea that the meteor was just a camouflage. It was really an aeroplane like a Zeppelin that looked like a meteor and the Germans were attacking us with gas bombs. The aeroplane was built to look like a meteor just to fool people.

Summarizing his findings, Cantril concluded:

> Critical ability alone is not a sure preventive of panic. It may be overpowered either by an individual's own susceptible personality or by emotions generated in him by an unusual listening situation.

stupidity" of the panicking listeners.

Sociologists disagreed. Hadley Cantril, professor of psychology at Princeton and author of the definitive study of the episode, demonstrated that intelligence or stupidity were secondary factors at best. Instead, he identified three factors:

1. critical ability—the ability to test for reality
2. personal susceptibility; some people are more suggestible than others
3. the listening situation—the actual context in which the broadcast was heard

No one of these three on its own was likely to cause a person to panic. For most people in most situations, possession of critical ability is sufficient insurance against being deceived. But

people are not all alike. Some have a lower suggestibility threshold than others, and more easily accept what they think they see or hear. We believe that testing for reality is an instinctive process, but circumstances may override it. Cantril found that one in three of those who panicked made no attempt to check the situation out, whether by phoning the authorities, switching to another radio channel, or checking with friends or neighbours.

Outside circumstances can play a critical part. An important factor in the Martian episode was the prevailing political climate. The *New York Times* accurately identified one important factor:

> Despite the fantastic nature of the reported "occurrences," the program,

We would do well to bear Cantril's finding in mind throughout this survey of otherworldly visitations, for what he says of the Martian panic is applicable to a wide range of experiences. What the Martian panic demonstrated was that you don't have to be stupid, or mentally ill, or in any other way exceptional, to be placed by circumstances in a situation in which you have difficulty distinguishing between fantasy and fact. If conditions favor it, a substantial portion of the population may hallucinate, misinterpret events or be deluded out of common reality.

While it would not be accurate to suggest that this is always the case in reports of otherworldly visitation, it is a possibility that we should always keep in mind, whether it involves contact with spirits of the dead or with abduction by extraterrestrials.

Clearly, though, any such possibility was far from Orson Welles' mind. Commenting the next day, he disclosed that, far from anticipating panic, he feared the radio audience might not be sufficiently entertained:

> It was our thought that perhaps people might be bored or annoyed at hearing a tale so improbable.

Like many before and since, Orson Welles underestimated humanity's ability to create a myth,and, having created it, to mistake it for reality.

FROM MOSES TO MARTIANS

It seems a far cry from God speaking with Moses on Mount Sinai to Martians landing in New Jersey. But both episodes are expressions of belief, whether founded or not. If no facts, or insufficient facts, are available, then we will fill the gap with fantasy, surmise and speculation. Our hopes and fears will direct our thoughts towards saviors or monsters. Myths and legends will be created, and rumors will fly. An example of this process at work can be seen in the "cargo cults" of the people of the South Pacific. From time to time on the scattered islands of the Pacific, a belief will arise that otherworldly beings are about to bestow on the native

population the goods that have been withheld from them by the selfish white man. In his book, *John Frum, He Come*, Edward Rice writes:

> South Pacific Cargo received its greatest impetus during World War II, after the arrival of American troops landed on dozens of islands with unlimited types of western goods, from war materials to … candy bars … whiskey and other luxuries undreamed of by people scarcely out of the Stone Age.

Mankind looks to otherwordly beings for many reasons. Some are as material as the South Sea Islanders hoping for candy bars and whiskey. Other people are looking for spiritual reassurance or for confirmation of their worst fears. But in one sense or another, we are all looking for our share of the "Cargo."

The day after the broadcast, producer Orson Welles defends his production against a storm of media and popular criticism.

34

Picturing the Martians

Early in the morning of June 30, 1908, an enormous aerial explosion, visible from a distance of 310 square miles, flattened some 77 square miles of pine forest near the Tunguska River in central Siberia. Vast numbers of trees were knocked down, and because they all fell away from a central point, it was easy to identify that point as the epicenter. But there was nothing there—not even a crater, just a marshy bog. Witnesses spoke of a huge fireball, and the most probable explanation is that a comet fragment entered Earth's atmosphere. Made of ice and dust, it would disintegrate, creating a fireball and blast wave, but no impact crater. Such is the scientific explanation for the unique "Tunguska Explosion." Because it is only a suggestion, alternative interpretations of the event have been proposed. Of these, the most intriguing is that the object that exploded in our atmosphere was a spacecraft from another world.

ANCIENT ASTRONAUTS

A similar explanation has been given for the Biblical account of the destruction of the cities of the plain, Sodom and Gomorrah. In 1960, a Russian professor named M. M. Agrest proposed that the event had been caused not by "fire from Heaven," as the Bible suggests, but by a nuclear explosion generated by extraterrestrial invaders 5000 years ago.

Geologists offer more mundane explanations. Neev and Emery, in a 1995 study, pointed out that "the cities are in an earthquake-prone belt and their area has been subject to severe changes of climate lasting hundreds of years." In other words, there is no need to look to other worlds for an explanation. To support his thesis, Agrest pointed to the megalithic monuments of Baalbek in Lebanon, which he suggested might have been

the launching platforms for interplanetary space ships.

Since then, the "ancient astronaut" concept has become a substantial subdivision of popular scientific speculation. Its champions point to the many

The heart of the devastation at Tunguska, where a huge area of forest was mysteriously flattened.

mysterious ruins and artifacts scattered about the world, and find explanations for all of them in terms of visits to our planet by otherworldly beings. Hundreds of books have been published with titles such as *Extraterrestrial Visitations from Prehistoric Times to the Present*, *Mankind—Child of the Stars* or *We Are Not The First*. Far fewer books have been published exposing the weaknesses of the suggested scenarios.

Folklore seems to provide a legitimization of this approach. The mythologies of many cultures contain legends of a "Golden Age" preceding the present, a time when people lived in peace and harmony with nature and with one another, when everything was better than it is now. The myths vary from one culture to another, but the fact that they are so widespread has encouraged some to think that there really was some form of civilization before our own, although its virtues may have been exaggerated.

Speculation about these earlier societies has spawned a vast body of literature. Some of it involves great physical changes in the world. The notion

LEFT: *With its big head and "wrap-around" eyes, Debbie Lee's classic "grey" represents aliens as perceived by witnesses of the 1980s and 1990s.*

ABOVE: *Many believe something other than natural causes destroyed Sodom and Gomorrah.*
LEFT: *This scene from the TV series,* The X-Files, *shows that Tunguska still captures the imagination.*

typical Von Däniken passage follows:

> Could this gold plaque be a message from alien astronauts to us? Who will decipher this code? What has it got to tell us?

Though the French writer Paul Misraki (writing as "Paul Thomas") may have been the first non-fiction author to link the idea of flying saucers and "ancient astronauts," it was von Däniken whose series of best-selling books did most to popularize the notion that today's UFOs are only the latest in a long history of visits from other worlds. We saw in the last chapter that many cultures have traditions of a god who imparted to them the secrets of art and civilization— for example, the Central American deity Quetzalcoatl. Now, authors such as Maurice Chatelain (*Our Ancestors Came from Outer Space*) and Robert Charroux (*Legacy of the Gods*) were proposing that those mythic gods were, in fact, visiting extraterrestrials, and devoted book after book to showing that "man's mysterious ancestry" had an otherworldly origin.

Scattered about our planet are a number of objects—ranging from small

that there formerly existed a large country, if not an entire continent, in the Atlantic, named Atlantis, is one theory. There are also reasons to believe that something of this sort existed in the Pacific. A vast body of myth supports the idea that Mu, or Lemuria, existed where now there is empty ocean.

Such legends have been retold throughout human history. It is indisputable that cultures have come and gone in the past, leaving behind monuments and other relics— Stonehenge, Baalbek, the Pyramids— which we do not fully understand. But only recently, with the beginning of our own first tentative explorations of space, has it been proposed that extraterrestrial visitors were involved.

The idea that beings from other planets might have visited Earth before the birth of humanity is not a new one. As is so often the case, science fiction writers got there first. In the November, 1934 issue of *Wonder Stories*, Philip Barshafsky tells a story of a Martian landing on Earth during the Jurassic Era. Mars itself had become unfit for

habitation, and the invaders are one of a succession of expeditions sent to other planets to see if any might provide suitable colonies for the Martians. They discover that Earth alone is suitable, or would be if it were not for the dinosaurs. For a while, the superior technology of the Martians enables them to hold off the attacks of the huge animals, but eventually brute force wins the day. The Martians are annihilated, their spaceship rusts away and nothing is left to show that aliens had ever set foot on our planet.

The scenarios sketched by Swiss author Erich von Däniken and other theorists twenty years later were somewhat different, but by then flying saucers had appeared on the scene. Authors such as Brinsley Le Poer Trench, Lord Clancarty, were inspired by the thought that today's flying saucers were part of an ongoing tradition of extraterrestrial visitation. While these theories were no less speculative than science fiction, their creators stirred fact into their speculation in a way that seemed to give them substance. A

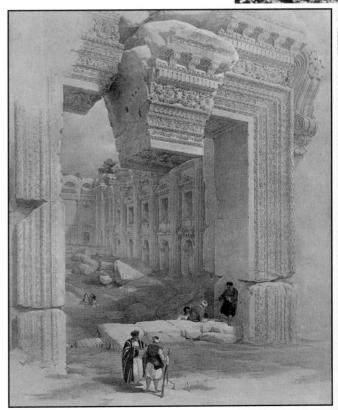

The Great Temple at Baalbek is so impressive that some writers insist aliens were responsible.

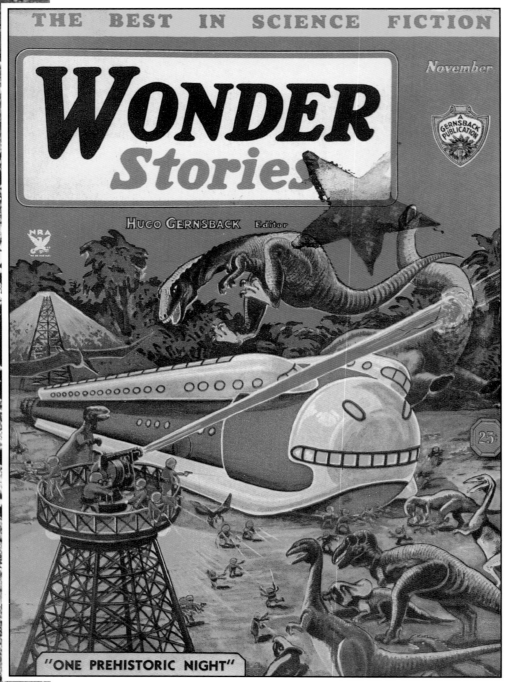

THE BEST IN SCIENCE FICTION

November

WONDER
Stories

A GERNSBACK PUBLICATION

HUGO GERNSBACK Editor

25

"ONE PREHISTORIC NIGHT"

Philip Barshofsky's 1934 story, "One Prehistoric Night," imagines what might have happened if aliens had landed on Earth during the age of the dinosaurs.

artifacts to vast building complexes, from massive markings on the ground to enigmatic drawings on cave walls—which can be interpreted as evidence that our planet housed other civilizations prior to our own. The boldness of these hypotheses is demonstrated by Robert Charroux, perhaps the least inhibited of the ancient astronaut proponents:

We have evidence that interplanetary rockets streaked across the heavens

millions of years ago; that atomic bombs destroyed one or more civilizations; that extraterrestrials left traces of their presence in several parts of our planet; that Moses was familiar with explosives and a death ray; that a man lighted his house with electricity in the time of Saint Louis; that an airplane flew during the reign of John V of Portugal; that secret societies forged the destiny of mankind ...

What requires cleverness is devising

a single, coherent story that embraces these many disparate ideas. A number of alternative scenarios are currently in circulation. Though each has its individual features, they can be roughly classified into groups:

- Humankind of a sort already existed, but we were incapable of development on our own. We required guidance from more advanced—i.e. extraterrestrial—civilizations to set us on the right track. In some scenarios, this guidance was limited to instruction; in others, genetic manipulation was needed to enable man to climb a rung of the evolutionary ladder. In still more, cross-breeding was required to let early humans acquire the genetic components necessary to become civilized creatures.
- We humans developed our own civilization, but the process was covertly masterminded by the more advanced extraterrestrials, in much the same way as a farmer oversees his livestock.
- We developed our own civilization, but things went wrong. So the extraterrestrials, in the spirit of cosmic cooperation, intervened to save us from the consequences of our mistakes.
- Humanity itself is of extraterrestrial origin, the Earth having been colonized by extraterrestrial explorers from whom we are descended.

Such speculation has been widely dismissed as irresponsible, and unquestionably a lot of nonsense has been written. Nevertheless, these theories have opened our eyes to possibilities we might not otherwise have entertained, inviting us to set our imaginations loose on the origin and nature of the universe. However silly many of the ideas may be, they remind us how much is still unknown about the early history of humanity.

But precisely because so little is known, it is difficult for these speculations to find confirmation. The theories flourish, but their roots are shallow. Though some proponents of the ancient astronaut hypothesis have sought a historical basis for their ideas in legendary writings, this is confined to speculation based on interpretation of such Biblical passages as this:

> And it came to pass, when men began to multiply on the face of the earth, and daughters were born unto them, that the sons of God saw the daughters of men that they were fair; and they took them wives of all which they chose … and also after that, when the sons of God came in unto the daughters of men, and they bare children to them, the same became mighty men which were of old, men of renown.
>
> GENESIS 6

A case can possibly be made that "the sons of God" are in fact extraterrestrial beings. However, the reference could also be to a terrestrial legend.

OUR AIRBORNE ANCESTORS

Whichever "ancient astronaut" scenario we choose to adopt, we must suppose that they traveled here in a spacecraft of some kind. Then, the astronauts flew away again or, if they remained here, destroyed their vessels, as Cortes burned his boats on the shores of Mexico so his men would not be tempted to sail back to Spain.

A number of believers in UFOs, keen to shore up their belief that it isn't simply a "space-age myth," have sought to establish a prehistory of the UFO. In his 1953 book, *Flying Saucers Have Landed*, Desmond Leslie writes:

> For as long as man has been able to write and record things, he has periodically noted the passage of luminous discs and fiery spindle-shaped objects in our skies. In ancient Rome, many references were made to "Flying Shields" … In China, they were called "fiery dragons" … Frescoes in a Fourteenth Century Yugoslavian church show little men in space capsules … Inscriptions on ancient stones depict spacecraft of the disk and spindle variety. There are cave drawings of men in curious-looking spacesuits, almost identical to the garb worn by modern astronauts.

Even if these interpretations are correct, they do not prove that there was any interaction with Earth people: less do they give any support to "ancient astronaut" theories.

The Bible is a favorite hunting ground for spacecraft. Numerous incidents, especially in the Old Testament, have been reinterpreted as UFO events. The vision of Ezeikel is a classic example, and references to "fiery chariots" can be interpreted as UFOs.

In June 1974, businessman Charles Silva had an interesting experience in Peru. In his book, *Date with the Gods*, he describes meeting an extraterrestrial calling herself Rama, who explains that she is on a mission to Earth to save humanity. When three flying saucers cross the sky, she says not to be surprised. "I see them all the time," she tells him, "They're all over the world." Then Rama adds, "If you want to know about flying saucers, the Bible is the place to go. There's a lot of evidence of flying objects in its pages." In the course of several meetings, Rama explains to Silva how extraterrestrials have been visiting Earth through human history. And Silva himself sees them and communicates with them telepathically.

If Silva, and others who have had similar encounters, can be believed, this is valuable evidence for the prehistory of UFOs. But can we believe them? Is Silva's story fact or fiction? We shall see in later chapters that it is not always easy to tell one from the other.

Andrew Tomas was one of the first writers to propose that "ancient astronauts" visited our planet in prehistoric times.

CHARIOTS OF THE GODS?

ERICH VON DANIKEN

Unsolved mysteries of the past
ERICH VON DANIKEN

venir

PHYSICAL EVIDENCE

Since so much remains unknown about humanity's distant past, it is hard to disprove the theories offered by the ancient astronaut proponents. Generally, it's a question of comparing their explanation to the conventional one, and choosing the more plausible of the two.

Sometimes, the weakness of the reasoning behind the ancient astronaut theories becomes evident. For example, it has been said said that the construction of the Pyramids, the building of Baalbek and the erection of the sculptured figures on Easter Island were beyond the skills available to our ancestors. This suggests that our ancestors were perhaps instructed in the appropriate technology by extraterrestrial visitors, or even that the visitors were themselves responsible for the constructions.

However, in all three of the instances cited above, it has been shown that the constructions *could* have been carried out using techniques involving comparatively simple skills that were probably available to our ancestors. Thor Heyerdahl, notably, carried out experiments on Easter Island showing that though erecting those massive figures calls for considerable ingenuity, it requires no sophisticated technology. While such demonstrations do not prove that these techniques were employed, they do make the notion of extraterrestrial assistance seem somewhat gratuitous.

One of the most notorious of the artifacts produced as evidence for visits by ancient astronauts is the carved stone lid of a sarcophagus in a temple at Palenque, Mexico, discovered by the Mexican archaeologist Lhuillier in 1949. Two French authors, Tarade and Millou, noted the resemblance to the pilot of a rocket ship, and the suggestion was taken up enthusiastically by others.

Raymond A. Drake, for example,

Discovered in 1949, this carving on a Mayan sarcophagus has been interpreted by some as depicting a space traveler, though it is a typical example of Mayan religious art.

writes, "There seems little doubt that it represents anything other than a humanoid piloting a rocket, even though it was carved thousands of years ago." In fact, it was carved just over a thousand years ago—the date carved on the tomb is the equivalent of A.D. 612.

Von Däniken adopted the same notion, without drawing attention to the fact that the tomb is not a unique object. In fact, there are many similar artifacts, though none are quite so striking. The scene is a religious one, embodying common motifs of Mayan religious art.

Dr. Peter White, Lecturer in Prehistory at the University of Sydney, says of the carved lid: "This scene is repeated elsewhere in Mayan carvings … it embodies various beliefs about the world and the afterworld." He also notes:

If we are dealing with an astronaut in a rocket, how does it come to be so like our own rockets in shape and propulsion? If the earth is being regularly visited by astronauts as part of an interstellar experiment, then surely we would expect the spaceships to be rather more developed, to use an atomic or magnetic drive on their intergalactic jaunts, to be pollution-free and computerized. Why is the Palenque astronaut using a superannuated Saturn Rocket?

Wall paintings at Tassili n'Ajjer in the Algerian Sahara—discovered by French archaeologist Henri Lhote in 1956, and dating from between 8000 and 6000 B.C.—have also been claimed by writers to be "space-suited figures." We are invited to imagine that our ancient ancestors drew pictures of visiting extraterrestrials, just as they did the bison and deer of the Lascaux cave paintings. Certainly, there is a superficial resemblance, but as critic Ronald Story points out, it is rather odd that the aliens would wear space helmets, yet be otherwise naked. Many have their sexual organs exposed, which to anthropologists suggests that they are intended to depict the ritual figures of fertility cults.

The same is true of wall paintings in Uzbekistan in the former Soviet Union, and elsewhere. In the absence of any direct evidence linking them to extraterrestrial visitors—and with good reason to suggest a more human explanation—these artifacts hardly constitute persuasive proof of long-ago alien visitors.

Often the champions of the ancient astronaut theories distort the facts to suit their purpose. The Nazca lines in Peru admittedly present a genuine mystery. Though many explanations have been proposed, the mystery remains unresolved. Von Däniken argues that, since the lines are clearly designed to be seen from the air, this implies that they were made for, or by, extraterrestrial visitors. But while it may be true that the markings are intended to be seen from the air, this could have simply represented a "message" to their gods in the same way that many of us offer prayers to our gods. It does not imply that extraterrestrials were physically present, still less that they were responsible for the lines. Von Däniken reproduces a photograph of the Nazca lines, but gives no indication of scale. It seems to back his suggestion that the lines could have been a landing field for extraterrestrial spacecraft until we realize that the scale has been

This drawing at Tassili n'Ajjer is seen by some writers as "the Great Martian God," though anthropologists view it as a fertility figure.

exaggerated. There is also the issue of whether extraterrestrial visitors would need a landing strip, any more than we did when we visited the Moon.

Further evidence concerns the possession of sophisticated knowledge. Maurice Chatelain, a NASA engineer, has made the striking discovery that lines drawn between (some of) the great French cathedrals match—provided one employs a flat projection—the constellation of Virgo. For Chatelain, this is evidence of a knowledge of astronomy far greater than that known to have been possessed at the time— knowledge which, he suggests, can only be of extraterrestrial origin. Exactly why the cathedral planners wished to reflect the celestial layout is something we can only wonder about.

Certainly, the more we uncover our past, the more reason we find to admire the skills of our ancestors. Patterns emerge to show that the positioning of a stone or the alignment of a monument may be design rather than chance. However, as has been shown in numerous examples—from the authorship of Shakespeare to the recently discovered

ABOVE: *The Great Pyramid and the Sphinx have attracted more theories than any other monuments.*
LEFT: *The stone figures of Easter Island have been seen by some as evidence of alien technology.*

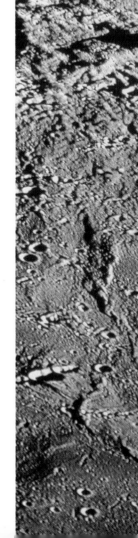

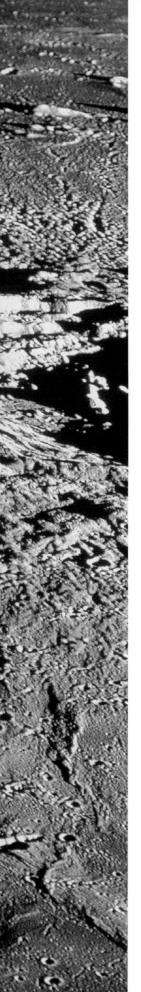

The destruction of Mu: The author James Churchward claimed in his book, The Lost Continent of Mu, *that the great Pacific continent was overwhelmed by a combination of flood and volcanic action.*

"Bible Code"—a combination of chance and careful selection of examples is often used to support flimsy hypotheses.

It is very likely that our ancestors possessed esoteric knowledge, and skilled craftsmen, then as now, no doubt guarded their trade secrets. It is all the more reason why we should view with skepticism theories that have their basis in the notion that long-ago people were incapable of wondrous technical feats.

ANCIENT WISDOM

There are many traditions asserting the existence of a body of ancient wisdom—running counter to established religious or scientific views—that has been secretly preserved by a series of extraordinarily gifted humans. Roger Bacon, Sir Francis Bacon, Nikolas Tesla and Albert Einstein are among those cited as such geniuses or "Lords of the Flame" working secretly in our midst. Robert Charroux asserts that there is:

a conspiracy of initiates whose purpose was to keep the people of the world in ignorance of their ancestors' prodigious adventure … The conspiracy must have existed for at least six thousand years, doling out such scientific knowledge as men could safely assimilate, but holding back what could not be divulged without danger.

Charroux and other theorists suggest that powers such as astral projection, telepathy, psychokinesis and psychic healing, which we tend to label paranormal, were commonly possessed by our ancestors, who obtained them from extraterrestrials. But even if we accept that such phenomena occur, the idea that otherworldly visitors are responsible is pure speculation. There have always been secret societies, but there are no grounds for supposing that they derived their knowledge from otherworldly sources. Moreover, the authors supporting such theories are remarkably reticent in providing useful details of their sources. James Churchward, who in a series of books has resolutely promoted the concept of

a Pacific continent of Mu, claims to have received his private information while staying in "certain Monasteries in India and Tibet whose names are withheld by request."

There are, in fact, sound geophysical reasons for believing that some such continent formerly existed, but Churchward arouses suspicion rather than trust by being so coy about his sources. Similarly, George Hunt Williamson, in offering some very esoteric ideas "linking ancient civilizations and the mysteries of their temple rituals with the remote beginnings of humanity and visitations from Outer Space," bases his theories on information obtained, he says,

from very ancient manuscripts preserved in the great library of one of the world's time-honored mystery schools, a "lost city" high in the mountains of Peru. In this city lives a master teacher, a survivor of the Elders …

But Williamson does not tell us what manuscripts, which master teacher, which mystery school, or which "lost" city he is referring to.

Peter Kolosimo, writing of an alleged tunnel built by extraterrrestrials under the Pacific from Asia to America, says,

> lamas who have been questioned about the tunnels have usually replied, "Yes, they exist: They were made by giants who gave us the benefit of their knowledge when the world was young."

Unfortunately, Kolosimo also does not tell us which lamas he is referring to, who they were speaking to, when and where they said so, or how dependable these commentators were on other matters.

These authors are entertaining to read and provide legitimate food for thought. Though they select only what serves their purpose—and exaggerate its significance—they frequently draw our attention to genuine puzzles. The authors invite us to question establishment explanations and received opinions. But without the backing of solid evidence, their speculations have little more substance than the fantasies of the authors who wrote in Hugo Gernsback's *Amazing Stories* twenty years earlier.

EXOTIC VARIATIONS

In addition to the various general theories about extraterrestrials, there have been any number of specific accounts. The thesis presented by Zecharia Sitchin in *The Twelfth Planet* and developed in later works is characteristic of the genre. Sitchin—like the ancient astronaut proponents—and like theological commentators for centuries before, had been puzzled by references to the Nephilim, the giant offspring of the unnatural union between visiting "sons of the Gods" and the "daughters of men," who figure in the Bible and other Middle Eastern traditions. How was it possible, Sitchin asked, for these beings to come and go so frequently between Earth and their home? The implication, he felt, was that they must have come from relatively nearby.

Sitchin agreed with orthodox science that none of the existing planets in the solar system was a suitable candidate. Instead, he produced legends, pointing to the existence of a twelfth planet, Marduk, whose orbit brings it close to Earth every 3600 years. Some 450,000 years ago, Marduk's inhabitants took advantage of just such a close orbit to land and colonize our planet. Eventually, needing a slave race to do their dirty work, they created mankind. Unfortunately, humanity didn't turn out to be quite the obedient second-class citizens their creators had in mind. And so the visitors left, expecting mankind to be wiped out by the tidal waves caused by the reappearance of the twelfth planet. However, they didn't reckon on Noah and his Ark.

Catastrophe of a different kind was involved in the story told by the Mann family of Gloucestershire, England, who reported being taken aboard a spaceship from Janos on June 19, 1978. Their abductors explained to them, in a scenario diametrically opposed to

Sir Francis Bacon's vast learning and far-sighted ideas caused many to include him in a group of extraordinarily gifted humans who it was believed possessed a body of ancient wisdom.

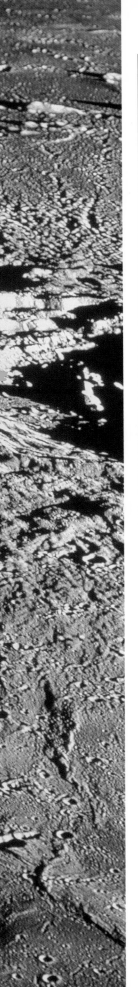

The "humming bird" image has been preserved for centuries on the arid plains of Nazca, Peru and seems as though it were intended to be seen from the air.

Sitchin's, that they themselves are the descendants of Earth people! Long, long ago, colonists from our planet had developed the technology to travel in space. They had settled elsewhere in the universe, including Janos, a planet several thousand light years from Earth. Unfortunately, their new home had come under threat of imminent destruction by natural forces, and they had to take refuge aboard giant spaceships. Now these prodigals were asking if we would take them back. They understood that our planet was already overcrowded, but surely we could find room for them somewhere. Norway, for instance, didn't seem particularly overcrowded, and there were only 10 million of them, drifting around the solar system in their saucers like planes stacked above an airport, waiting for permission to land.

Frank Johnson presented his account of "The Janos People" in 1980, and since then, nothing has been heard of them. Presumably, they are still out there,

wandering about the skies, extraterrestrial refugees. Maybe some other planet has been more welcoming.

Although every year new theories of this kind are published, their authors have generally failed to establish a firm basis for tales of extraterrestrial visitation. As a result, the theories tend to be put on hold. In addition, several skeptical books have been published demonstrating the weakness of the theories. Though the books did not get onto the bestseller lists, they have had a general effect of disparaging any and all stories of visits by extraterrestrials.

In short, the case is far from proved. The mysteries are there, no question. The Nazca Lines, Stonehenge and many other artifacts continue to challenge us. But the fact that we cannot explain them in the light of our current knowledge does not mean that we should invoke beings from other worlds, for there is not a scrap of evidence that they are responsible. Our remote ancestors, when they did not understand

the thunder, attributed it to the anger of the gods. We have now abandoned that explanation, but, it seems, we are still disposed to look beyond this world to explain what we can't understand.

WHAT HAPPENED TO THE ASTRONAUTS?

Even if beings from other worlds visited our planet in the remote past, they evidently did not choose to settle here, or, if they did, they were wiped out. This calamity not only destroyed them, but must have removed every trace of them and of their existence and handiwork, with the exception of a few controversial monuments.

Not everyone agrees. Some have suggested that the aliens *did* remain in some form. In a 1957 book, the

American writer Morris Jessup speculated:

> There are "little people" in African and New Guinea jungles today ... but *nobody* knows their origin or ancestry. Were these isolated tribes "planted" in the tropical jungle from UFOs thousands of years ago? Did UFOs land, or crash, and establish colonies?

In support of this somewhat improbable suggestion, Jessup cited a newspaper story:

> During construction work on the Cathedral of Saint John (New York), workmen left a high scaffold in place over a weekend. When they returned, they found lying on the scaffolding the body of a little man with one eye in the middle of his forehead. A *New York Times* reporter is said to have written it up, but his story was "killed" to avoid the charge of sensationalism. Army authorities were said to have removed the body.

Jessup does not tell us what makes him conclude that this "little man" should be a solitary survivor from a race of prehistoric alien visitors. But in any case, it requires a big leap of faith to believe that tribes currently living in remote jungle areas are related to aliens who visited Earth long ago to bring us art and civilization.

This and other intriguing scenarios have their champions, but remain unsupported speculation. It seems more likely that, if there ever were any "ancient astronauts," they didn't like our planet enough to want to stay here. For all practical purposes, any question of visitors to Earth before human history must be placed in the "pending" file until some really convincing evidence turns up.

THE STAR PEOPLE

During the 1980s, new claims were made that otherworldly people were present on Earth, but this time the scenario was a very different one. It was proposed that thousands, perhaps millions, of people who appear to be normal human beings are, in fact, extraterrestrials.

The most visible exponent of this notion has been the American writer Brad Steiger. He, alone and in collaboration with his wife, Francie, has authored a series of books stating that many people on Earth are extraterrestrials, though even they may not realize it.

The concept did not originate with the Steigers, of course. The idea of extraterrestrials mixing with humans and living among us may be as old as the Bible, and has surfaced over and over again in different contexts. When we come our discussion of contactees, we shall find that Howard Menger and his wife, Connie, are two of the most prominent to claim an extraterrestrial origin—he from Saturn, she from Venus. Dana Howard, too, considers herself an "Earthborn Venusian" and, in addition to telling of her own adventures *(She Came From Venus)*, has written a fiction story in which her Venusian heroine becomes the first woman president of the United States.

As we shall see, the contactee phenomenon was essentially one of individuals selected because of their personal qualities. This was certainly the case with Dana Howard and the Mengers. But by the 1990s, the notion of a chosen elite had given way to a mass phenomenon. As abductions escalated from isolated cases to thousands, and then to millions, so more and more people came to realize that they, too, were "Star People."

In his 1995 book, *From Elsewhere: Being E.T. in America*, Dr. Scott Mandelker invited his readers to contemplate the fact that:

> There may be as many as 100 million extraterrestrials living on Earth. Most of them are what could be called Sleeping Wanderers.

The number is not mere guesswork, but was arrived at from what the author says are channeled messages received from the extraterrestrials themselves. Mandelker explains that by "Wanderers" he means:

> ... those E.T. souls who have been extraterrestrial since birth, but who've forgotten who they are and live under a

kind of veil of their true being, and then slowly—if they're fortunate— begin to awaken.

The Wanderers are born of human parents, according to Mandelker. Some may never realize their extraterrestrial origins, though this seems like a waste of their talents, since they have supposedly been placed on Earth to carry out a mission. Those who have not yet awakened to their extraterrestrial origin are known as "Sleeping Wanderers," which makes them sound more like zombies than emissaries of a superior race. Mandelker does not make it clear whether he gave them these labels, or if this is what the people call themselves. Although Steiger writes the introduction to Mandelker's book, the author does not himself use Steiger's "Star People" label.

The Earth-born Wanderers are not the only kind of aliens living in our midst. There is another category, the "Walk-ins." These are "real" aliens of extraterrestrial origin who have taken over the physical bodies of Earth people, who voluntarily relinquish life on this planet in favor of life elsewhere, for a time at least.

So what are all these extraterrestrials doing on our planet? They are here to help us, say their proponents. Unlike the aggressive abductors we shall be meeting later, these are benevolent citizens of the cosmos who are genuinely concerned about the way our Earthly civilization is developing, and who have come among us to help from the inside. This has been going on throughout history—Americans will be proud to know that Benjamin Franklin and Thomas Jefferson are both said to have been extraterrestrials. On the other hand, it could be said that if the representatives of these superior civilizations are here to help our ailing Earth, they are certainly taking their time about it.

The curious thing about the Star People is that they don't immediately know what they are. They have to find out. Sometimes finding out comes in the form of a revelation from "the Beyond," sometimes from a vision. Presumably quite a high proportion learn of their true nature by reading books like *The Star*

IMAGINE THE JOY OF FINDING OUT
THAT YOU ARE ONE OF

THE STAR PEOPLE

BRAD & FRANCIE STEIGER

The startling truth about the thousands
of "aliens" now awakening among us!

People by Brad and Francie Steiger, which says on its cover:

> IMAGINE THE JOY OF FINDING OUT THAT YOU ARE ONE OF THE STAR PEOPLE!

It is, evidently, a joyful discovery. You learn that, as you always suspected, you are not quite like other people. You are someone special; in fact you are someone superior. You are not here on Earth simply to be a population statistic, but to fulfill a high purpose, that of saving the Earth!

Still, it does seem rather remarkable that, with so important a mission to accomplish, those whose function it is to carry out that mission should learn of their role in such a haphazard, uncertain way. Steiger tells us:

> Ever since I was a child, I have felt as though I were really a stranger here on Earth. I felt that I was an observer, rather than a participant, of this alien land in which I found myself.

Similarly, Steiger's wife Francie says:

> I believe I am one of the Star People. When I was $4\frac{1}{2}$ years old, two men, one dark-haired and the other blond, came up to me. These mysterious messengers told me I was here on earth for a special mission that I would come to understand later in life.

This would seem a very casual method of recruitment. You might think it would be better to be sure of your identity and mission as a Star Person. But most Star People say they are comfortable knowing who they are; and many claim to have been told the good news by an apparition of some kind. For Dr G. H., a psychologist from Texas, it was an angel; for C. L., a teacher from Arizona, it appeared to be a Native American; S. S., a New York psychotherapist, learned it from a goddess named Bast, and P. B., a Pennsylvania psychiatrist, had an encounter with a beautifully-robed entity resembling Jesus.

These entities are not necessarily who they seem to be. H. L. L. of California had a vision of Jesus at age 11, but:

LEFT: In Brad and Francie Steiger's book, the authors reveal that they, and many others, are in fact "Star People" of extraterrestrial origin.

"FASCINATING RESEARCH...IMPECCABLY DONE... A TOPIC NO ONE ELSE HAS DARED TO TOUCH." —Kenneth Ring, Ph.D., author of *The Omega Project*

ARE YOU— OR IS SOMEONE YOU KNOW— AN E.T.?

FROM ELSEWHERE

BEING E.T. IN AMERICA

Scott Mandelker, Ph.D.

With an Introduction by Brad Steiger

Like the Steigers, Scott Mandelker reveals in his book that he himself is an extraterrestrial, one of millions who have been sent to help the people of Earth.

I realized later that it was actually a guide who appeared to me as Jesus, because at that time I was very religious and would only accept a guide in that form. The entity used big words which I could not understand at that time, but I remembered them until I could. The gist of what he said was that I was to grow to become aware of all things.

Certainly the Star People do seem to possess exceptional talents. Few people can remember words they do not understand, especially when heard at an early age. They seem to live more deeply than most people, even when young. Professor Leo Sprinkle of Laramie, Wyoming, an investigator who came to realize that he is a Star Person, recalls:

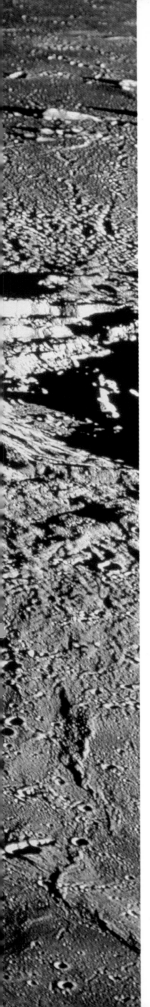

at five or six, I felt a "pull" toward another world, as if I had a mission to accomplish here before I could rejoin my "true home." I was sad and apprehensive in my task.

Because Star People are as precocious in their feelings as in their intelligence, it is perhaps not surprising that so many of them are visited by their guides at a very tender age and told that when they are adults, they will understand. It seems a rather odd procedure, but doubtless it serves some purpose, if only to make it less of a shock when they are subsequently briefed on their role.

Interestingly, this is something the Star People have in common with the UFO contactees and abductees we shall meet in Chapter Five. Many of them, too, receive "previews" during childhood of their later roles as involuntary guests of the aliens. This may, simply be the otherworldly forces making sure of their human associates. On the other hand, a psychologist might think that all these people who claim to have been contacted during childhood share a common psychological disposition. Whether that disposition is bestowed on them by the aliens or springs from the depths of their personalities is another question.

Most extraterrestrials on Earth who realize their true nature are convinced that they have a mission to accomplish. One that I met told me that she had exchanged bodies with a 12-year old Earth girl because she had a vital mission to carry out. She was the captain of a crew, a person whose job description sounded very similar to that of James Kirk, captain of *Star Trek*'s "Enterprise". Indeed, I was privileged to be present when she was reunited with a member of her crew, a Texan woman who was attending the same get-together. The two women immediately recognized each other as ETs (extraterrestrials), which was nice. She told me, not without humour, about the difficulties of adjusting from being an ET to being an Earth person. But there are compensations, it seems. Another Star Person, Inid, says that the human sex procedure is one of the "perks" of being incarnate in a physical Earthly body.

Some Wanderers have very specific roles to play. Vikram was attending a channeling meeting when he suddenly realized that he was a member of the Council of Twelve that the speaker was channeling a message about. The Council of Twelve is connected with Ashtar Command, an extraterrestrial organization that has many links to Earth people. A well-known American contactee, George Van Tassel of California, was privileged to receive many messages from the same source, as have other contactees. Inid—the alien who finds Earth sex such fun—is certain that "at one time, she was the sole representative on Earth of a confederation of extraterrestrial races."

What seems odd, though, is that—setting aside the references to Benjamin Franklin and Thomas Jefferson—none of these Star People seem to be actually doing anything to justify their claim to be on a mission. Here they are, supposed to be saving our planet, and, according to Mandelker:

> ...for these people, time is spent ...[engaging in] reading, meditation, channeling, group membership, personal spiritual exploration ... these were the activities that I heard mentioned most often. About a third of those I spoke with said they felt closer to nature, even to animal and plant life, than they did to people. And about a third of those who hail From Elsewhere surprised me by stating they simply didn't feel very connected to people at all and didn't think much about it. They enjoy their solitude and have no deep yearning for personal relations.

This is all very well for the spiritual development of the individual Star Persons, but it doesn't sound as if it's going to help our planet very much. Mandelker tells us that there is a tendency for the Wanderers, once they become aware of their destiny, to move into caring professions like social work and teaching. That's better than making bombs and killing people, but is it really worth coming all the way from a distant planet just to become a social worker on Earth?

Interestingly, though, this again mirrors closely the experiences of the abductees we will meet in Chapter Five. In 1980, during the early days of abductions, American authors Judith and Alan Gansberg made a study of the after-effects of being abducted. They found a strong tendency for abductees to direct their lives towards healing, teaching and caring. This is certainly borne out by those that I have met personally. John and Sue Day, who were abducted at Aveley, England, on October 27, 1974, experienced similar after effects. John had a breakdown and had to give up his job, eventually finding more congenial work helping the mentally handicapped. He took to writing poems, gave up smoking, and became a vegetarian. His wife, Sue, followed a similar course.

Mandelker also tells of two women who shared an apartment in San Francisco. Although both were lesbians, they were not on good terms. However, both were undergoing past-life therapy, and among the revelations each experienced was that they were both extraterrestrials. It created a bond between them, enabling them to enter a shared relationship, and their former mutual hostility turned into a love affair. Once again, one must ask that while this may have been wonderful for them, was it for this that they were sent to Earth?

How do you know if you are an extraterrestrial? Steiger and Mandelker both provide lists of the tell tale clues, and other lists have appeared elsewhere. Here are some of the indicators. You are most likely a Star Person if:

- You feel somehow "different" from others.
- You find life on Earth boring and meaningless.
- You dreamed about UFOs and space as a child.
- Your family have always thought you were "a bit odd."
- You feel your parents aren't your true parents.
- You are not interested in money.
- You see good in people, to the point of being naive.
- You sincerely wish to improve the world.

RIGHT: *At Aveley, in Essex, England in 1974, John and Susan Day and their child are abducted and taken with their car, aboard a UFO, where the adults undergo a physical examination by the aliens.*

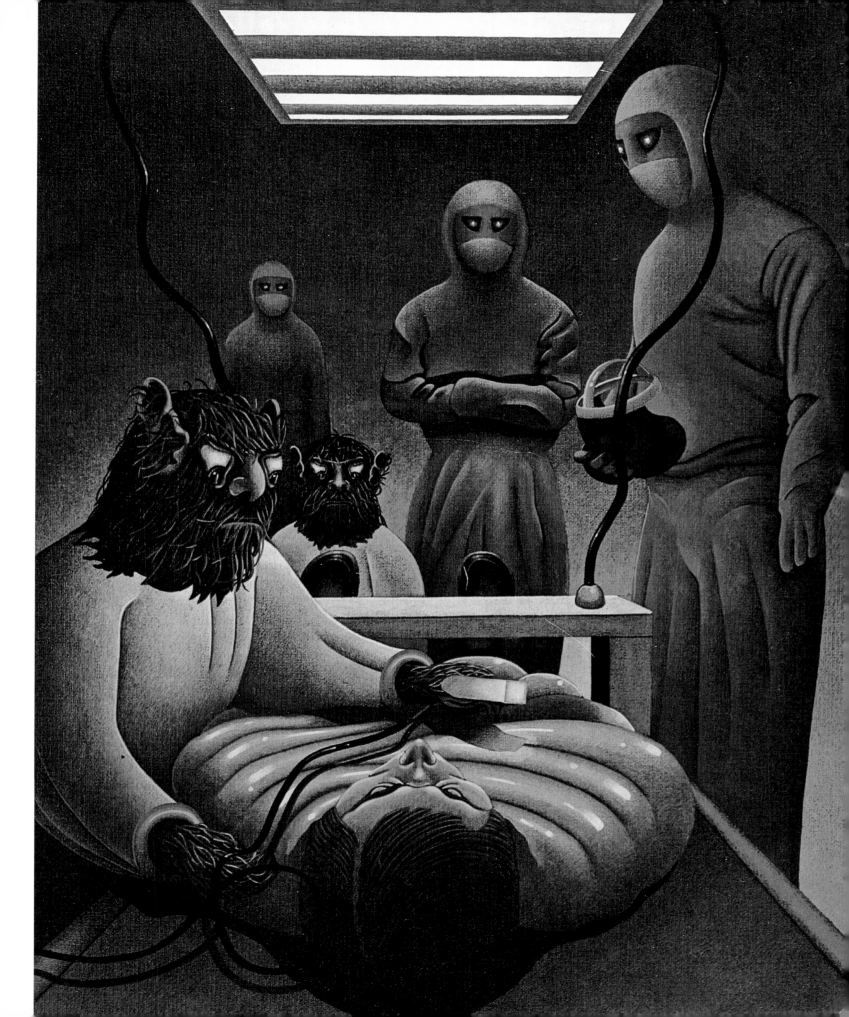

- You easily get lost in fantasy fiction.
- You feel drawn towards Atlantis, Lemuria and other civilizations.
- You are interested in enhancing your spiritual powers.
- You don't require as much sleep as most people.
- You are hypersensitive.
- You are subject to headaches and migraines.
- You had unseen friends as a child.
- You seem to recall previous lives.

Steiger himself, as we have noted, felt early in life that he was somehow "different" and this led to the realization that he is a Star Person. He was lucky enough to meet and marry another. Fellow author Scott Mandelker, too, has come to recognize that he is a Star Person. When we look at contactee and abduction experiences, we shall see that many who investigate abductions discover, in the course of investigating the experiences of others, that they themselves have been abducted.

However, identifying yourself as a Star Person is very much up to the individual: For example, how do you define "feeling different from others" when each of us is unique? As a result, many Wanderers do not feel totally confident that they are extraterrestrials. There is no exclusive biological indicator such as pointed ears or webbed feet that would at once settle the matter; instead, what is felt is a "subjective certainty." Unfortunately, while this may satisfy the person in question, it is not likely to carry much weight with others—unless, of course, they are themselves extraterrestrial.

The realization that one is a Star Person is similar to religious conversion—a similarity we shall notice in other contexts. It varies with the individual, ranging from a gradual realization that he or she is "not like other people" to a sudden flash of recognition.

However—as William James observed in connection with religious conversion—even when there seems to be a sudden moment of recognition, there has generally been a long process of subconscious development before the realization the surfaces. Clearly, this ties in with the childhood conditioning we have referred to.

THE LORDS OF FLAME

If we go along with people's claims that they have extraterrestrial origins, we have to ask "Where do they come from?" It turns out that they all claim to come from actual civilizations on other worlds. Various locations are mentioned. Betty is from Antares in the Scorpio constellation, but with a base station on Venus. Julie and Linda are both from

... and in that moment he knew he was a Space Brother sent to awaken humanity

"A Space Brother sent to awaken humanity." Illustrator Gwen Fulton pokes gentle fun at the "Star People."

Sirius. But who, precisely, is masterminding the operation? There are references to a Council that meets on Saturn. This conjures a picture of Council members arriving in their spaceships—like earth committee members in their chauffeur-driven cars—and congregating in some celestial boardroom.

But probably it isn't like that. If these people are so much more technologically advanced than us, they would not need to "meet" anywhere. Virtual conferencing via computer should make a physical gathering unnecessary. Those who manage the Universe will do so without needing to leave their home planets.

The Star People seem to be assigned guides, who have the job, first, of telling them during childhood of their future mission, and then reinforcing that assurance when necessary. But the guides are never very explicit about who they are; they don't say exactly where in the universe they come from, and they are disturbingly vague about what they have in mind for Earth.

However benevolent these aliens may be, there is no assurance that they really know what is best for us Earth people. There is always the possibility that what they say doesn't reflect their real intentions and that this is in fact the beginning of a sinister plot to take over the Earth.

Some Star People have received insights concerning the ultimate authority behind the project. Dr. Elsa von Eckartsberg—who teaches German, Comparative Literature and Stress Management at Harvard—claims to come from Venus, and is confident that we Earth people will connect ourselves to "the cosmic dimensions" in the not-too-distant future. She believes that "The Lords of Flame" projected sparks of consciousness into mindless men and awakened the intellect within them.

This takes us back to the ancient astronauts, and the ancient legends of gods who brought knowledge of the arts and civilization to mankind. One of the great enigmas of life is how and when Man developed the self-consciousness which distinguishes him other living creatures. Some proponents of the ancient astronauts scenario credit extraterrestrials with this achievement, and if Dr. von Eckartsberg is correct, they are right to do so. It wasn't the result of evolution; it was literally a gift from the gods. If this is the case, it is they who are responsible for the fact that things haven't turned out as well as they might. Perhaps that is why they feel the need to send missionaries to our planet to get us back onto the right track.

According to Brad and Francie Steiger, the ancestors of the Star People first came to Earth about 40000 B.C. During most of that time, they kept a close control over human activities. It was only during the last 4000 years—what we think of as recorded history—that we have been left to run our own lives, for better or worse. Unfortunately, this means that there is no historical record of the Star People's existence. We have to rely on what people like Francie Steiger tell us.

Fortunately, if there's one thing the Star People are happy to do, it is to give us messages from the beyond, even though they are usually sadly short on fact and often contradictory. Francie Steiger tells us that what happened to the aliens was that the messages "etherealized" into "pure energy." We are told that "they joyously accepted their elevation from physically dense matter to a finer vibratory frequency." They were not so preoccupied with their newly-found transcendence that they neglected their responsibility towards the Earth people, however. This is why people like Francie and Brad Steiger and Scott Mandelker have been sent—to "accelerate the process for the dwellers of Earth"—so that we, too, may rise to a higher and less material state.

We have already noted the similarities between the Star People's experiences and those of contactees and abductees. There are also similarities with other types of experience. The seeing of visions is a frequent accompaniment to religious conversion, and to the lives of those individuals, such as Saint Teresa of Avila, who are called to a higher life of religious mysticism. Visions seem to play much the same role in both cases.

Another curious similarity is exemplified by a Star Person who asked to be called "Barbara," who has had not one "walk-in," but three—very like the experiences of people who suffer with multiple personalities.

The "walk-ins" play different roles. The first "walk-in" led her to break with her mother, but the third healed the old family traumas. Once again, the thought arises that if the point of these extraterrestrials being on Earth rather than home—wherever that may be—is to save our world from catastrophe, they should have better things to do than sort out family problems. That is particularly true in this case, as it is a problem for which Barbara was initially responsible. Barbara had told her husband that she was an extraterrestrial over a candlelit restaurant meal. He was unconvinced, and after an argument, walked out of the restaurant and out of her life. Perhaps it was necessary for the accomplishment of Barbara's "mission" that she be freed from the encumbrance of a husband. However, to achieve her freedom from all constraints, including those of family, Barbara also told her little girl, "You are not my daughter." This can't have been very nice for the child and seems a strange way for a superior person who is trying to improve the world to behave. On the other hand, it *is* quite characteristic of a person who is facing a personal crisis.

If the Star People really are who they think they are, then this is of momentous importance to mankind. One of the Star People, Barbara Marx Hubbard from Washington, D.C., feels "a deep consciousness of having volunteered to come to this planet at this moment of evolutionary transition." If Star People like her are truly here to help our planet and its inhabitants solve our problems, it is a welcome change from hostile aliens who want to colonize us or enslave us

Private visions, such as this manifestation of the Sacred Heart of Jesus, play an important part in the spiritual life of mystics such as Teresa of Avila.

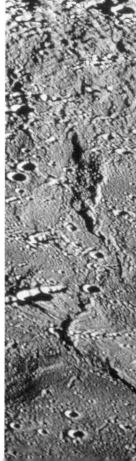

or wipe us out so they can seize our planet.

Providing the Star People are genuine, then we can at least say that they are probably doing more good than harm. But some aspects of the Star People phenomenon make one uneasy: Some have already been mentioned—the concern with trivia and the lack of any marked progress. Another is the fact that virtually all of them are Americans. Perhaps the rest, scattered over the globe, are Sleeping Wanderers who don't yet know their heritage. Maybe if Brad and Francie Steiger's books were to be translated into Swahili, we'd see more extraterrestrials coming forth. If the Star People are here to change conditions on Earth, Africa needs them even more than the United States.

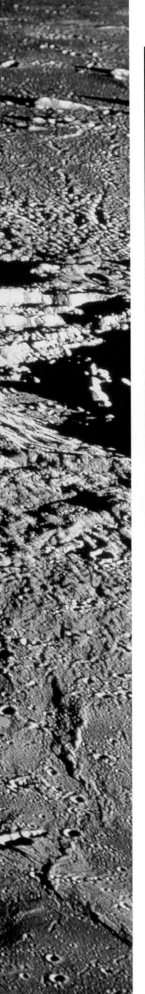

Secret societies, such as the Freemasons (seen here), the Rosicrucians and the Templars are often suspected of possessing "secret wisdom" handed down from one generation to the next.

WHY NOW?

If there are indeed millions of "Star People" living among us, and if they have been doing so all along, it is odd that it is only in the late Twentieth Century that they have been revealed.

There may be a good reason for this. We have already noted the ages-old belief that there exist schools of occult teaching—the Rosicrucians, the Templars, the Masons, the Synarchy, and hundreds more—who are believed to be the guardians of a body of secret knowledge. This knowledge is held by just a few, who carry on the tradition from one generation to the next, and who are, supposedly, waiting for something momentous to occur. Could these be Star People?

Another theory is that it is only now, when man has acquired so much new and dangerous knowledge, that it has

become appropriate, even vital, for the rest of the universe to step in. Often, UFO contactees are told by the aliens that Earth has become a source of concern to the rest of the galaxy.

A third alternative is that mankind has developed intellectually, and now the time has come to graduate to a more spiritual awareness of things. According to this view—which we will come across again in connection with the contactees—mankind is being prepared, gently and unobtrusively, for a total change.

Those who promote this possibility point to "New Age" thinking, to the upsurge in concern for the environment, and to the widespread interest in alternative medicine, folklore and the like. Which is all very well, but if outside forces could put a Star Person in the White House in 1801, it seems a shame that they don't do it again.

"GODS AND SPACEMEN THROUGHOUT HISTORY"

In a book with this title, and six other volumes, author W. Raymond Drake has collected evidence that extraterrestrial visits to our planet did not cease when the last of the ancient astronauts left, nor did they begin with the flying saucers of our own day. According to Drake, and many other researchers, there has been a succession of incidents which, rightly interpreted, point to the fact that these phenomena have been continuous throughout human history.

Unfortunately, the phrase "rightly interpreted" indicates the weakness of the case. Strange lights in the sky, accounts of aerial battles, ships seen in the heavens—these are all intriguing, but we can never be certain that there isn't a more down-to-earth explanation.

One possible explanation is that in earlier times, we didn't have the same capacity to recognize evidence of otherworldly visits. Perhaps it is only now, with our awareness of UFOs, that we can look back and see that they have been with us throughout history. Two French researchers, Olivyer and Boëdec, have searched through the *Histoires Admirables et Memorables of Simon Goulart* (1543–1628), a French chronicler who in 1600 made a record of all the remarkable events of the prior century. They found 93 unusual aerial phenomena:

July 4, 1554: There appeared in the air, about 10 p.m., in the region known as the High Palatinate of the Rhine, towards the Bohemian forest, two men in full armor, one considerably taller than the other,

having on his belly a brightly shining star, and a flaming sword in his hand, as also had the smaller one. They began a violent fight, at the end of which the smaller one was beaten down and could not move, whereupon a chair was brought for the victor, on which he sat, and never ceased to threaten with the sword he held in his hand the one who was lying at his feet, as if at any moment he would strike him. Finally, the two of them disappeared.

What are we to make of this remarkably detailed account? Unfortunately, we are not told how many witnesses observed it, but I doubt if Goulart would have thought it worth recording if it was a single person's vision. It is hard to believe that everyday celestial objects—stars and planets—could have given rise to so circumstantial an account.

Several authors wanting to establish UFOs as an ongoing historical phenomenon have seized on such

accounts as evidence. Indeed, Olivyer and Boëdec themselves subtitle their book, "The UFO Wave of 1500 to 1600." Belgian writer Christiane Piens compiled one of the more thoughtful collections. She concluded her 1977 book by writing:

In their broad outlines, the ancient cases are no different—apart from the frequency of their occurrence—from the modern ones. If we have succeeded in demonstrating their existence, we can no longer see the UFO phenomenon as a recent event. But this raises the complication that the beings (are they always the same species?) have been visiting us for many centuries without making official contact with mankind. We have to face the fact: The problem of non-contact is a great puzzle.

Since then, Piens says, she has become less sure that these sightings are evidence of extraterrestrial visitation. But that doesn't alter the fact that these

In July and August, 1566, curious aerial phenomena were seen over Basel, Switzerland. The fact that they occurred at sunrise and sunset indicates a natural phenomenon, but others see them as early UFOs.

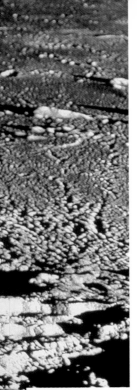

events occurred, and that chroniclers thought them worth recording. They serve as a reminder that strange things have been seen in Earth's skies throughout history.

As with the mysteries of ancient civilizations, these early UFOs present a problem on more than one level. Did they really take place as recorded? If so, how are they to be interpreted? The dual problem is presented strikingly in the following case.

ALIENS
BUZZ NICE

If certain documents in the city's archives can be taken at face value,

something happened in 1608 in the Italian town of Nizza—today the French city of Nice—that strongly suggests a visit by extraterrestrial spacecraft.

Around 8 p.m. on August 5, 1608, the citizens of Nice saw three luminous shapes over the Baie des Anges, heading at high speed towards their city. Arriving in front of the citadel that overlooked the harbor, the three objects suddenly stopped, then began to maneuver slowly about 3 feet over the water. The low altitude and the slowness of their movements meant the watchers could examine the strange arrivals in detail. What they saw changed their curiosity into anxiety.

The machines were of long oval shape, flattened, and topped with a sort of mast. Hovering almost motionless, they caused the water beneath them to

seethe, giving off a dense orange-yellow vapor accompanied by an infernal noise. From one of the machines a living being emerged, followed by a second. They were approximately human in appearance, dressed in a kind of red outfit with what seemed to be silvery scales. Their heads were huge, and two luminous circular openings took the place of eyes. Holding two tubes attached vertically to a kind of harness, they plunged into the water up to their hips and proceeded to move around their machines for a couple of hours. Then, near 10 p.m., the two visitors got back into their machine, and with a formidable rumbling, all three moving objects raced off towards the east, becoming in a few seconds three luminous points in the starry sky.

For the people of Nizza, these

In 1608, mysterious flying machines approached the Italian Mediterranean town of Nizza—today's Nice, France— and greatly alarmed the populace.

From the harbor of Nizza (now Nice), observers see the strange flying machines settle on the surface of the Baie des Anges.

portents could only be a warning from God. Terrified, they processed through the streets carrying the figure of Jesus, praying and imploring forgiveness for their sins, until the next day dawned with no further sign from their mysterious visitors.

But the visitors had not gone far. On August 22, they appeared further round the coast, at Genoa, Italy. But the Genovese, who had heard what had happened at Nizza, reacted more violently. From the citadel, a salvo of artillery fire volleyed towards the three craft. Some 800 cannonballs were fired in hope of driving the visitors away. They did not cause the slightest damage to the machines, though, nor distract them from their maneuvers. However, it seems that the gunfire did discourage the occupants, for none emerged into the open on this occasion.

After about an hour, one of the machines left the others and positioned itself over the town. The populace went into panic, and many injuries occurred. Several deaths were reported. Some people were trampled by crowds, others overcome by fear, but some were also said to have died as a result of radiations emitted by the vessel. After a while, the machine rejoined the others, and all three headed to the east at top speed.

On August 25, a single vessel appeared above Martigues, a fishing village close to Nizza, and maneuvered overhead for an hour and a half. Two people got out, and were similar in appearance to the two who had been seen at Nizza. They flew around their craft. It seemed to the watchers as if they were engaged in a kind of airborne duel.

This was the last manifestation of the machines. But the following week there were abundant falls of colored rain in the area—red rain, like blood. It was certainly considered to be blood by the locals, who saw it as a warning from God, as any unusual event tended to be interpreted at that time. A more prosaic explanation is that the local soil, rich in bauxite, has a red dust which may have been stirred up by the movements of the machines. For forty days, churches were packed with crowds begging to be spared whatever disaster the mysterious machines might portend.

What are we to make of all this? The entries in the local archives, from which these accounts are taken, are couched in the language of the time, and much of the wording is ambiguous. This was an age when there was widespread belief in aerial visions. Impressive accounts of "armies in the sky" frequently occur in ancient chronicles, and there is no doubt that ignorant people were apt to misinterpret natural

French astronomer Camille Flammarion, writing in 1904. Who should know better? For if people all over the world—in 1904 as in 1998—are talking about Mars, it is in large part his doing. In his popular books and articles, Flammarion for many years presented life on Mars as a scientific possibility. With so respectable an authority to guide them, every man or woman in the street felt authorized to contemplate the prospect that, any day now, we would find that we humans are not the only intelligent inhabitants of the universe.

One day in 1894, professor Auguste Lemaître of Geneva, Switzerland told his colleague Théodore Flournoy, professor of psychology at Geneva University, about a remarkable spirit medium, in the same city, whose career he had been following for some six years. Flournoy, intrigued by what he heard, attended a seance with Catherine Elise Muller (named "Hélène Smith" in the accounts), which led to an investigation spread over several years. This culminated in a book which has become one of the great classics of psychological literature.

Muller was a Swiss woman in her thirties, who had a responsible job in a store in Geneva. She was intelligent, gifted and modest. In her leisure time, she was as a non-professional medium who, in her seances, described what she saw and heard and what was communicated to her by spirits through rapped messages. Though Flournoy maintained a consistently skeptical attitude, openly disagreeing with Muller about how her experiences should be interpreted, he nonetheless retained her friendship and cooperation.

Muller received a series of astonishing revelations that caused her to travel spiritually, in time and place. In one scenario, she was controlled by Victor Hugo; in another by a certain Leopold, who was really Cagliostro. Later, there was Marie Antoinette. What made them exceptional was that these were not simply "messages" from the past, but episodes in which Muller actively participated—living scenes and events that are vividly described as first-person experiences. This was true of all Muller's experiences—those on Mars as well as those in ancient India or

The strange occupants of the flying machines that invaded Nizza (Nice) in 1608.

happenings. But these detailed observations seem to be more than that. Could so many people, in three separate locations, have imagined the whole affair, space ships and all, at a time when aerial flight was not even considered as a possibility?

On the other hand, if these events really did take place as described, it is a remarkable event worthy of a place in history. Why haven't we heard more about it? One reason may be that the event is so ambiguous. There is no real interaction between the visitors and the Earth people, and the purpose of the aliens' visit remains obscure.

The same is true of all the anomalous events which have been seized upon as evidence of continued extraterrestrial visits. There is no pattern, no evidence of purpose and, above all, no contact.

But this was to change dramatically as the Nineteenth Century progressed. The growth of spiritualism, following on the experiences of the Fox sisters, led to new channels of communication with other worlds. For the most part,

this communication was with the surviving dead, but some of it seemed to go further, and to open up ways to access other worlds.

THE GREAT MARTIAN TERROR

Mars is now as much a subject of conversation as politics or art. In Buenos Aires, Mexico, Caracas, as well as in Paris, St. Petersburg, Budapest and Stockholm, the latest telescopic investigations are discussed, for it is known that this neighboring world is actually approaching the earth … The discovery of canal-like lines in the planet has led to the question of possible inhabitants of Mars, and of the probability of a future communication with them.

The words are those of the eminent

Eighteenth Century France.

To explain how Muller's Martian adventures started, we must go back to Flammarion, who had recently asserted:

What marvels the science of the future is keeping for our successors! Who will dare to deny that Martian humanity and terrestrial humanity may one day enter into communication one with the other?

Flammarion's ideas had been much discussed among Muller's circle of friends. One day in 1894, Lemaître expressed the wish that communication with Mars might really come about. This casual remark was clearly the trigger which sparked Muller's space adventure, for she prefaced her first revelations with the words, "Lemaître, here is what you wanted so much!"

What Muller then proceeded to do, over a long period, was to produce a chronicle of Martian adventures. Because she personally participated in them, the encounters had all the clarity of first-hand descriptions. Some took place while she was asleep and some while she was awake, though doubtless in some altered state. So involved was Muller in her Martian experiences and so continuous was the succession of episodes that Flournoy came to the conclusion that *a part of Muller was "living" her Martian existence every moment of the day or night.* Whenever she passed into another state—whether trance or sleep— she switched from her terrestrial existence to her Martian existence.

For example, on September 5, 1896, Muller was awakened by a high wind that she thought might be harmful to the flowers she had put out on her bedroom windowsill. After she rescued her flowers, instead of going straight back to sleep, she sat on her bed— except that it was no longer a bed and it had become a bench. In the place of her window, looking out on the storm-swept streets of Geneva, she now saw before her a landscape crowded with exotic people. The bench was at the edge of a lake of pinkish-blue, with a bridge whose edges were transparent and constructed of yellow tubes, like organ pipes. She saw a male figure who was carrying a small machine like a lamp, which emitted flames and enabled him to fly. The vision lasted

some 25 minutes, during which time Muller was convinced that she was awake, not asleep.

As episode succeeded episode, they built up into a fairly comprehensive picture of life on Mars—how the Martians traveled, what their homes were like, and so on. What gives the visions their power, though, was the vividness of Muller's descriptions. For example, we learn about Martian flowers from the detailed description she gave of the table ornaments at a great feast which took place in one of her visions. So clearly did she remember these scenes that she was able to depict them in detailed drawings.

But the most remarkable aspect of her Martian experiences—the feature which makes her case of unique interest for our understanding of the human mind—is that Muller learned to speak the Martian language. This was revealed when, after having been inspired to draw a Martian house, she received what seemed to her a meaningless message:

Dode ne chi haudan te mechemetiche astane ke de me veche.

It wasn't till six weeks later that her Martian friends explained to her in a vision, what this message was telling her—that the house she had drawn

Catherine Muller's own drawing of herself, accompanied by her guardian angel.

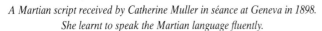

A Martian script received by Catherine Muller in séance at Geneva in 1898.
She learnt to speak the Martian language fluently.

impression. After an interval of weeks, she would use the same word with the same meaning. Nor were the words arbitrary, as though they had no meaning outside that particular utterance. It was a fully structured language with a coherent syntax. Indeed, it was precisely that fact which bothered Flournoy—the Martian language was structured in the same way as French, Muller's native tongue.

The coincidence of Martians speaking a language structured in the same way as French was too great for Flournoy. He concluded that, incredible as it seemed, the language had been created by Muller herself. Not, of course, in her conscious mind; this would have been virtually impossible for someone of her educational level, even given time, and there had been no time for preparation. The Martian language had made its appearance almost overnight. It was clear to Flournoy that it was a subconscious operation, but he found that even more significant than if she had indeed learned the language from her Martian friends. Muller's command of the Martian language showed that her subconscious mind was capable of creating an entire, grammatically consistent language and holding it in memory as surely as the language she had been speaking since she was a child.

Needless to say, this is not how Muller herself saw the matter. Though she did not for a minute believe that she had visited Mars in her physical body, she was convinced that she had visited Mars in spirit. The clarity of her descriptions, the wealth of detail she was able to provide—which to Flournoy were evidence of her remarkable subconscious creativity—were to her convincing proof that she had indeed traveled to Mars in some manner. As interesting as Muller's Martian adventures would be to the psychologist, they are hardly less fascinating to the sociologist. For they were not an isolated phenomenon, but occurred at a time when the "idea" of Mars was very much in the public's mind. There can be no doubt that Muller's Martian wanderings were inspired by the public context created by Flammarion and others.

belonged to Astane. It was further revealed that he had been the male figure she had seen with the mini-jet in her waking vision. From this point on, the Martian language made its appearance in her communications more and more.

The extraordinary thing is that Muller used the Martian language consistently. There was no question that this was a "nonsense language," in which she just jabbered to make an

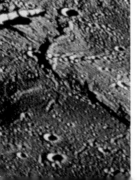

MRS. CLEAVELAND

In 1901 the most eminent psychical researcher in America was probably James Hyslop, a professor of philosophy at New York's Columbia University. That year, he was contacted by the Reverend Cleaveland, a clergyman, whose wife had experienced some psychic phenomena which he thought Hyslop might find interesting.

Mrs. Cleaveland (known as "Mrs. Smead" in the accounts) had been having psychic experiences all her life—seeing apparitions, doing automatic writing and so on. In 1895, at about the same time that Catherine Muller started her Martian adventures, Mrs. Cleaveland began to receive messages from some dead relatives. Three of them were her own children, and a fourth was a brother. Inevitably, one of the first things Mrs. Cleaveland wanted to know was where they were. She received an utterly unexpected answer from one of her daughters, Maude. She learned that "some spirits are on Earth and some are on other worlds."

Five weeks later, the brother reported that Maude had gone to Mars. Soon, Mrs. Cleaveland was receiving messages from Maude that gave an account of her life on Mars. Compared with the vivid communications of Catherine Muller, these accounts were all on a very simple level. However, a detailed map was drawn showing various zones and naming them, and Maude confirmed that the canals of Mars were indeed constructed artificially by the Martians. This was very interesting, because the question of the canals of Mars was the subject of lively debate at that time. Indeed, articles on the subject had appeared earlier that very year in the *Atlantic Monthly*, though the Cleavelands insisted that they had not read them.

Maude was able to tell her mother details of life on the planet and of the lifestyle of the Martians. Specimens of the Martian language were provided: "Mare" = man, "Maren" = men, "Kare" = woman, "Karen" = women. Though not nearly so developed as Catherine Muller's Martian tongue, it was structured like an earthly language, though in Maude Cleaveland's case, it resembled English, rather than French. Indeed, it resembled English more closely than it did the Martian language spoken by Muller. Of course, just as there are many different languages spoken here on Earth, so it may be that there is more than one language spoken on Mars. However it is a curious coincidence that French-speaking Muller's Martian language resembled French, whereas English-speaking Cleaveland's Martian language was similar to English.

Maude gave a particularly interesting account of an airship, a propeller-driven vessel with flapping, inflated wings. The power source was electricity. This was a period when there was intense activity in aerial research, reflected in the "great airship scare" which swept through America at this time. Two years later, the Wright brothers would demonstrate the first airplane, but all kinds of alternative methods of flight were being discussed, and it is interesting that Cleaveland's messages reflect this excitement.

In many ways, life on Mars, as described by Maude, was not so very

Two Martians drawn by Mrs. Cleaveland, as communicated by her daughter, Maude, who went to live on Mars after her death.

WILLS'S CIGARETTES.

IMAGINARY LANDSCAPE ON MARS.

At the start of the Twentieth Century, it was widely supposed that Mars was crossed by "canals," and this was confirmed by alleged communicators from the planet.

different from life on Earth. The houses, furnishings, clothes and so on were variations on ours, just as they had been in Catherine Muller's descriptions. Nor would we have found it difficult to adapt to a Martian lifestyle. Aristocratic young humans might not feel too happy about having to work in the fields, but all young Martians were required to do so until they married.

Though Hyslop was apt to be a believer when it came to communication from spirits, he was not so credulous when it was a matter of messages from otherworldly beings. Like Théodore Flournoy in Geneva, Hyslop came to the conclusion that these message came from a secondary personality of Mrs. Cleaveland:

> We find in such cases evidence that we need not attribute fraud to the normal consciousness, and we discover automatic processes of mentation that may be equally acquitted of fraudulent intent while we are also free from the obligation to accept the phenomena at their assumed value. Their most extraordinary characteristic is the extent to which they imitate the organizing intelligence of a normal mind, and the perfection of their impersonation of spirits.

HÉLÈNE PREISWERK

A third person from the same period who reported contact with alien beings was another young Swiss woman, Hélène Preiswerk, both a cousin and a patient of the Zurich psychologist Carl Gustav Jung. In 1899, Helene was a somewhat disturbed 15-year-old girl. Her family history included many relatives who had experienced hallucinations and other visionary experiences, somnambulism, prophetic utterances, hysterical episodes and nervous heart attacks. Though she herself displayed no outwardly hysterical symptoms, Hélène was moody, absent-minded and distracted.

Like Catherine Muller in Geneva, Hélène had found a distraction from her unsatisfying home life in spiritualism. She, too, turned out to be an excellent medium. Jung was invited to witness for himself the states of "somnambulism" in which Helene performed remarkable feats of impersonation.

Even when not in spirit trance, Hélène would report visits by "spirits"— "shining white figures who detached themselves from the foggy

brightness, wrapped in white veil-like robes …" They were "generally of a pleasant nature." However, she also had terrifying demonic visions. Good or evil, she accepted them as the sort of thing a spirit medium must encounter in the course of her activities. She was very happy in what she believed to be her true vocation, and she made it clear to Jung that she was unshakeably convinced of the reality of her visions:

> I do not know if what the spirits say and teach me is true, nor do I know if they really are the people they call themselves; but that my spirits exist is beyond question. I see them before me, I can touch them. I speak to them about everything I wish, as naturally as I'm talking to you. They must be real.

Not surprisingly, she refused to accept that these experiences meant that she was in any way ill. She was hurt by Jung's scepticism, so, like Flournoy had with Catherine Muller, Jung learned to be discreetly diplomatic with his subject.

Hélène's trances frequently involved journeys to spirit worlds in the beyond— "that space between the stars which people think is empty, but which really contains countless spirit worlds." Some of these she was able to describe:

she told us all the peculiarities of the star-dwellers; they have no godlike souls, as men have, they pursue no science, no philosophy, but in the technical arts they are far more advanced than we are. Thus, flying machines have long been in existence on Mars; the whole of Mars is covered with canals. The canals are artificial lakes and are used for irrigation.

Hélène's account of life on Mars is less detailed than that of Catherine Muller or Maude Cleaveland. But unlike them, she had one otherworldly experience while on Earth:

She once returned from a railway journey in an extremely agitated state. We thought at first that something unpleasant must have happened to her; but finally she pulled herself together and explained that "a star-dweller had sat opposite her in the train." From the description she gave of this being, I recognized an elderly merchant I happened to know, who had a rather unsympathetic face.

Subsequently, Jung tells us, Hélène Preiswerk abandoned spiritualism, and nothing more was heard of her "star-dwellers."

MIREILLE AND THE ELECTRIC FIELDS

In 1895—the same year that Mrs. Cleaveland began to receive her messages from Mars—the noted French researcher Colonel Albert de Rochas was, like Jung, asked to help a family friend. Mireille, now age 45, had been known to him since childhood. She had a troublesome ailment, and knowing that he had success with healing by hypnosis, she hoped he could help her.

The therapy was successful, and in return, Mireille agreed to help him with his experimental work, having proved herself a good and willing hypnotic subject. Though intelligent, she was not highly educated, but she moved in circles where current ideas were discussed. Although not herself interested in the paranormal, she would

certainly have heard her friends discussing subjects such as the possibility of extraterrestrial life.

In one of her hypnotic sessions, she described how she seemed to be rising in space, which she said was brightly luminous and peopled with "phantoms." Among these, she noted a childhood friend, Victor, who had been dead for ten years. During subsequent sessions she told of visits to Mars and other planets. She was unable to give detailed descriptions—only vague references to the canals which, as we have seen, were an everyday source of discussion at the time. All she could say of the Martians was that they were physically superior to Earth people but less intelligent.

In fact, little out of the ordinary occurred until the day when, instead of telling of her own experiences, Mireille seemed to be possessed by Victor, who presented himself in the role of her guide and protector. Victor told de Rochas that he had nearly "lost" Mireille, owing to the electric fields she had to penetrate in order to reach Mars.

From that point on, Mireille served almost entirely as Victor's channel of communication. De Rochas was immediately aware when Mireille had given place to Victor. Normally, he would hold Mireille's hand while she was in a trance. Victor didn't think it right for two males to hold hands, though, and as soon as he took over Mireille's body, the hand was withdrawn. While Mireille didn't smoke, Victor did. Moreover, Victor insisted that de Rochas explain to him why he was wearing female clothing.

There may have been another reason why Victor found it embarrassing to hold hands. Describing life on other planets, he explained that it is primarily arms above all that are the organs of affection, and manual expressions of tender feelings are the rule.

Consequently, the arms tend to become highly developed, and are sometimes mistaken for wings when angels and other spirits are seen. This was a stupid idea, Victor pointed out, for ethereal beings such as angels and spirits had no need of physical wings to fly!

Practical comments of this kind were typical of Victor's no-nonsense communications. De Rochas soon found it quite natural to hold

conversations with Victor—speaking through Mireille—as if he was indeed the living, intelligent being he claimed to be. This led to some amusing misunderstandings:

One day, I revealed to Victor my doubts as to the reality of his existence outside the imagination of Mireille. I told him that what made me suspicious was that the alleged communicators, though they might be talking about the same subject, often contradicted one another.

"Happily," Victor replied, "your doubts as to whether I exist don't prevent me from existing! As for the matter of contradiction, you need to distinguish carefully where the revelations are coming from. If they are from a spirit which is more or less detached from its astral body, it can and often will take for reality what is actually no more than the objectivization of its own thoughts and memories. This is why every ecstatic has visions which conform to his own religious beliefs.

"You are mistaken if you think there exists any profound difference between the world of the living and that of the dead, or any hiatus separating them. The spirit life continues beyond the tomb with no more transition than if, in the life of flesh, the inhabitants of a house being at first gathered in a ground-floor room dimly lit by narrow windows, a few should separate from the others and go upstairs to where the rooms are illuminated with light."

Though Victor put up strong arguments for his existence, de Rochas retained his doubts. But as in the case of Catherine Muller's Martian language, even though the facts may not be what they seem to be, that does not make them any the less remarkable. If, as de Rochas suspected, Victor was a projection created by Mireille's own unconscious, it was remarkable that this poorly-educated lady possessed the sophistication to support his fantasy existence with such clearly thought-out arguments.

In the 1890s, Mars was an idea whose time had come. It inspired not only scientific speculation, but also individual fantasies claimed as actual experience. If this was true of "the great Martian terror," we must ask

MICHEL CARROUGES

LES APPARITIONS DE MARTIENS

FAYARD

ourselves whether it may be equally true of other claimed experiences that mimic prevailing notions.

THE MARTIAN MYTH

The fiction writers knew they were creating a mythical Mars peopled by mythical Martians. The spiritualists believed they were telling the truth about Mars, though most of us will probably agree with Flournoy, Jung, Hyslop and de Rochas that we need look no farther than the limitless creativity of the subconscious human mind. As for the scientists, though they based their speculations on fact and observation, they could sometimes be just as wide of the mark as the others. The American astronomer Percival Lowell believed that Mars was criss-crossed with canals, but the introduction of more powerful telescopes has shown this to be false. The Martians that Flammarion hoped we would one day meet have been proven non-existent, as was probably always the case.

But the Martian myth is more than a mere weaving of wishes and imaginings. The fact that Catherine Muller, Mrs. Cleaveland, Hélène Preiswerk and Mireille could each create a personal Mars of the mind is an impressive tribute to the human imagination. Moreover, the myth has shown a remarkable survival value. In France, the term "Martien" is virtually a synonym for extraterrestrials. When, in 1963, Michel Carrouges wrote his telling study of the UFO phenomenon, he entitled it *Les Apparitions de Martiens* in tribute to the myth.

So, although the term "Martien" was frequently used by the French during the great wave of sightings they experienced in 1954, this did not mean that they really believed the UFOs were of Martian origin. However, in that same year was published in England one of the few UFO books to claim that the extraterrestrials do really come from Mars. An amateur ornithologist named Cedric Allingham

was bird-watching in the north of Scotland when he saw and photographed a UFO and met its pilot, who told him he came from Mars. The photograph Allingham took, as the pilot walked back to his spaceship, shows a very human-like being, not at all like the monsters dreamed up by science fiction illustrators.

Cedric Allingham disappeared from the public eye after his book was published and, indeed, there are allegations that he never really existed. Another theory persisted that he existed under the name of Patrick Moore, a

popular English astronomer with a reputation for practical joking. Moore has always denied this allegation, and so the possibility remains that this is a genuine photograph. If so, it is probably the only photograph of a Martian in existence.

Even if the Martians do not exist outside our own imaginations, we should not belittle them. They have provided us with a wonderful "straw man" to embody our hopes and our fears. H. G. Wells' great fantasy still has the power to spark our imaginations, as demonstrated by the one of the latest

In 1954, Cedric Allingham, an ornithologist, took this unique photograph alleged to be a Martian near Lossiemouth in northern Scotland.

LEFT: *In France, Martians were the archetypal aliens, so the term covered all extraterrestrials.*

The success of the film Independence Day, *and others like it, is proof that the myth of hostile aliens is still a powerful source of anxiety.*

reinterpretations, the blockbuster movie *Independence Day*.

For Catherine Muller and the others, the Martians symbolized the wider, richer realms that lie beyond the reach of our earthly senses. It seems that we all subconsciously crave the excitement which Barthel and Brucker—analyzing the French 1954 wave—named *La Grande Peur Martienne* or the great Martian terror!

THE MARTIAN STEREOTYPE

In 1997, American writer Patrick Huyghe published *A Field Guide to Extraterrestrials*, which seeks to do for flying saucer occupants what bird-spotters' guides do for birds. In other

words, it identifies and classifies the various types of aliens that witnesses have reported so that we, too— should we be fortunate enough to meet one—will know what species we are encountering.

Huyghe is careful to point out that he can only tell us what the witnesses themselves report. Often, they were alone at the time of their sighting, and because they were usually taken by surprise, they tended to be frightened and confused. Thus, the testimony on which Huyghe bases his categories is of uncertain reliability. But though that might tend to make his book of limited value if one encountered an extraterrestrial—one cannot, somehow, picture oneself rapidly flipping through the pages till we identify our companion as a "Humanoid, Short Non-Grey, Variant 5"—it shows that a kind of consensus has been reached as to what UFO occupants look like. This inevitably leads to the feeling that this is

what they *should* look like, which in turn influences what people see, or think they see. In Chapter Seven, we shall look more closely at this process, which applies also to séance-room materializations and other perceived beings.

The imagination of the science fiction writers of the 1920s and 1930s was matched only by that of their illustrators. The aliens they drew range from humanoid look-alikes to creatures with no pretensions of resembling Earth people. Tentacles were very popular with monsters. Some of the humanoids differ from us in having more arms or fewer eyes. Giant insects and fish-scaled mammals occur from time to time, but the preference is for various forms of reptilian lizardry. Comparing the science fiction illustrations with the aliens depicted in Huyghe's book, there is little difference. Both feature predictable variations on the human body, such as

In H. G. Wells' The First Men in the Moon, *space traveler Cavor is taken prisoner by insect-like inhabitants of the Moon.*

These "consensus" aliens generally possess two eyes, though they tend to be larger than ours and are often described as "wrap-around." Since nature bestowed two eyes on most Earthly creatures, including mammals, birds, fish and insects, the same reasoning seems to apply here. In addition, the eyes are positioned as ours are. No alien has eyes in the sides of its head like our birds, or on stalks, though this is sometimes found on science fiction monsters.

There is less uniformity with regard to the other organs. Various combinations of ears, nose and mouth— or the absence thereof—have been reported. When they are present, they are invariably located where ours are. The aliens rarely have hair.

Wells had made his Martians closer to cephalopods than to anything resembling a human. However, in John W. Campbell Junior's *When The Atoms Failed* (1930), artist Wesso (Hans Waldemar Wessolowski) perceives the Martians as gnome-like creatures. They are humanoid in configuration, with disproportionate heads and staring eyes, very much like those described by recent abductees. Unlike the later Martians, though, these have very prominent ears. The alien invaders depicted by Leo

one might expect to find on a nearly parallel world, but also monsters which are, more often than not, extrapolations from earth species. The diversity of life on Earth is more than sufficient to provide models for otherworldly life.

There is one species, however, which has gradually established itself as the dominant alien type. It is an essentially humanoid entity. It has a body which presumably contains the essential organs, to which are joined two legs for walking and two arms for performing, topped by a head which appears to house the senses and the organs of communication. The head is generally larger in proportion to the body than with adult humans, often giving this species the look of the unborn human fetus. Since

aliens are generally perceived as being more highly developed intellectually than ourselves, their heads may be larger to accommodate greater brain capacity. Perhaps it is with them as with the creatures discovered by *The First Men in the Moon* in H. G. Wells's 1901 novel:

> If, for example, a Selenite is destined to be a mathematician … his brain grows, or at least the mathematical faculties of his brain grow, and the rest of him only so much as is necessary to sustain this essential part of him … His brain grows continually larger, at least so far as the portions engaging in mathematics are concerned; they bulge ever larger and seem to suck all life and vigor from the rest of his frame.

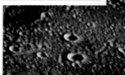
"WABBLING JELLIES OF KNOWLEDGE."

Worker Selenites carry an intellectual who is no longer capable of walking due to his huge brain.

¶ *They obeyed in some little trepidation, drawing near the strange conveyance and stopping as a small square opening appeared in the side nearest them*

Travelers from Earth in this 1930 fiction are alarmed to find Neptune inhabited by powerful creatures who trample on their spacecraft.

Morey for Harl Vincent's *Microcosmic Buccaneers* (1929) are even more similar to today's abductors. They have human shape, big heads and staring eyes, but no nose or mouth. When they land on Earth and see some Earth people watching them, they wave their arms in salutation just as we do!

Some exobiologists—those who speculate about life on other worlds— hold that, to produce life at all, conditions comparable to Earth's are needed. This seems an unjustifiably anthropocentric view, but if they are right, then it would not be surprising if life developed elsewhere along more or less similar lines. Aliens would then be more or less similar to ourselves—bipedal, with four limbs, body, head and the usual sense organs.

But are they necessarily right? Those other worlds might have conditions vastly different from Earth's, and yet be inhabited. In this case, we would encounter creatures whose forms are adapted to life on their planet. They might be much bigger or much smaller,

depending on the force of gravity. Even if we assume an atmosphere much like ours, variations in atmospheric pressure might necessitate enormously larger lungs or even some other system for taking in whatever chemicals are necessary to sustain life. Very slight differences in the atmosphere would affect sight and sound, requiring appropriate modification of the sense organs. The disproportionately large ears of the extraterrestrials encountered (and shot at) by the Sutton family at Hopkinsville, Kentucky, in August 1955, could mean that the aliens come from a planet where sound needs to be amplified more than here on Earth.

Overall, neither the science fiction illustrators nor the claimed witnesses have departed very far from existing species on Earth. Yet they might well have done, without seeming indulgent or extravagant. For example, humans have often been reported as "seeing" with parts of their anatomy other than the eyes. Biologists scoff, since even if visual perceptions could be obtained by the stomach, as has been claimed, it is difficult to explain how those perceptions could be transmitted to the brain and processed in the same way as images from the eyes. But the concept of perception distributed over the entire body is not totally ridiculous. It might just be an adaptation to life in another world, like the body fueling itself with different chemicals.

If the physical configuration of the consensus aliens remains surprisingly close to our own, the same is true of their behavior. When Catherine Muller and her contemporaries described the Martians, they never implied that their conduct was in any way different from

ours. We have seen that, by and large, the same is true of the science fiction writers. Often, they produced sophisticated theories about aliens, seeing them as dispassionate superior species to whom we Earth people are little more than cattle. In Eando Binder's The *Impossible World* (1939), the invading intelligences "brainwash" Earth people with sophisticated technical instruments, not unlike what sinister Earthly forces, like authoritarian governments, have been accused of doing. The psychology of the aliens is frequently presented in the same manner as that of the evil scientist who wants to take over the world in Earthly stories—cold, calculating and unfeeling.

As we shall see, this is also the impression that is given to those who report being abducted onto extraterrestrial spacecraft. They feel themselves to be no more than guinea pigs, involuntarily assisting the aliens in their research. However, the contactees of

The years pass, but aliens are still frequently seen as monsters. Here, a 1953 movie poster.

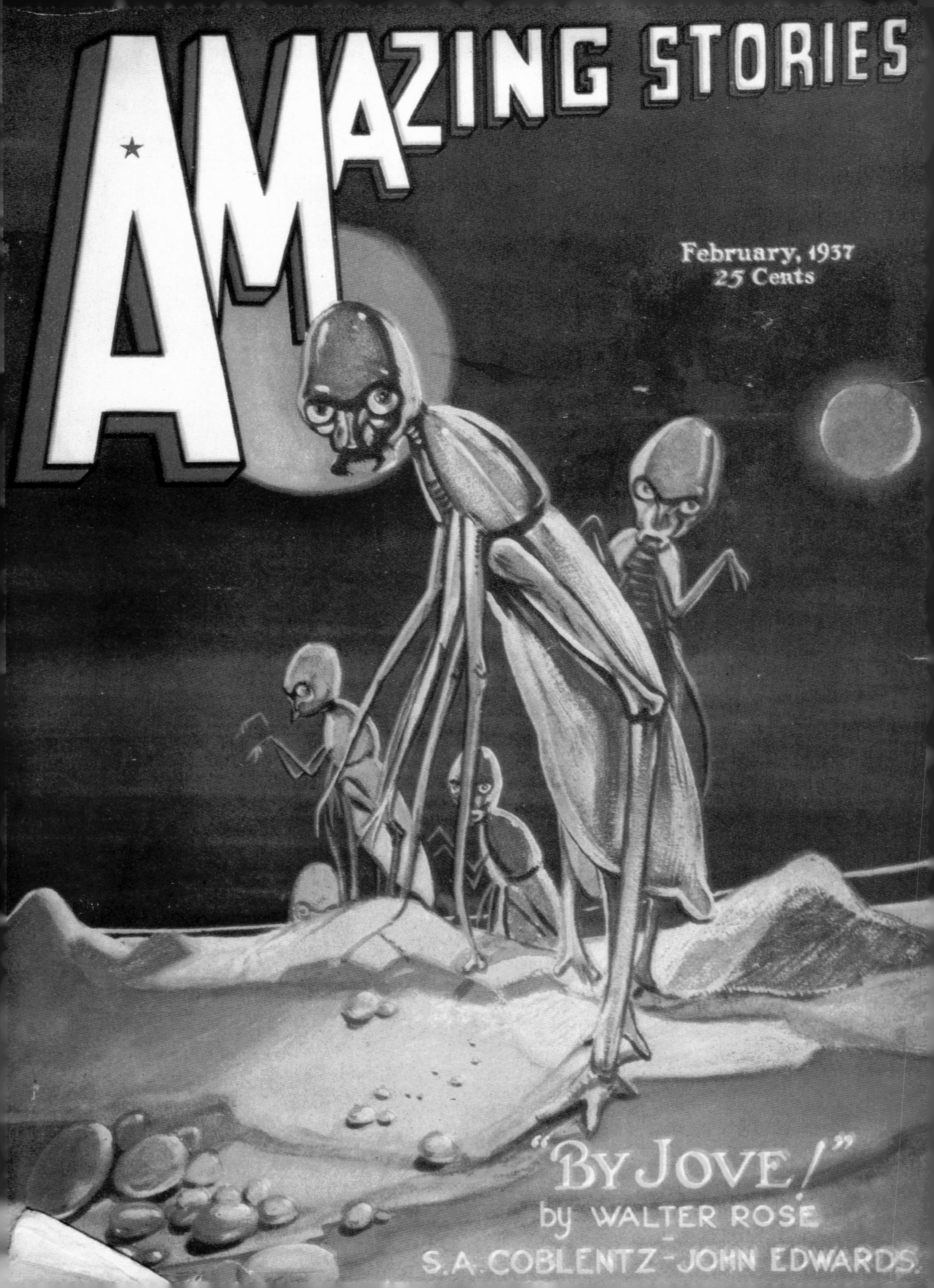

AMAZING STORIES

February, 1937
25 Cents

"By Jove!"
by WALTER ROSE
S. A. COBLENTZ – JOHN EDWARDS

At their home in Hopkinsville, Kentucky, in 1955, the Sutton family is besieged by alien creatures who are not hurt, even when hit by bullets.

the preceding era presented quite a different picture. These were caring, sensitive beings, concerned about the way we are treating our planet and offering their services to help us do better.

These fluctuations in the way we perceive our extraterrestrial visitors may reflect reality. Perhaps different Earth people are meeting different aliens. Alternatively, perhaps they reflect our own attitudes, our hopes, expectations and fears. What is most remarkable, though, is the fact that we are able to perceive them at all. It is by no means certain that people from other worlds exist, yet any schoolchild, invited to draw a space person, will reach for a pencil and draw a space person—and you and I would at once recognize it as such. Some would argue that so widespread a consensus must reflect reality. To others, it is a tribute to man's genius for mythmaking.

In 1979, the French researcher Eric

LEFT: *Giant insects were featured in science fiction pulps like this 1937 story, and were a favorite of Hollywood horror movies. However, they are a comparative rarity in UFO reports.*

Zurcher published a survey of extraterrestrial beings, entitled: *Les Apparitions d'Humanoïds.* He presents a comparative study of their morphology, dress, activity and comportment. What strikes him first is how human-like most aliens are, and second, how they reflect human preoccupations— a legionnaire sees Ufonauts dressed in khaki and carrying back-packs; a farmer sees Ufonauts examining plants; a retired soldier sees a Ufonaut carrying a sword! This doesn't make much sense, until you look at the aliens in context with folklore. Traditional entities like the Irish *leprechaun* and the Breton *korrigan* not only resemble aliens physically, but also seem to mimic human behavior. Yet they do so in the way that seems to be most appropriate to the age in which they are seen. Similarly, the illustrations to Hugo Gernsback's science fiction pulps could not have been created at the time of Catherine Muller and H.G. Wells. Zurcher suggests:

> Everything takes place… as if the key themes of mankind's dreams are somehow kept in some kind of store, from which the phenomenon of the flying saucer can draw directly on its models and its manifestations.

As he points out, we are close to Jung's notion of a "collective unconscious" with its universal archetypes. Jung himself recognized this when he subtitled his own study of flying saucers "a modern myth of things seen in the skies."

We began this chapter with the suggestion that otherworldly beings visited our earth long before human history: We conclude it with the suggestion that we should think of them as outside history altogether, as timeless beings embedded in the human subconscious.

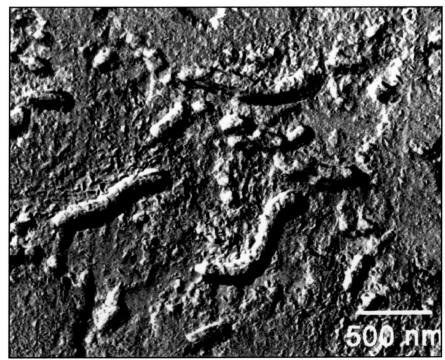

Evidence of life on Mars? Microscopic tube-like structures from a Martian meteorite could be fossilized bacteria-like organisms.

Aerial Beings

We live at the bottom of an atmospheric ocean. Is it possible that other organisms may live above us? If the seas of our Earth are swarming with varieties of living things, both great and small, is it not logical to assume that the "sea" of our sky abounds with sundry forms of living things, likewise both great and small, of varied shapes, but adaptable to their celestial environment?

So wrote American author John Philip Bessor in 1955. Similarly, in 1983, the astronomer Fred Hoyle wrote:

> To me, it seemed preposterous that NASA should be spending hundreds of millions of dollars in a mission to discover if there was life on Mars, while leaving unresolved the question of whether there was life a mere 30 miles above our heads.

The idea that Earth's atmosphere may sustain its own race of beings, independent of life on the planet's surface, is one that has intrigued many speculative thinkers. Although there is little evidence to support the idea, there have been some tantalizing hints.

In 1917, during the First World War, a strange story was submitted by an anonymous airman to a respectable monthly, *The Occult Review*. The writer told of an unusual experience that happened to a fellow aviator, who did not wish his name to be cited in connection with so strange a story, but who is described as "a very experienced airman:"

> He told me confidentially that at a very great height he had seen a curious colored dragon-like animal apparently floating in

the air and approaching him rapidly. Understandably, the pilot had become a little unnerved and at once descended to earth; but for fear of being ridiculed and accused of over-indulgence in alcoholic refreshment, he had said nothing. Had it been an isolated experience, he might have ended by doubting his own eyes; but that first sighting was confirmed by subsequent experiences of the same kind. He suspected that other pilots may have had similar experiences, but like him were reluctant to tell their stories for

In Conan Doyle's Horror of Heights, *an aviator flying at 40,000 ft. above the the earth encounters mysterious life forms.*

fear of being laughed at by their colleagues.

Well, a story told by one unnamed aviator to another does not carry much scientific weight. What makes this one particularly interesting is that it seems to have been anticipated a few years earlier by none other than the creator of Sherlock Holmes. Arthur Conan Doyle's fictional story, "The Horror of the Heights," was published in the popular weekly, *The Strand,* in its November, 1913 issue. Though told with Conan Doyle's usual vivid touches and convincing detail, it makes no pretensions to be anything other than an exciting piece of science fiction. It is a typical example of the speculative writing with which H. G. Wells and others were thrilling the reading public.

The story tells of an aviator who is determined to explore the upper atmosphere in his flimsy monoplane, a machine pretty much like the plane in which Louis Bleriot had crossed the Channel only four years earlier. Flying at about 40,000 ft. the hero encounters:

> the most wonderful vision that ever man has seen ... Conceive a jellyfish such as sails in our summer seas—far larger than the dome of St Paul's cathedral. It was of a light pink color veined with a delicate green; from it there descended two long drooping tentacles ...

LEFT: *A mysterious ball of light shines brightly above the Earth. Could our own atmosphere contain life forms unknown to us?*

RIGHT: *Aliens take the form of gargantuan jellyfish on the cover of this UFO magazine from 1972.*

"In the Abyss," a science fiction story by H.G. Wells, told of divers encountering strange creatures in the ocean. Like Conan Doyle, Wells fascinated the public with fantastical stories of other worlds.

RIGHT: *Aliens take the form of gargantuan jellyfish on the cover of this UFO magazine from 1972.*

It becomes clear that these are living creatures that are inhabiting the upper atmosphere. Beautiful they may be, but they are also dangerous. They resent the intruder from Earth's surface, who barely manages to escape their evidently hostile maneuvers.

Despite their hostility, however, he is determined to continue his explorations. Leaving behind the record of his first encounter—which provides the basis for Conan Doyle's story—he sets off again, but this time he is never seen again. He disappears, along with his plane, to a fate unknown. Conan Doyle can only speculate that he "had been overtaken and devoured by these horrible creatures at some spot in the outer atmosphere."

Conan Doyle was writing simply to entertain us, and it would be reasonable to suppose that his fantasy possesses even less substance than the story by the anonymous contributor to *The Occult Review*. However, not for the first time, it seems that a science fiction writer was ahead of the scientists themselves.

In July, 1993, two NASA observers flying above a thunderstorm made a major contribution to meteorology when they scientifically established a fact that had long been reported by flyers. Not all lightning flashes are from the clouds to the earth; they occur also above the clouds, rising rather than descending.

The NASA observers logged 19 flashes, but it was the term they used to describe them that concerns us. They likened them to—of all things—jellyfish:

> They appear brightest where they top out, typically about 40 miles high, so you have the jellyfish body at the top with tentacles trailing down.

Was this what the World War One aviator saw and what Conan Doyle was describing in his fiction? But if so, how could he possibly know that the mysterious "aerial dragons" would resemble jellyfish? For at that time, no aircraft had been constructed capable of reaching an altitude at which an aviator could have seen this phenomenon firsthand.

GOLD KEY®

90259-211

UFO FLYING SAUCERS

15c

UFO FLYING SAUCERS

ARE THEY ALIVE?
STRANGE EVENTS—OMINOUS ENCOUNTERS— THAT CONFRONT AND BAFFLE MANKIND!

THE COUNTESS' THEORY

An intriguing contribution to these ideas was offered in 1955 by the Austrian Countess Zoe Wassilko-Serecki, a well-known investigator of the paranormal. In an article entitled "The Biological Explanation for Flying Saucers," she explained that she was convinced that flying saucers existed, but the more she read about them, the less was she satisfied by the explanation—which by 1955 was widely accepted—that they came from Outer Space. Instead, she put the case for living creatures inhabiting our atmosphere.

Why had they only recently come to our attention, she wondered? Partly, no doubt, because only recently had air-craft been able to fly at high altitudes. Or perhaps the creatures had also

been disturbed by experiments with the atom and hydrogen bombs. Among other things, her theory provided an explanation for the falls of mysterious jelly-like substances which are periodically reported. These, she suggested, are the dead bodies of these aerial beings, fallen to Earth. She cited a report written in 1652 that told of a huge mass of this kind that fell near Rome soon after a huge luminous body had passed overhead and then compared it with a more recent account:

On October 1, 1951, four police officers in Washington saw and touched with their hands a sort of plasma which stuck to their fingers but gradually disintegrated, and in the course of about half an hour disappeared completely.

The Countess submitted her theories to "the official American investigators" —probably the NICAP organization—

but there is no record of her having received any response.

It is certainly true, though, that a great many strange things fall from the sky. Some are clearly natural. The falls of "blood" and "flesh" which seemed such ominous "Signs from Heaven" in the Middle Ages can today be attributed to such mundane causes as airborne sand from the Sahara. Others are clearly artificial, such as the metallic and plastic fragments that are reported from time to time. While certainly bizarre, these can presumably be considered to be of human origin.

However, "blobs" and "slime" are another matter. In 1984, Hilary Belcher and Erica Swale of Lucy Cavendish College, Cambridge, England, published a paper in "Folklore," in whichthey traced a curious old belief about meteorites, described thus by Sir Walter Scott:

A bizarre "rain of blood" alarms the inhabitants of Nice in the Seventeenth Century. At the time, such occurrences were seen as warning signs from a higher power. Today, such happenings can often be explained scientifically.

It is a common idea that falling stars, as they are called, are converted into a sort of jelly. Among the rest, I had often the opportunity to see the seeming shooting of the stars from place to place, and sometimes they appeared as if falling to the ground, where I once or twice found a white jelly-like matter among the grass, which I imagined to be distilled from them, and thence foolishly conjectured that the stars themselves must certainly consist of a like substance.

The authors quote a number of accounts of a similar nature, relating to a substance variously known as "star-slime," "star-jelly," "star-blubber" and many other names. The fact that it has been given so many different names is in itself an indication of how widespread the idea is. They give instances from several European countries, the United States and Brazil. In 1678, Dryden and Lee wrote: "The shooting stars end all in purple jellies," and so many cases have been reported from Wales that their name for it, *Pwrdre Ser*, has become a standard label for the phenomenon.

The blobs invariably decompose fairly rapidly, leaving little trace if any, so it is rare that any kind of analysis is possible. However, on August 11, 1979, Texas housewife Sibyl Christian found three "purple blobs" on her lawn, and managed to have them collected by the police and frozen before they disintegrated. They were submitted to NASA, Houston, for analysis. The NASA scientists found that nothing more exotic was involved than waste matter from a nearby battery reprocessing plant.

Sometimes scientists are more easily satisfied than independent researchers. Investigator Ted Schultz found some weaknesses in the battery-waste explanation. The Christians' material decomposed rapidly; the waste lies outdoors without changing. The two differed in appearance, color and texture. The waste was rock hard, whereas the Christians' was "like smooth whipped cream." He also found that NASA had not carried out the tests that would have established whether or not the two substances were made from the same chemical ingredients. The basic tests that were carried out revealed the presence of some unlikely materials:

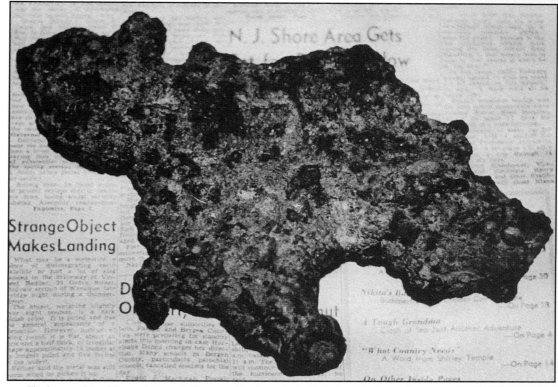

This bizarre object fell on a driveway in Wanaque, New Jersey in the 1960s. It weighed more than 8 pounds and was over 10 inches long.

Alcohols were found that are not used in battery reprocessing, and the company explained that material discarded as waste went through a process that eliminates many of the elements found in Mrs. Christian's material. The Heard Natural Science Museum, describing the substance, said that a pattern of lead specks was "like nothing on Earth."

In short, no satisfactory explanation for the substance was forthcoming, nor for why it should have turned up on the Christians' lawn after a neighbor had seen a meteorite falling in their direction. William Corliss, compiler of the world's most comprehensive catalogs of scientific anomalies, records dozens of cases in which the association of "falling stars" with "fallen blobs" is a recurring feature. These reports, together with abundant reference in literature and folklore, puts the matter beyond coincidence.

But the complications do not stop there. On the one hand, there is the fact that meteorites—if that is what the "falling stars" are—do not normally consist of material resembling pink whipped cream. If it did fall from space, we can only speculate as to how it survived the fall through Earth's

atmosphere, and wonder if it was in that form when it started its fall, or whether the form in which it was found on the Christians' lawn is the consequence of the fall.

Then there is the fact that the blobs are seldom exactly alike. Among the recorded accounts we find great variety of descriptions: from 1638, thick, slimy and black; from 1796, of the color and odor of varnish; from 1819, of a bright, buff color, with a fine nap similar to milled cloth; from 1833, like soft soap; from 1844, a gelatinous mass which trembled all over when poked with a stick; from 1950, a glowing purple gelatinous mass 6½ ft. across and 1 ft. thick at the center; from 1958, a substance that seemed made up of thousands of minute cells resembling a honeycomb, pulsating over its entire body; from 1973, a black jelly-like blob with thick bubbles all through it, which changed color when punctured, and from 1978, a mass the size of a football, with the consistency of a jelly.

Many of the supposed star falls are quickly recognized by experts as natural phenomena—generally unusual fungi. The 1973 case mentioned above was reported as multiplying 16 times in over two weeks. This is the only recorded instance of a blob which not only did not decompose, but actually grew, so perhaps it was a natural growth of some kind. Medieval commentators ascribed them to natural causes of a different kind. A manuscript dating from the Eleventh or Twelfth Century explained that winds, when they collide, may cause sparks that fall to Earth like falling stars, leaving masses of a poisonous phlegm-like substance in the fields. The Swiss physician and alchemist Paracelsus quoted, though he may not have believed it, that the substance was the natural result of the "cleaning" of the stars.

Others have followed different paths of speculation. Commenting on the 1950 case, Curtis Fuller, editor of *Fate* magazine, wrote:

> Here is new confirmation of theories that some kind of space creature, or at least stratosphere animal, may exist which science has not yet discovered. What the creature's metabolism is we cannot know, but the fact that when seen at night the "thing" seemed to glow, and in the daytime looked as though made of shining crystals, is extraordinarily significant. Scientists, please note!

This drew an interesting letter of comment from a reader:

> Your recent articles on the subject of "vanishing glop" interested us for the reason that we are quite familiar with this substance. Not everything that comes from interplanetary space is a space ship, as can be proved by this entirely foreign substance. "Glop" is a substance that people of our neighboring planets (or spacemen) are sending to our planet to help neutralize our now-contaminated atmosphere. Our angelic brothers in space are far superior to Earth people in wisdom (due to their great age). They love the people of Earth and consider helping us their duty to the Infinite Creator.
> —GEORGE L ROBERTSON, INGLEWOOD, CALIF.

This explanation clearly had not occurred to the NASA scientists. Nor are they likely to have accepted a theory proposed in rudimentary form at the beginning of the Twentieth Century by the Swedish scientist Svante Arrhenius, and more recently developed by astronomers Fred Hoyle and Chandra Wickramasinghe of University College, Cardiff, Wales. They suggest that micro-organisms exist in space. From time to time, these fall to Earth, where they may be responsible for diseases such as flu epidemics. They think it possible that life itself may have originated when our planet was seeded with organisms from space.

Russian probes of the upper atmosphere suggest that it abounds with life, albeit in the relatively simple form of bacteria. Could the falls of "star-jelly" be derived from these primitive organisms? Could anything exist at that altitude which could be regarded as a living creature? It seems an extravagant extrapolation from the facts, but two things are certain: First, the micro-organisms which would provide the starting point do indeed exist. Second, there seems little doubt that these substances do indeed fall from the skies, and that they do not originate on the surface of our planet.

Because they decompose so rapidly, analysis of the blobs has rarely been attempted, and their nature remains a mystery. Countess Wassilo-Serecki's suggestion is intriguing, but as evidence for the existence of airborne or even space-borne life forms, star-jelly is still too much of an unknown quantity.

BESSOR AND CONSTABLE

John Bessor is a sturdy champion of the "organic UFO" hypothesis. Writing in *Fate* magazine in 1967, he recalled:

Trevor James Constable standing amid a UFO shower in the Mojave Desert, April 26, 1958.
The images were captured on infrared film by Jim Woods.

In July, 1947, I expressed to the Air Force my belief that "flying discs" are various species of extraterrestrial, highly attenuated life forms or craft propelled by telekinetic energy or by sheer will or thought. Possibly originating in the ionosphere, I believe they have been forced to "migrate" to denser atmospheres periodically because of solar or cosmic disturbances in space … Facts substantiate my theory that typical flying saucers are sky animals of an "ectoplasmic" substance and are capable of materialization and dematerialization. In August, a reply from Air Material Command commented: "Your theory concerning the flying discs is one of the most intelligent we have received."

In 1955, Bessor wrote an article entitled "Are the Saucers Space Animals?" In it, he argued the case for his theory. Three years later, a new book offered photographic evidence that seemed to support this view. The jacket blurb of the book—*They Live in the Sky!*—by New Zealand author Trevor James, who later changed his name to Trevor James Constable, told readers:

> The author describes his own telepathic contact with an invisible being, and how, at the suggestion of this invisible intelligence, he began experimenting with infrared film in conjunction with elementary principles of spiritual science.

The book contained some 30 photographs, taken on infrared film, which did indeed show strange shapes in the sky. They were, frankly, little more than shapeless blobs—far from traditional flying saucers. One also has to wonder, why no one else has ever reported these creatures.

It turns out that others besides Constable have photographed the sky creatures. In May, 1977, Richard Toronto armed himself with four rolls of infrared film and set off into the Yucca Valley–Giant Rock area, since desert conditions provide the clean, clear sky that seems most favorable for photographing the creatures. He succeeded in taking two frames in which UFOs appeared. This encouraged further experiments, and he obtained further photographs of the

Brightly colored balls of light (BOLs) of the type witnessed by Trevor James Constable have left many UFO observers wondering about their origin.

"gelatinous meteors," but was never able to learn anything more about them.

However, these jellyfish-like creatures are not the only observed phenomena which support the idea of airborne life forms. When he originally set out his theory, Bessor wondered if there might be a connection between his "organic UFOs" and the "balls of light" (BOLs) which recur so frequently in UFO accounts:

> A number of good reports of UFO landings describe red- or blue-colored globes of light floating several feet off the ground in the vicinity of the landed UFOs. Are these blobs of light the ghostly occupants themselves?

As far as I know, no one else has proposed that BOLs are the actual occupants. However, the behavior of these mysterious lights often suggests that some degree of intelligence is involved.

For many UFO researchers—myself included—they are the most interesting category of UFO sightings, if only because they are the most susceptible to scientific study.

BALL OF LIGHT PHENOMENA

A curious episode of World War Two, which has never been resolved satisfactorily, is that of the so-called "Foo Fighters." These were enigmatic aerial objects which were observed by pilots on both sides, in both the European and Pacific theaters of war. In appearance, they were no more than balls of light (BOL), comparable to other BOL phenomena such as feux follets, St. Elmo's Fire and ball lightning. But the Foo Fighters were paradoxical both in their behaviour and in the circumstances of their manifestation. For example, on December 22, 1944, an American bomber crew over Germany saw two very bright lights climb toward them from the ground. On reaching the plane, the lights leveled off and stayed on the plane's tail for about two minutes. They were huge, bright and orange-colored, and they seemed to be under perfect control.

During a mission over Austria and Yugoslavia in the winter of 1944, USAF bomber pilot William Leet reported a BOL which suddenly appeared alongside his plane "like a light switch being turned on." He estimated that its distance from the wing tip was 250 to 300 ft. laterally, and about 16 ft. to the rear. It seemed two- rather than three-dimensional, like the light of a traffic signal, but not like any earthly light. The estimated diameter was 10 ft. It stayed with the plane for about 45 to 50 minutes, then suddenly was gone. It was seen by all the crew:

> Our gunners wanted to shoot it down, but I ordered them not to. I told them if it was hostile, it would already have shot us down. Let's try to figure out what it is, I told them.

A duration of more than 45 minutes far exceeds the life-span of ball lightning or any other scientifically accepted BOL phenomenon. Leet himself, in his 1979 book, was sufficiently influenced by UFO thinking to ask, "Could it possibly have been a space craft piloted by advanced beings from another world?" He theorized that perhaps the BOL could have somehow protected his plane from enemy attack. However, he does not propose this suggestion with any conviction, and really it does no more than express his bafflement at the experience.

The explanation which comes immediately to mind is that it might have been a plasma created by the aircraft's progress through the atmosphere. If so, it is curious that only one wing tip created such a plasma, and it is hard to account both for its extended duration and for its intense luminosity in the night sky, as there was nothing for it to reflect from. It was

"Foo Fighters" photographed during World War Two.

An American B-24 "Liberator" encounters Foo Fighters during a daylight bombing raid over Germany.
Initially, these phenomena were believed to be secret weapons.

bright enough for Leet and his crew to suppose their plane had been picked up by German searchlights. But they saw no beams coming from the ground. One crew member reported "a blinding glare that seemed to come from above," and more than one spoke of intense heat which may or may not have been associated with the BOL.

This is just one instance of several such reports that came mainly from the European theater of war, but also from the Japanese. The most puzzling feature of the Foo Fighter phenomenon, however, is that it was mostly limited to a brief historical period—two or three years of World War Two—and even then occurred only occasionally, in the course of operations in the German and Pacific airspaces. Because the historical context is so clearly a determining parameter, we are constrained to look to the historical circumstances for an explanation.

I think it is legitimate to speculate that some kind of artifact, generated by military activities or associated hardware, was interacting with natural factors to produce the phenomenon.

Dr. Richard Haines, in his important study of reports made by pilots during the Korean war, includes many BOL-type observations. Here is one of them:

> February 10, 1952: Lieut. Perez, flying a B-29 bomber, reported a globe-shaped object, estimated size 3 ft. across ... color resembled the sun, a light orange, occasionally changing to bluish ... the outer edge appeared to be fuzzy and it seemed to have an internal churning movement like flames or fiery gases ... it came in on the same level as the B-29, remained in the same relative position for approximately one minute, then receded on the same path, fading in the distance ...

If the Foo Fighter is a naturally occurring phenomenon related to mechanical flight, why does it not occur more frequently? There are occasional references to similar phenomena in a non-military context, such as the following incident which took place on April 23, 1964: The crew of an aircraft flying over Bedford, England, reported a loud bang and a whitish-blue flash of light. A ball of blue light the size of a football appeared on the starboard wing tip. It vanished in two seconds.

The great majority of accounts—particularly those in which a long duration is cited—relate to military flying. We have to ask, are there any special features of military flying which distinguish it from civilian flying? The 2-second duration of the incident just cited falls a long way short of Leet's 45 or more minutes. Can we be sure that we are dealing with the same phenomenon in both cases? Then again,

During the Korean War, the crew of a United States Air Force B-29 bomber reported a UFO over Wonsan, Korea.

while military aircraft are different in many respects from civil aircraft, they are surely not so very different. The wartime air crews are liable to be in a state of unnatural tension, but there are many circumstances in civilian flying which would also lead to unusual stress and provoke the same psycho-physiological responses. Yet they do not seem to trigger the same BOL reports.

It seems beyond doubt that the Foo Fighter phenomenon is a real one, in the sense that it comprises a number of observations which are similar to one another and distinct in some respects from other comparable phenomena. But we cannot be sure how much of the recorded details are accurate, and which result from over-interpretation by witnesses in tense psychological situations. As they are described to us, the objects do seem to manifest more intelligent control than we would expect from a purely natural phenomenon.

However, this may be a question of reading more into their behaviour than is warranted. The Foo Fighters remain an intriguing phenomenon, but they do not strongly support the theory of atmospheric creatures.

PIEDMONT, YAKIMA AND HESSDALEN

At first sight, the phenomena experienced at the three locations mentioned above are unexciting. Even when photographs from BOL incidents at these places are enlarged, they show points of light that could be stars or aircraft lights, or shapeless blobs that could be Constable's "space animals," but could just as well be something

entirely different. At the same time, they are evidently something, because there are many hundreds of photographs that constitute evidence.

Equally, it is by no means certain that the phenomena at Piedmont, Missouri are related to those at Yakima, in Washington State, or that either are linked to those at Hessdalen in Norway. But all three have in common one extremely important feature—each involves low-level BOLs observed within a relatively limited region over an extended period of time. This makes them almost unique. The vast majority of UFOs and other anomalous aerial phenomena occur spontaneously. A witness happens to see them, then reports the sighting to the authorities, the media or to a research organization. Any investigation that is carried out is done after the event—often a long while after—and most often there is no evidence whatsoever, beyond the testimony of the witness, that anything happened at all. The original description is typically the only material the investigators have to work with.

At these three locations, on the other hand, because the phenomena have been recurrent, the investigators were able to observe them first hand. Moreover, the observers were not random members of the public, but persons with some degree of knowledge and experience, and in some cases scientific qualifications. In other words, these were people who were mentally prepared to see the BOLs rather than being taken by surprise, and who were frequently armed with cameras and other appropriate scientific equipment. Consequently, the phenomena have been observed on instrumental records. There are many hundreds of photographs, which constitute our best objective evidence for the existence of a BOL phenomenon unrecognized by current science.

They are, therefore, the most comprehensively studied of all UFO sightings. It is of special significance, therefore, to note that in all three cases, but particularly at Piedmont and Hessdalen, there were indications of intelligent behavior on the part of the phenomena.

At Yakima, the observations were made in a largely forested area that requires continuous surveillance against the danger of fire. This meant that there were observation posts manned 24 hours per day located at particularly strategic sites—as well-placed for observing UFOs as fires! The observers here were experienced and were able to discount the usual natural phenomena, so when they reported things they considered to be anomalous, they had every right to a serious hearing.

Some reports say structured objects were seen, but most sightings—and all the available photos—show only BOLs. Nevertheless, one 1972 witness described an object the size of a two-story house, and one reported that the object she saw responded to her flashlight. A farmer who saw one of the same lights reported that it affected the instruments on his tractor when it passed overhead.

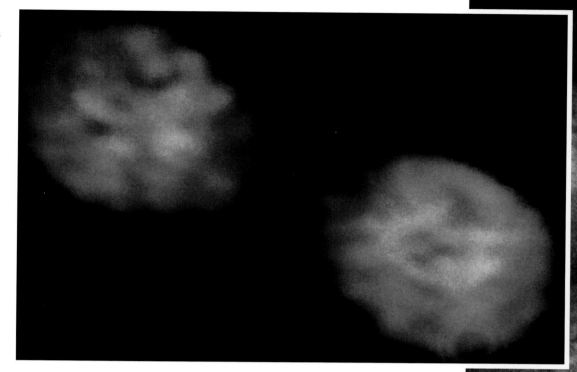

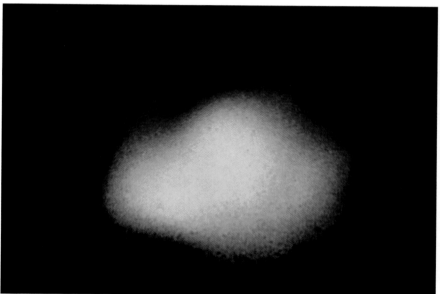

Ball of Light (BOL) phenomena photographed in the sky above the remote village of Hessdalen in central Norway, between 1981 and 1984.

Unfortunately, though we know more about these three sets of lights than we do about any other kind of BOL except ball lightning itself, that is not saying very much. In the 1984 series of observations at Hessdalen, for example, though 188 observations were recorded, only two of them were made in conditions which left no reasonable room for doubt that an anomalous event had occurred.

At Piedmont, Missouri, lights were observed in nearby hills which were investigated by physics professor Dr.

Harley Rutledge over a seven-year period. By 1981, when he published his findings, the project had recorded 178 anomalous objects on 157 occasions, under circumstances which seem to rule out either natural phenomena or man-made artifacts. By using triangulation methods based on simultaneous observation from separate posts, the investigators were able to determine the course, distance, speed and movements of the objects. They could consequently eliminate all obvious explanations such as aircraft, satellites, meteorites, car headlamps, street lights, refraction effects, mirages, etc.

What is of particular interest is that on at least 32 recorded occasions, Dr. Rutledge and/or his colleagues recorded a high degree of synchronicity between the movement of the object and the activity of the observers. This activity was sometimes as physical as switching a car lamp on or off. Other times, it was a verbal or a radio message, or even an unspoken thought in the mind of one of the observers. There is no way of substantiating this last category, of course. Nevertheless, if we accept the investigators' word in other respects, we must at least give them a hearing with regard to these remarkable claims.

Of these three sets of phenomena, those most thoroughly observed and documented have been the ones in the remote valley of Hessdalen, in central Norway. From this sparsely populated area have come, since 1981, reports of luminous objects in the sky whose physical existence has been confirmed by more than 500 photographs, along with other instrumental recordings and hundreds of visual sightings.

Although Project Hessdalen has been studying the phenomenon for more than 15 years with the co-operation of scientists from Japan, Russia, America and elsewhere, no satisfactory explanation is yet forthcoming. The lights often seem to be 3 ft. or more in diameter; can be observed for more than half an hour at a time, and have been seen to travel

RIGHT: Charles Victor Miller was an American medium who held dramatic séances in Paris. This image shows the materialization of a figure during a séance in 1908.

over distances of 12 miles. Some have been photographed in front of nearby mountains, establishing their exact location. Some very remarkable behavior has been observed. When la laser beam was directed towards a periodically flashing "UFO," the flash period immediately doubled, only to resume its previous flashing pattern when the laser was switched off. When the laser was again directed at it, the flashing doubled again. This occurred a total of eight times out of nine.

Needless to say, there is no phenomenon known to science that behaves in this manner. American

A flying saucer, alleged to have landed in Hessdalen in Norway in 1996.

Louis Malteste

UFO researcher J. Allen Hynek concluded that this "suggests intelligent behavior." Indeed, though the automatic quality of the response does not imply that the object was consciously responding, it does imply something more controlled than, say, the reaction of an animal when a torch beam is directed at it.

The sightings at Yakima, Hessdalen and Piedmont do not, of themselves, prove the existence of "space animals." However, they certainly suggest there are stranger things in the Earth's atmosphere than we normally suppose.

HELPFUL AND HOSTILE

The Balls of Light at Piedmont and Hessdalen may have indicated a response which may be interpreted as an indication of intelligence. However, it doesn't take very much intelligence to respond to a stimulus by modifying

your flashing rate. Yet, there have been instances where something more seems to have been involved, approaching the level of positive interaction with the human observers. A disturbing case is reported from the Caucasus Mountains in 1978.

Victor Kavunenko was one of party of five climbers camped at around 13,000 ft. During the night, he woke with the feeling that there was a stranger in the tent. Looking out from his sleeping bag, he saw a "bright yellow blob" floating about 3 ft. from the ground. It disappeared into a fellow climber's sleeping bag. The man screamed in pain. The ball jumped out and circled over the other bags, hiding now in one, now in another:

> When it burned a hole in mine, I felt an unbearable pain, as if I were being burned by a welding machine, and blacked out. Regaining consciousness after a while, I saw the same ball which, methodically observing a pattern that was known to it alone, kept diving into the bags, evoking desperate howls from

the victims. This indescribable horror repeated itself many times. When I came back to my senses for the fifth or sixth time, the ball was gone. I could not move my arms or legs and my body was burning as if it had turned into a ball of fire itself. In the hospital, where we were flown by helicopter, seven wounds were discovered on my body. They were worse than burns; pieces of muscle were found to be torn out to the bone. The same happened to three of the others; the fifth was dead, possibly because his bag had been on a rubber mattress, insulating it from the ground. The ball lightning did not touch a single metal object, injuring only people.

Were the observers being fanciful when they detected hostility on the part of the BOL? Possibly, but there are other cases where there can be no question whether the BOLs were motivated. A remarkable story was told in 1956 by Peggy Hight, who had been prospecting with her husband for uranium three years earlier in the New Mexico desert. Her husband had gone off on a week-long exploration and Peggy became very ill, to the point where she felt herself to be on the verge of death.

As she lay there one afternoon wondering what would become of her, a small light appeared in one corner of the cabin. It grew larger, until within a few minutes it had expanded to a large glowing light. It moved slowly towards her, changing from a solid ball into a wheel consisting of a centre axle out of which radiated seven spokes, encircled by an outer rim. It whirled through her body, leaving a wonderfully clean and refreshed sensation, then disappeared. She felt a surge of vitality and well being. She got up, and realized that the light had completely restored her health.

Frau Elsa Schmidt-Falk, a German lady, wrote to me describing an experience she had while climbing in the Bavarian Alps in the 1950s. She had accidentally lost her way:

> You will understand that this is rather a heavy mountain tour. There is a good way up and down, but one must not miss it, as I did. Having started a little late for the return, with light beginning to fade, all

Ball Lightning photographed during the summer of 1978 by Werner Burger at Sakt Gallenkirch, Voralberg, in Austria.

Captain Kirk, Spock and crew are transported in the popular television series, Star Trek. *Similarly, do the mysterious entities that help and harm transport themselves in balls of light?*

of a sudden I found myself in a really dangerous position. As a matter of fact, one year later, a young girl fell to death exactly on the spot where I realized myself to be in an almost hopeless position. All of a sudden, I noticed a sort of a big ball of light, and this condensed to the shape of a tall, rather Chinese-looking gentleman. Extraordinarily, I was not a bit frightened, and also not astonished; it all seemed then quite natural to me. The gentleman bowed, spoke a few words, led me a small path to the tourists' way, and disappeared as a ball of light.

Just as it is no ordinary ball of light that heals a sick woman, so it is no ordinary one that guides a strayed climber down a mountain. It is not likely that occult powers maintain mountain rescue services in case of emergency, so we must suppose that this helper came to the lady because of her need. Various scenarios suggest themselves, but the simplest one is that her subconscious mind sent out a mayday call, to which the BOL/Chinese gentleman responded.

What was this ball of light which turned into a figure? The simplest explanation is that it was the mechanism by which the entity could transport itself

to where it wanted to be, much like the shimmering columns of the transporter in the *Star Trek* television series. If so, we must see the BOL not so much as a thing in its own right, but as something else in a transitional phase.

CHARLES VICTOR MILLER

That this may be the case is supported by many records in occult literature. Remarkable phenomena were produced by the American medium Charles Victor Miller, especially Paris in 1906, where Octave Beliard described:

The medium Miller made about 30 phantoms appear in succession in front of about 100 people, myself included. They were large and small, of every age and every sex, and often one saw two at a time. The way in which the phantoms arrived was very strange. In the darkness, above the platform where Miller was lying in trance, we saw a vague luminosity floating near the ceiling, pretty much like a lump of cotton wool, about the size of a fist. This slowly dropped until it touched the floor, then suddenly it expanded into a

human form, surrounded by a thin gauze. And this form spoke, gave its name, in a distant voice and like a dream. A conversation then took place with it. I remember a colossal man wearing bracelets shining like diamonds. He strode across the platform in great strides and jabbering incomprehensible words ... a woman asked the audience to sing a ridiculous song ... a little girl danced ...

Beliard, like many others who attended Miller's séances, was impressed by the show, but not entirely convinced. Miller, who was never a professional medium, is not known to have continued his demonstrations, and the question of what he was doing remains unresolved. But if they were genuine, then there is an obvious similarity to the German widow's story.

This story seems to draw us into the world of psychic phenomena. Indeed, in Chapter Six we shall find that many of our visitors from other worlds come under this heading, when we consider ghosts and spirits of the dead. But the following incident doesn't seem to fall into either of those categories:

My elderly cook has told me that on many occasions she has awakened suddenly during the night and has seen a round or oval patch of red, or sometimes white, light on the wall of the room, which disappeared after a few minutes, but after each of these appearances a death has occurred, either in her family or among her neighbors. On one occasion the globe of light left the wall, proceeded slowly across the ceiling and descended near her bed to about the level of her eyes. The day following, her son died in the hospital ... One night a girl was sleeping in her room, and they both saw two lights, and two deaths took place among their friends shortly afterwards ...

When BOLs start to share attributes with guardian angels, we may despair of finding a scientific explanation. On the face of it, a blob of light on a cook's bedroom wall doesn't have much in common with organisms inhabiting the upper atmosphere of our Earth. All, or some, or none, may be intelligent entities sharing our universe. But all have some kind of existence beyond the reaches of our current knowledge.

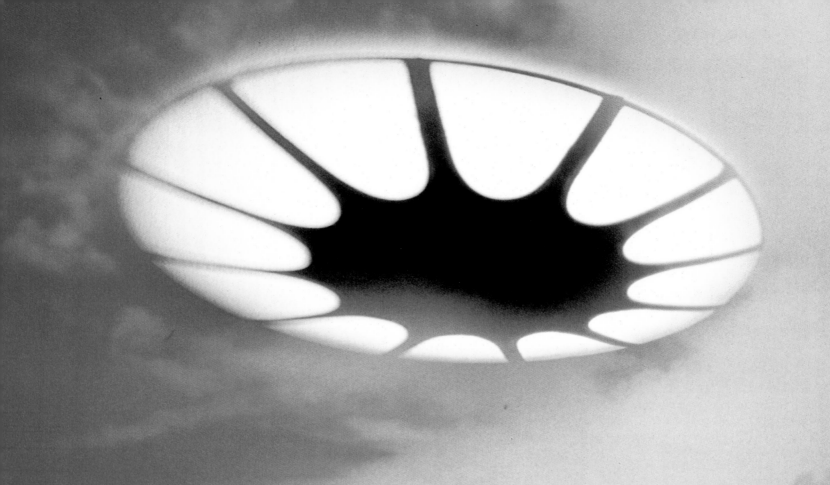

The Coming Of The UFOs

In 1947, it happened at last. For as long as anyone could remember, there had been talk about the Martians. There had been books, magazine stories, radio broadcasts. But on June 24, 1947, the "maybes" and the "sometimes" were suddenly right here and right now: Fiction became fact, and dream became reality.

Or so it seemed. But was it, rather, that the world found the ingredients with which to create a new myth of otherworldly visitation? Was it more satisfying than that of ancient astronauts because it was happening here and now, more credible than the Star People because it derived its authorization from mankind's own developing technology?

Whatever the facts of the matter, the coming of the saucers was a landmark event. Significantly, too, it was a media event. The term "flying saucer" was itself a media creation—a newspaperman's label—coined from the words used by pilot Kenneth Arnold to describe a formation of flying objects which he had not been able to identify while flying over the mountains of Washington state in June, 1947.

Throughout the "Age of the Flying Saucer," which was born that day, the media would be in on the act— sometimes supportive of the believers, sometimes derisive, but always watching, commenting in a way that was not true of any of the other landmark events we have considered in this book. Previously, the people in the street had been largely indifferent to new views of the universe made possible by technological innovations even when they had been aware of them. Advances

such as the invention of the telescope, then that of the balloon and, later, heavier-than-air flight, attracted little attention. In America, where the first controlled heavier-than-air flight was made by the Wright Brothers in 1903, there was almost total indifference to their achievement—so much so that the brothers, today two of the brightest stars in the American pantheon, took their invention to France.

But with flying saucers, it was different. The media saw to it that the

The COMING of the SAUCERS

By Kenneth Arnold & Ray Palmer

UFO phenomenon got coverage on an unprecedented scale, and this had significant repercussions for the phenomenon itself.

One unfortunate effect of media interest was to give the impression that UFOs, which are essentially a haphazard assortment of anomalous events, constitute a single phenomenon. Commentators, who like to have everyone and everything tidily classified and labeled, stuck the "flying saucer" label onto the whole assortment of unexplained events. This turned it into a category, with the result that anyone who sees anything strange in the sky is liable to ask "Is it a flying saucer? Is it a UFO?" Every time this happens, the witness makes a contribution to the communal myth.

This all-or-nothing approach, encompassing rubbish of every kind along with genuinely puzzling events, has meant that the UFO never achieved scientific recognition. As it has evolved, the phenomenon ranges across the spectrum from fact to fantasy, incorporating Nazi bases under the Antarctic ice, mutilated cattle in the American midwest, Men in Black knocking on the doors of witnesses, circular marks in cornfields interpreted as cosmic messages, government conspiracies, abductees beamed up into spaceships for the purpose of inter-species breeding, and more. It's a rich and wonderful myth, but it's not the

Fact or fiction? A typical flying saucer hovers above an unsuspecting human.

The Coming of the Saucers *was a landmark account of the experiences of pilot Kenneth Arnold.*

The Daily Scare

MYSTERIOUS

AIR-SHIP

SEEN

EVERYWHERE

BY NIGHT

Bernard Partridge.

stuff of which science is constructed. Yet it is important to bear in mind that, within the soft flesh of the myth, there remains a hard kernel of genuine scientific anomaly.

THE HISTORY OF THE UFO

We know now that UFOs did not suddenly start to appear on June 24, 1947. Of course, there has never been a time when people did not see things in the sky that they could not identify. In earlier chapters, we saw how scattered observations provided historians of this subject with the material for a "prehistory" of the UFO. Periodically, there have been clusters of reports which, while they are perhaps more easily accounted for in socio-cultural terms, have also been interpreted as flurries of extraterrestrial activity:

- There was a wave of sightings of mystery airships across the United States during the 1890s. This was at a time when experimentation with flying machines was widespread, and the competition to be the first to achieve controlled flight was feverish. But there were no airships flying in the American skies that could have accounted for the sightings.
- Other airship scares followed, notably in Britain just before World War One. At this time, general apprehension of the imminent hostilities was symbolized by Germany's Zeppelin, a sinister menace that seemed more threatening as war loomed closer. There were so many "sightings" that the popular alarm provoked anxious questions in the British Parliament. Similar scares took place in New Zealand.
- A wave of more than 1000 sightings of "mystery aircraft" was reported from Scandinavia during the 1930s, often observed flying in conditions which at the time were considered impossible. This was a time when rearmament was contributing to

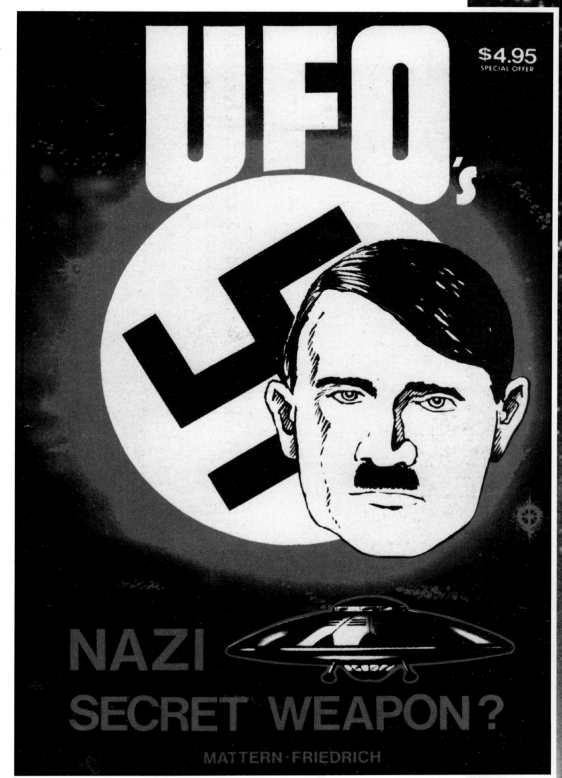

The 1965 book, UFOs, Nazi Secret Weapon, *capitalized on the idea that the Nazis developed all kinds of mystery aircraft. It is known that they had built a prototype of a saucer-shaped craft.*

international tension—and international tension was inspiring further rearmament—and when both Nazi Germany and Soviet Russia represented unknown potential threats.

- In the tense postwar summer of 1946, a time that was made uneasy by the Cold War, some 1600 reports were made of "ghost rockets" hurtling through the skies of Scandinavia.

THE AGE OF THE FLYING SAUCER

Kenneth Arnold's 1947 sighting—and the "Age of the Flying Saucer" that it ushered in—tended not to be seen in the perspective of these former manifestations, as part of a continuing phenomenon. As far as the public was concerned, flying saucers were something totally new and unparalleled. Whether the occupants were welcomed as friendly visitors bearing greetings from other inhabited parts of the universe or feared as alien invaders, it soon came to be taken for granted that they were of extraterrestrial origin. The terms "flying saucer" and "alien spacecraft" became interchangeable.

This is not to say that the world rushed headlong into the idea that these things came from beyond Earth. Other possibilities were seriously considered—in particular, that the objects were secret military devices of the Americans or the Russians. As American researcher Martin Kottmeyer has pointed out:

> Polls from 1947 into the 1960s show that the secret weapons idea had clear dominance in the minds of the general public. One from 1968 showed that 57% thought most UFOs were due to secret defense projects either in the U.S. or another country. Only 40% thought people were seeing space ships from another planet.

More than one theory was derived from the military experiments of German scientists, who were known to have developed a saucer-shaped aircraft at least to the prototype stage. An elaborate theory, backed by fact, was developed by the Italian writer Renato Vesco. His conclusion was that the flying saucers should be credited to the British and Canadian governments, who had developed secret disc-shaped devices based on German wartime research. An equally impressive array of circumstantial evidence was produced by Germans in Canada, creating a strong alternative scenario in which the Nazi scientists escaped from Germany after World War Two to previously-prepared bases in the Antarctic.

Both explanations were plausible, and incorporated a substantial body of suggestive, if circumstantial, evidence. Other theories moved from the possible, through the improbable, to the bizarre. One school of thought suggested that the UFO occupants were traveling in time—that they were actually our own descendants and had come to look at their ancestors. Another popular theory stated that UFOs were vehicles carrying demons. With such a wealth of alleged sightings of every shape, size and configuration, there is hardly any limit to the scenarios that can be constructed if the ingredients are carefully selected. Some years ago, a UFO periodical invited readers to submit UFO explanations that no one believed in. So strong a case can be made that UFOs

are sent by Masters of Wisdom hidden in the Himalayas that I almost convinced myself! Other such theories were put forward seriously, and the books are there to prove it: *Flying Saucers from the Fourth Dimension* (Kurt Glemser, 1969); *God Drives a Flying Saucer* (R. L. Dione, 1969), and *Flying Saucers from the Earth's interior* (Raymond Bernard, 1958).

One by one, though, these alternative scenarios were set aside—largely because there was no real evidence for them. Yet, ironically, neither was there any evidence for the scenario that came to predominate—the extraterrestrial hypothesis that flying saucers came from other worlds. So long as the flying saucers were objects seen afar, there seemed no way of resolving the

Alleged alien remains from the 1948 crash of a flying saucer near Aztec, New Mexico.

question. If only we could meet their occupants, though, that would settle the matter. The world waited for the moment when a flying saucer would land on the White House lawn and Little Green Men would step out and say to the nearest bystander, "Take me to your leader!" Or, if the flying saucer occupants were reluctant to initiate a voluntary meeting, perhaps one would make a forced landing, or even crash.

THE SAUCER CRASHES

One of the more bizarre manifestations of the UFO phenomenon is the persistent rumor that a flying saucer has crashed, and that it—together with the bodies of its occupants—is being held in secret by the United States Government.

Stories of crashed UFOs began to be told almost as soon as the idea of "flying saucers" became prevalent. At one time or another, saucers have been said to have crashed in Spitzbergen (1952), Heligoland (1955), Mexico (1948, 1950 and 1964), Bolivia (1978) and in various locations in the southwestern United States, including Salinas, California (1947) and Aztec, New Mexico (1948). Each of these stories created a flurry of interest at the time, then faded when no confirming evidence was produced. Some may have been deliberate hoaxes, others rumors and misinterpretations.

Then, in the 1970s, the subject was revived when veteran American investigator Leonard Stringfield began to collect statements from individuals who claimed to have been involved in official investigations of crashed saucers in the late 1940s. In a series of dossiers, he brought together dozens of personal stories which—though they were mostly circumstantial, nearly always anonymous and frequently contradictory—nevertheless converged towards a common theme. They said that a flying saucer had crashed in a desert area in the southwestern United States, that alien bodies—and perhaps even survivors—had been recovered, and that the crashed discs, together with their occupants, had been taken away by the authorities for top-secret examination and analysis.

ROSWELL

In 1980 Charles Berlitz and William Moore published *The Roswell Incident*, which offered evidence that complemented Stringfield's findings and, moreover, focused on a specific time and place. The time was July, 1947—that is to say, within weeks of Kenneth Arnold's landmark sighting—and the place was, Roswell, New Mexico. In the words of the jacket blurb:

… after extensive research and considerable detective work, Charles Berlitz and William Moore have pieced together the strongest evidence to date that a manned UFO actually reached earth—over thirty years ago!

The head and torso of a replica of an alien on an autopsy table. The "alien" is an exhibit at the International UFO Museum and Research Center in Roswell, New Mexico.

Two "aliens" watching the the comet Hale-Bopp in the night sky over Roswell.
Many inhabitants of the town still believe that aliens landed in the area in 1947.

The extraordinary legend that then grew up is a magnificent example of myth-making in action. There was no official starting point, and no official record of the incident—no government documents whatever—were known to exist. At the same time, there could be little doubt that *something* had come down from the sky near Roswell in July, 1947; that the authorities were well aware of this, and that some kind of official action had been taken. In the initial confusion, an official press release was issued, announcing the crash of a "flying saucer." Though it was retracted a day or two later, it was enough to set rumors flying. Gradually, the few known facts were embellished. Witnesses were found and scenarios were constructed, until something approaching a consensus history of the event was created, along with a shelf-full of book-length treatments offering individual perspectives on the basic theme.

Critics pointed out that no two versions of the story matched. The witnesses contradicted one another, and sometimes themselves. They noted that many of the allegations could not have been true, if only because they were incompatible. But by now the story had acquired sufficient momentum to keep going despite all criticism. It was admitted that not all the testimony was reliable; however, that was only to be expected when half a century had elapsed and many of those who had participated in the events were no longer alive to testify.

While most versions of the myth were honest attempts to uncover the truth, some of the variations were curious, not to say bizarre. Perhaps most remarkable was the story told by a senior U.S. Army officer of high repute, Philip Corso, in 1997. He confirms the basic fact—that an extraterrestrial craft crashed in the desert near Roswell—and claimed that he saw physical evidence of it. Further, he describes in detail how he was personally responsible for handling of much of the debris from the crash, which he was instructed by his superiors to pass on to selected commercial companies for the purposes of "back-engineering." We are asked to believe that, as a result of analyzing the scraps of wreckage from the Roswell desert, several important breakthroughs were achieved that significantly accelerated the progress of technological research. The laser, microcircuits, fiber optics and night vision devices are just four of the applications that the author mentions.

Skeptics were quick to point out the glaring improbabilities, inconsistencies and outright impossibilities of Corso's story, but this only fueled the mystery. How did so senior an officer, of hitherto unblemished reputation, come to be publishing this nonsense? What authorization, if any, did he have to go public with these revelations? Deliberate hoax? Fiction pretending to be fact? The truth has yet to be revealed, but the real importance of Corso's claim is to show how—by absorbing the facts, twisting them, stretching them, and extrapolating from them—the mythmakers feed the myth.

In fact, the actual events were much simpler than the mythical scenario, and not nearly so exciting. There was, indeed, a "crash" at Roswell, in the sense that something came down from the skies. What came down was a weather balloon, which would have, sooner or later, come down somewhere. It was of a secret type which—because it might be used for

An artist's impression of the flying saucer that allegedly crashed during a thunderstorm at Roswell, New Mexico on July 2, 1947. The next day, many pieces of debris were said to have been found on a sheep farm nearby.

espionage over other countries—had to be kept from public knowledge.

How did a weather balloon come to be announced as a flying saucer? This was unquestionably the result of the prevailing emotional climate. The Arnold sighting had sparked off a wave of world-wide interest just weeks before, and during those first months, before a more realistic assessment could be made, thousands of sightings were reported. The Roswell "crash" occurred at a time when, all over the United States, people were reporting seeing the mysterious "flying saucers." Every unknown object was liable to be perceived as a saucer, and the thing that came down at Roswell was an "unknown". With the benefit of hindsight, it can be seen that people overreacted and rushed to premature judgement, but given the mood of the time, their mistake is not so surprising.

Another aspect of the Roswell phenomenon is the way in which the myth was sustained in the face of continued official denial. Government sources, by making it obvious that something was being concealed, gave free rein to the amateur theorists to claim that a cover-up—if not a conspiracy—was in progress and this was, in a sense, true. Scores of theorists went into action, producing article after article, book after book. It is significant of the crash stories—and we shall see that the same is true of contactees and abductees—that most of the revelations are made not by official pronouncement or authoritative statement, but by individuals writing books sold by commercial publishers. Under such circumstances, it should not be expected that a neutral, honest presentation of the facts will take

place. A large part of the Roswell controversy consists of rival theorists bashing one another's claims.

The town of Roswell itself is thriving on the myth. A substantial income is derived from tourism, and two museums attract visitors from all over the world. Though its present notoriety is unlikely to endure, Roswell has earned its place in history. But if so, it will not be as the place where the aliens landed, but as the location for one of the classic legends, along with Loch Ness and Avalon.

Neither Roswell—nor any of the other stories of crashed saucers—offer any evidence whatsoever of visitation from other worlds. Rather, they demonstrate what happens when the myth-making process is allowed to follow its own course, unhampered by inconvenient fact.

A "SPACE AGE" MYTH

Clearly, the earlier UFO waves had their roots in the social and political climate. Similarly, it is more than coincidence that UFO reports became a matter of public concern just at the time when we inhabitants of Earth were making our first tentative ventures into the cosmos.

Is the entire flying saucer phenomenon a fantasy generated by our space age preoccupations? There is support for such a view in the cluster of extraterrestrial encounter tales that we saw occurring in the 1890s. If the "Martians" of Catherine Muller, Mrs. Cleaveland and the others were fantasies created by the cultural climate, then could not "flying saucers" be the same?

This was the conclusion reached by one of the few people to have played a part in both the turn of the century "Martian Scare" and the latter-day "Age of the Flying Saucer"—the Swiss psychologist Carl Gustav Jung. His 1958 book *Flying Saucers: A Modern Myth of Things Seen in the Skies,* remains one of the most perceptive commentaries on the UFO phenomenon. This is despite the fact that it was written when the UFO phenomenon was only ten years old, when the case file was only a fraction of its present size. Indeed some of the most striking features of the UFO phenomenon—including the remarkable outbreak of abduction claims—had yet to occur. Nevertheless, patterns were already beginning to emerge. In the book, Jung notes how often the report insists that

> the witness is above suspicion because
> he was never distinguished for his lively
> imagination or credulousness but, on the
> contrary, for his cool judgement and
> critical reason.

To Jung as a psychologist, this was an important clue, because he knew from his clinical work that it is in people of

LEFT: Brigadier General Roger M. Ramey, commanding officer of the 8th Air Force, and Colonel Thomas Dubose, 8th Air Force Chief of Staff, look over the metallic debris found at Roswell, New Mexico in 1947.

Cover artwork for Carl Gustav Jung's 1958 study of the UFO phenomenon, Flying Saucers: A Modern Myth of Things Seen in the Skies.

this kind that the subconscious has to resort to particularly drastic measures, if it wishes its contents to be perceived by the *conscious* mind. The most effective way by which it does this is projection. The individual externalizes his inner preoccupation as an object outside himself. The flying saucer is the outward representation of the subconscious hope or fear, chosen because it symbolizes the benefits or the menace presented by the otherworldly visitors.

At the time that Jung wrote his book, contact with flying saucer occupants had only just begun. The only contactee case known to Jung—apart from that of Adamski, on whom he heaps sarcastic comments—was that of California factory worker Orfeo Angelucci, who claimed to have been

chosen by beings from another world as their evangelist on Earth. Jung found this case to be of the deepest interest: "Without having the faintest inkling of psychology, Angelucci has described in the greatest detail the mystic experience associated with a UFO vision."

Angelucci's fairy tale encounter was, for Jung, a perfect example of myth perceived as reality. To Jung, whether or not the encounter experience had any physical reality was only of secondary interest. The primary question was to discover what, in the course of the experience, was released from the individual subconscious. The question of whether flying saucers existed was essentially irrelevant to the encounter phenomenon, because encounter experiences occur on a different level of reality to UFO sightings.

FLYING SAUCERS FROM OUTER SPACE

The astonishing fact is that there is not a scrap of evidence for the otherworldly origin of UFOs. The popular conception whereby they have come to be perceived as extraterrestrial spaceships is supported by nothing but conjecture.

However, it has to be said that the conjecture is a perfectly logical one. If UFOs are truly behaving as witnesses say they are, there is nothing on Earth that can behave in that way, so it makes sense to suppose that their origin is elsewhere. The weak point in that argument is, of course, the question of whether UFOs are truly behaving as witnesses claim. In his 1979 work, *The UFO Handbook*, American investigator Allan Hendry showed how easily an honest and well-intentioned witness can misinterpret what is seen:

- A witness who saw a balloon said, "It looked like the saucers you read about."
- A witness who watched a star for an hour said, "It made a whirring noise."
- A witness described an advertising plane as "something out of *Star Wars.*"
- A woman scared by an ad plane screamed for her husband to get back in the car.
- A witness who saw Venus and Mars for a whole week said she was "scared so bad, could hardly breathe [and] lost sleep."
- Police officers who saw stars said they had "never seen anything like it all of our lives."
- A woman who watched a star changing color over a period of hours thought, "Oh my Lord, it's the end of the world! I'd better get down on my knees and pray!"

Hendry's findings, echoing the response to the H.G. Wells/Orson Welles *War of the Worlds* broadcast, reveal that there are virtually no limits to how

Triangle-shaped UFOs were observed by many people over the outskirts of Brussels, Belgium.

people will classify what they see to match what they expect to see. In fact, the history of the UFO phenomenon is largely a chronicle of things turning out to not be what they seem. From the start, it was recognized that at least nine out of ten of the cases reported turned out to have some explanation—sometimes prosaic, sometimes truly bizarre. Sometimes, too, the explanation was on the secret list. There is no doubt that clandestine aviation developments would have explained a number of sightings, if they had been public knowledge. For example, a massive wave of sightings was reported over Belgium in 1989. On November 29, 150 eyewitness reports came from the small town of Eupen alone. Even making allowance for excited imaginations, there seems no doubt that the sightings, —2000 or more in all—related to some unknown object flying over the country. Since its behavior was unlike that of any

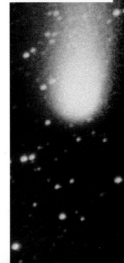

known aircraft, many believed they had no choice but to ascribe the sightings to something out of this world.

The only viable alternative was that the Americans were testing secret aircraft over one of the most densely populated places in the world. Could they really be so stupid as to do something so dangerous? It is hard to believe, yet investigation shows that this is the least improbable of all the explanations offered.

June 1966: An experimental disc made by Paul Villa to a design that he claims was offered to him by visiting aliens from Coma Berneices.

THE VARIETY OF UFOS

Once the idea had been accepted that flying saucers might come from beyond Earth, it quickly became the explanation of choice. Soon, for the majority of people, flying saucers—and later UFOs—came to be synonymous with extraterrestrial spacecraft. It was the simplest scenario, because it was a transposition of our own first tentative ventures beyond our own atmosphere. The simplicity was deceptive, however. The moment the claims were seriously evaluated, problems came thick and fast.

In the first place, there was the fact that hardly any two UFOs looked alike. Investigators did their best to prepare charts of the various kinds, much as, during World War Two, charts of aircraft types had been prepared for spotters. The diversity of descriptions was so great, however, that only a portion could be fitted into any pre-prepared category. Hundreds of sightings were one-of-a-kind events, defying classification. How could one make sense of this variety? One way was to break them down in terms of size and function:

- The very small ones—too small to contain a human-size occupant—were perceived as unmanned probes, or remote-controlled information-gatherers. Paul Villa claimed to have photographed some of these near Albuquerque, New Mexico in the 1960s.
- Small discs, which might be equivalent in size to a car were perceived as "scouts." They were considered to be manned, because occupants were sometimes seen, as in the 1970 Cowichan case.
- Larger discs, often described as being about 65 ft. in diameter, were probably the most frequently reported, even though they varied greatly in appearance. The sighting at Helena, Montana in 1966 was a classic instance of this type.
- Cigar-shaped craft, resembling airships—often described as very big—were perceived as "mother ships." These did not themselves come close to the Earth's surface. Instead, they housed "scout ships," which emerged and came closer to the ground. George Adamski claimed to have photographed some of these, together with their scouts.
- Finally, there were the truly massive UFOs, often said to be "the size of a football field." A group of witnesses in 1977 at Partington, in Lancashire, England, described the object they saw in these terms, although one of them compared it to a floating restaurant.

A classic domed disk with windows and four-piece landing gear hovers over a house in Helena, Montana. This "flying saucer" was reportedly seen in April, 1966.

This rough-and-ready classification made sense when compared to our

A UFO magazine from 1977 depicts a huge cigar-shaped extraterrestrial craft crashing down to Earth.

technology on Earth. When the time came for us to start exploring space, the first ventures would be made with unmanned "probes." The first manned spacecraft were very small, carrying one astronaut. As technology developed, spacecraft grew larger, carrying more passengers and equipment. But should this technological progression be applied to spacecraft from other worlds? If so, it presupposed not only that the aliens would go about things in the same way that we did, but that they were pretty much the same size as us, and similar to us in many other respects.

THE OCCUPANTS

In Chapter Two, we saw how ideas of otherworldly beings changed and developed. Even as late as the 1930s, science fiction writers and artists were contemplating all kinds of monsters that varied from the human norm in almost every respect. What a relief it was to find, when the first sightings were made of flying saucer occupants, that they were not so very different from ourselves:

• Near Hopkinsville, Kentucky, on the night of August 21, 1955, the Sutton farming family found themselves "besieged" by a group of short humanoid creatures, about 3 ft. tall. They had the oversized heads so frequently reported, very long arms and huge, taloned hands. The eyes were large and glowing, and their bodies had a silver metallic appearance, though whether this was flesh or clothing, the terrified witnesses could not be sure.

• At Socorro, on April 24, 1964, American police patrolman Lonnie Zamora saw a landed UFO. Nearby were "two small figures in what resembled white coveralls ... they appeared normal. Small, though— maybe the size of boys."

UFO FLYING SAUCERS

GOLD KEY®

90259 701

UFO FLYING SAUCERS

30¢

Have aliens crashed on Earth?

© WESTERN PUBLISHING COMPANY, INC.

• On July 1, 1965, French lavender farmer Maurice Masse had a similar experience when he arrived at his fields near Valensole. A UFO the shape of a rugby ball was among his bushes. Nearby, according to Masse, was

a human being of the height and build of a child of about eight ... wearing a one-piece suit, but no helmet. Inside the machine, I could see another being. ... The one who was down on the ground ... saw me, and he immediately jumped into the machine.

EXOBIOLOGY

July 1, 1965: Working early in the morning in his lavender field, Maurice Masse came across an alien craft and its occupants.

Later Masse added that the alien, on becoming aware of him, immobilized him with a hand-held tubular device before re-entering the UFO.

Although there are many variations, the flying saucer occupants in these three cases are typical of the first close encounter stories. Clearly, they could not be mistaken for humans. Equally clearly though, they were not monsters.

We have no reason to suppose that this would be the case. In principle, extraterrestrial visitors could easily be very much smaller or very much larger than we are. There is no reason to suppose that conditions on other worlds are anything like our own, but even if we assume that this is so, even very minor differences would affect the appearance of its residents. Our own Earth supports beings as varied as the ant and the elephant, the shrimp and the whale.

A great many science fiction plots involve non-human creatures with human or even superhuman intelligence. Giant ants are a Hollywood favorite, and all kinds of creatures have at one time or another been recruited to send shivers down sci-fi readers' spines. Suppose we set these aside and make the assumption, which we have really no right to make, that only creatures

fundamentally similar to ourselves—bipedal, walking rather than crawling or swimming, with brains contained in bony cases at the top of a spinal column—have been endowed with the necessary mental equipment to start exploring space. Even so, that still leaves open a wide variety of options. A very small difference in gravity could lead to marked differences in size. Differences in light would affect sense organs, so that visiting aliens might find Earth blindingly bright or gloomily obscure. Differences in atmospheric make-up would lead to different-sized breathing organs, and so on. Unless our visitors came from a planet precisely made up like ours, we should expect them to differ in appearance to a greater or lesser degree.

Which, of course, they do. Paradoxically, though, the appearance of alien visitors, as described by witnesses, does not involve differences which can clearly be attributed to environmental variations. Knowing how our own biological parameters are dictated by our environment, we ought to be able to infer, from the appearance of visiting aliens, what conditions prevail on their home planet. But no clear indications of this sort have hitherto emerged.

Exobiology—the study of the biology of extraterrestrials—is about as far from being an exact science as it is possible to get. There is, indeed, no certainty that there is any actual material for the science to study. The data are all derived from witness testimony, and the evaluation is wholly speculative. It amounts to little more than academic game-playing, albeit with a serious underlying intention.

Exobiologists necessarily take as their starting point the fact that the visiting aliens seem to adapt very readily to Earth's environment. Though this may seem "natural," it is really somewhat astonishing. It implies, for example, that they do not find our planet either too cold or too hot, though we know that temperatures on the planets of the Solar System vary enormously. Even here on Earth, many people find it difficult to adapt to Saharan heat or Polar cold. Again, the visiting aliens breathe our atmosphere quite happily, adjusting to it more easily than Earthpeople do to the rarefied air of, say, the Peruvian uplands. They do not seem to be troubled by whatever level of humidity they encounter, though most Earthpeople find our own jungle or rainforest conditions extremely difficult to cope with.

Is it simply that we are less adaptable than our alien visitors, or do they indeed come from a planet exactly like our own? Perhaps they are much less sensitive than we are to minor differences in environmental conditions. Perhaps they are wearing protective clothing which compensates for any difference. Or maybe the beings we meet are not the aliens in their true form, but in a form they have adopted for the specific purpose of visiting Earth, and adapting to it. Whether any of these or any other explanations are valid, the paradox of alien compatibility is not easily accounted for.

But that is not the only paradox of alien appearance—there is also the problem of their variety. In a 1966

RIGHT: *Through the looking glass: the basically humanoid features of a "short gray" alien.*

The massive head and huge "wrap-around" eyes of the stereotypical "Short-Gray" alien as identified by the writer Patrick Huyghe.

conditioned our own structure. In short, they conclude, "this creature will be basically like an ape, a human or, perhaps, the frequently reported little men observed in connection with UFO sightings."

In fact, descriptions of UFO occupants vary as much as the descriptions of the craft themselves. In Patrick Huyghe's authoritative *Field Guide to Extraterrestrials*, by far the largest section comprises bipedal beings more or less similar to ourselves. The remaining sections—Animalian, Robotic and Exotic—have markedly fewer specimens. All the varieties he presents are taken from actual cases, but this is precisely the weakness of attempting any such classification. The "identikit" drawings are artist drawings made from descriptions—sometimes verbal, sometimes witness' sketches. They are subject to all the shortcomings of eye-witness testimony—faulty observation, misinterpretation, defects of memory, the tendency to rationalize and to replace the unknown with the known. Moreover, the majority of descriptions of the more exotic varieties rest on the testimony of single witnesses. Most aliens were seen on one occasion only, by a solitary individual.

That aliens should vary so much in appearance is even more surprising than that the UFOs should vary. After all, our aircrews use a wide variety of aircraft for different purposes, but the people who fly them are roughly similar. Are we receiving visitors from a great number of different worlds? Or do many different races live on the worlds that visit us, with great physical differences between them?

The situation is not simplified by the fact that some stereotypes have emerged. You will have noticed that in the three cases I mentioned earlier—Zamora, Masse and the Sutton family—the aliens were all short humanoids, with a tendency to have large heads. This style of alien gradually evolved—so far as Earth witnesses are concerned—into the type which Huyghe labels "Short Gray." Originally reported by the abductees Barney and Betty Hill, whose adventure we shall consider in the next chapter, this has become—with minor variations—a stereotype for abductees. They are fundamentally human in

magazine article, Jack and Mary Robinson outlined the basic requirements for an intelligent alien being, showing that the most probable type would be carbon-based rather than silicon or crystalline-based. It would also have a hydrogen-oxygen cycle, as opposed to chlorine-fluorine-methane or a hydrogen-fluorine cycle, both of which—whatever their advantages as a source of energy—would have serious drawbacks in terrestrial environmental conditions. Consequently, they argue, any alien capable of surviving on Earth would have to conform basically to the same parameters as those which have

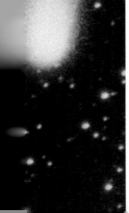

appearance, with two legs, two arms, trunk and head. The major differences are the very large head and the big black "wrap-around" eyes. The nose, mouth and ears are optional. If the beings are naked, there is no indication of navel or genitals. The number of fingers and toes may vary, but by and large, the Short Grays barely fall outside the parameters of human appearance.

Does this mean that we can say that—setting aside the countless variations—we do have, in the Short Grays, an identifiable alien species? Unfortunately, this is not particularly realistic. For the differences between them, though minor, are nonetheless very real. We might try to set them aside by blaming defective observation—the witnesses, in the excitement of the encounter, might well have mistaken a detail like a nose or ears. But we are still left with the problem of deciding which version is the correct one.

There is always a further possibility, that of confabulation—that witnesses are seeing what they expect to see, and what they expect to see will be based on what others have seen. For example, researcher Nick Pope mentions the case of "Mary," an Irish abductee:

> Mary saw a copy of Whitley Strieber's book, *Communion*, and stopped in her tracks. The artist's impression of Whitley's alien, which was on the front cover of the book, was identical to the fairy that she had seen all those years ago. It was this incident that first caused her to suspect that some of the incidents from her childhood might not be due to fairies, after all.

While at first sight such cases seem to have a literal interpretation—that seeing the artist's depiction of Streiber's entity reminded Mary of the entity she had herself seen but forgotten—there is also the possibility that she was responding to an archetype embedded in her subconscious. Though this sounds far-fetched, it conforms to the patterns of human behaviour observed by Jung that were discussed earlier. It is also confirmed by such findings as the Lawson-McCall experiment in "imaginary abductees," which we shall look at in Chapter 7.

ALIEN AGGRESSORS

Reports of UFOs run into millions; reports of their occupants into thousands. But when it comes to figuring out what those occupants do, what their intentions are, and why they are here, we have very little useful to go on. All information comes from the contact and abduction cases that we shall look at more closely in the next chapter.

Yet if the alien visitations are genuine, they must have a purpose. Simply to know that purpose would be an immense step forward in our understanding of the universe. Are otherworldly beings driven by the same motivations as ourselves, or are their actions governed by a wholly different agenda, one which we might never understand, even if we were told?

As we have seen in earlier chapters, our own thinking as to why beings from one world should visit other worlds has been dominated by two ideas, one positive and the other negative. On the one hand, there is scientific curiosity and exploration; on the other, aggression, invasion, and domination. Jules Verne's space travelers were on a strictly scientific mission of exploration, but H.G. Wells portrayed both his Selenites and his Martians as dangerous, and he set the pattern for most subsequent writers. It is true to say that the vast majority of science fiction, when dealing with interaction between ourselves and the extraterrestrials, involves conflict to a greater or lesser extent. Even that great television series, *Star Trek*, had the ongoing hostility with the Klingons as a background to incidents which all too often involved some kind of armed confrontation.

So, when the Flying Saucers came, suspicion was uppermost in most people's minds. Brad Steiger, who we have seen coming out of the closet to identify himself as one of the "Star People," was clearly unaware of his alien origins in 1967. That year, he and Joan Whritenour wrote *Flying Saucers are Hostile* and, two years later, *Flying Saucer Invasion: Target Earth*:

There is a wealth of well-documented evidence that UFOs have been responsible for murders, assaults, burnings with direct-ray focus, radiation sickness, kidnappings, pursuits of automobiles, attacks on homes, disruptions of power sources, paralysis, mysterious cremations, and destruction of aircraft.

Their books are as full of horror stories as any science fiction collection. By contrast, the French group GABRIEL, in their wide-ranging survey of the phenomenon, found only six cases of alien aggression. One took place in 1897, and involved a Michigan farmer being hit by a "Martian." Three related cases occurred in Venezuela, with the testimony of the young men concerned open to question; a 1958 case in Hoganas, Sweden involved an attack by "fluid" creatures who fled when a motor-horn was sounded: And a 1965 case from Argentina concerned three

Steiger and Whritenour's book in which UFOs are perceived as aggressive invaders.

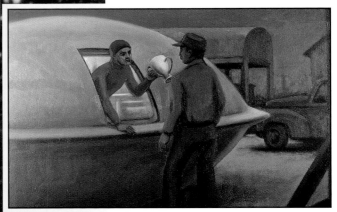

Joe Simonton is visited by aliens who ask him for some water; in return they give him pancakes.

schoolboys, and no UFO was sighted.

If that is the worst we have to fear, it is hard to take General MacArthur's 1955 warning seriously: "The nations of the world will have to unite, for the next war will be an interplanetary war." More than forty years later, we can be thankful that no war of the worlds has broken out, no alien invasion has taken place. The only aspect of alien behaviour that can be construed as aggressive is the habit of abducting humans and subjecting them to medical examinations. Even that is seen as benevolent by many commentators.

ALIEN CURIOSITY

As we have seen, even Brad Steiger changed his mind about the aliens and came to think of them as benevolent. Most researchers have dismissed the aggression stories as exaggerated; though we don't know what aliens want, it doesn't seem as though they mean us harm. But that only makes it harder to understand what motivates them. Most of the time, they simply fly overhead. They waved at Father Gill and his flock at Papua New Guinea in June, 1959. In April, 1961, they presented Joe Simonton with four pancakes. At Cennina, Italy, in November, 1954, two of them grabbed Rosa Lotti's flowers and try to take her stockings. At Vilvorde, Belgium, in 1973, a 3-ft. high humanoid appeared to examine a suburban garden with something like a metal detector. Simple aggression we could understand, but most of the aliens behavior is ambiguous to the point of

absurdity. That hasn't stopped a lot of people from guessing at their motives, though.

It is possible that the aliens are simply curious, just as our own space exploration is motivated largely by scientific curiosity. Yet, though this may seem to us the most plausible motive, there is little evidence to support it. Occasionally, sightings are reported in which the aliens are apparently collecting soil samples, but if that's what they are doing, they do not seem to be going about it very enthusiastically. There are no signs of any methodical exploration, such as we make on our own expeditions to the Moon and Mars.

No alien has ever been seen using a camera, a theodolite, or even a tape measure ...

The most evident indications of scientific curiosity would seem to be the abduction reports, in which examinations of human physiology, the taking of sperm samples etc., suggest a biological interest. But as we shall see, there are serious problems with the abductees' testimony. In any case, it raises the question that if the aliens are motivated by scientific curiosity, is it reasonable that the only form that curiosity takes is examining the bodies of abducted humans? Why do they seem to show no interest in our engineering

Rosa Lotti, an Italian housewife, encountered aliens while she was walking through the woods to church in 1954. The aliens grabbed the flowers she was holding and tried to take her stockings!

achievements, our cities, our monuments? Do they have so many pyramids of their own that they won't spare ours a glance?

But the moment we use a word like "reasonable," we are reminded how little right we have to impose our notions of what is reasonable on these otherworldly beings. This is particularly true since we don't even know for sure that they exist.

HERE TO HELP US

The best way to understand the aliens' motives would be to have them tell us in their own words. According to those who claim to have met them, they are often happy to do this. For example, Gloria Lee, a contactee we shall meet again in the next chapter, quotes her extraterrestrial contact, J.W. from Jupiter:

> We have come to your planet to help with your evolvement … We bring you the way to a new life. We can help your planet immensely with the knowledge in our possession. We come in peace and brotherly love.

The great majority of the contactees we shall encounter in the following chapter insist that the aliens they meet have benevolent intentions. Hundreds of books have been written, messages obtained from these beings by channeling, dictation or automatic writing. They tend to share the same message—inviting Earthpeople to qualify for Cosmic Brotherhood by learning to live in peace and love, caring for the environment, giving up war, and the like. The general principles are fine, but unfortunately, they are not accompanied by any practical advice on how they are to be realized. The fact that they are given to people who are not in any position to implement them is also regrettable. Random members of the general public, however enthusiastic, are not likely to bring wars to an end.

On a more immediately practical level, there have been, throughout the history of the UFO phenomenon, reports of individuals being healed by UFO occupants. A Canadian lady told

me she received daily visits from aliens who were actively cooperating with the Mexican Government to find a cure for cancer. American author Preston Dennett collected more than 100 cases in his book, *UFO Healings*. The author admits to having previously been skeptical about UFOs but, says he became convinced of their existence due to the number of cases in which individuals claim to have been healed thanks to alien intervention. Picking one case at random, we read how Licia Davidson of Los Angeles—who had been having UFO contacts for as long as she can remember—was in 1989 diagnosed as having terminal cancer and given three months to live. Soon after, she was abducted by aliens who operated on her. The next time she visited her doctor, all traces of her cancer had gone.

The cases quoted by Dennett cover a wide range of ailments, and a variety of treatments are used by the alien doctors. Some 30% of patients are healed with more or less conventional surgery; 21% with a beam of light; 13% with unfamiliar instruments; 9% with pills, salves or other medication, and 5% by "alien mind power." A good many of these healings take place aboard UFOs. Others are healed while observing a UFO—usually in the form of a beam of light—or in the course of house visits by aliens.

There are even cases in which some kind of "absent healing" seems to occur. A particularly puzzling case is that of an American woman, Beryl Hendricks. At home one day in 1978, Hendricks joined her husband on a couch. There, she appeared to pass out. It seemed to her that she was on some kind of operating table, with a number of figures around her. They removed a tumor from her breast.

During the entire time, however, she was watched by her husband. He saw that she did not move from the couch. In other words, the operation did not take place in physical reality. Yet, if we can believe her subsequent claim, the operation was performed, and the tumor was really and truly gone when she woke. Psychologist Kenneth Ring, who investigated the case, was baffled. Though no believer in UFOs, he asked "What on earth—or in heaven—do we

have here? Is this a Near Death Experience, or some kind of UFO encounter?"

If we accept the physical reality of extraterrestrial visitors, we are obliged to credit them with the healing. In addition to the cases collected by Dennett, many others have been recorded from all parts of the world. However, we should bear in mind that preoccupation with our physical health not only plays a large part in our daily life, but is intimately bound up with our beliefs. For instance, healing is a recurrent theme in Christian religious belief. Jesus himself is credited with many healings, and a healing miracle—either during the person's life or as a result of a pilgrimage visit to a shrine—is virtually essential for any candidate for sainthood.

This does not invalidate healings by extraterrestrial visitors, but it does require us to consider them in the wider context that all visitors from other worlds—except those specifically

Gloria Lee, founder of the Cosmon Foundation, who starved herself to death on alien's instructions.

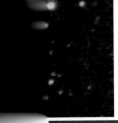

The fairy Melsuine who, once her true nature was discovered by her husband, resumed her fairy shape and left him.

evil or hostile—are credited with healing. This is tantamount to saying that they are expected to perform healings. Any visitor from another world who carries a cure for cancer in his briefcase can be sure of an immediate welcome.

To counter skepticism, the medical authorities at Lourdes now require very strict evidence for a healing miracle attributable to Bernadette's vision of Mary. At the very least, they require thorough medical documentation of the patient's state before and after the visit. Thus, the sick who go to Lourdes, can make sure before their visit that such records are available, as they go there in deliberate hope of a cure. But UFO-related healings come out of the blue. Because the patient is taken by surprise, it is rare that satisfactory documentation is available.

This is true even of the best-documented instance, the classic case of "Dr X." On November 2 at 4 a.m., in the morning, Dr X. saw, from the terrace of his home, a pair of linked UFOs unlike any reported elsewhere. They directed a beam at him, then left with a loud bang. He woke his wife, who noted that an ankle wound, sustained three days

before while chopping wood, had gone. The next day, he found himself cured of a war injury, that had for years partially paralyzed his right arm and leg. He also had a strange triangular mark on his belly, as did his 14-month-old son.

Although investigated by Aimé Michel, France's most eminent ufologist, the case rests largely on the testimony of the witness. Taken at face value, it implies that the occupants of two UFOs, knowing of Dr. X's predicament, made a special journey to his neighborhood, carried out various maneuvers, then directed a beam at him which, among other things, instantly cured both a paralysis and a physical injury. In other words, the supposed beam of light somehow transferred to Dr. X's body the equivalent of medication. It performed manipulation if not surgery, provided whatever was needed for instant regeneration of tissue, and so on … This is aside from diagnosing the complaints in the first place. Some beam of light! If this is what actually took place, then the cure is as miraculous as any reported in a religious context.

Another disconcerting case occurred in 1984. *The Weekly World News* told how Australian yachtsman Steve Palmer, sailing in the Bermuda Triangle, was too sick with an infected appendix to sail to shore, though he knew he needed urgent treatment. Fortunately, a ball of white light appeared in the sky, changing into a trio of 6 ft. tall men in metallic green bodysuits. He fell asleep, and when he woke, the aliens told him his appendix was gone into the sea. They cooked him a warm white broth to recover his strength. There was a surgical incision on his right side. When he got back to the Bahamas, a doctor told him he had had a professional appendectomy done on him within the past 2 to 4 days.

The absence of convincing medical records for these alien healings is unfortunate. If we could be certain that they did really take place as claimed by the patient, we would know for sure that the extraterrestrial visitors exist on the same plane of reality as ourselves, able to operate in the material world that we inhabit. Moreover, we would know that their intentions are benevolent.

SEX WITH ALIENS

Romances between humans and otherworldly beings are a traditional feature of legend. Mermaids, in particular, have a distressing habit of falling in love with humans, leading to difficulties—often fatal—when it becomes a question of "My place or yours?" Frequently, such stories involve the Cupid and Psyche motif, whereby one must not see the other, or utter their name, etc. The fairy Melusine was just one of many creatures whose relationship with a human came to a sad end for this reason. When Melusine was forced to leave, her husband retained custody of their children, though she came to revisit them at night when he and their new stepmother were asleep.

The question of whether humans can have sexual relations with aliens obviously depends on how human-like the aliens are. This brings us back to the questions we had to consider earlier in this chapter. If there is to be crossbreeding between aliens and humans, they must be genetically similar to us. Dr. Michael Swords, in an article entitled "Extraterrestrial Hybridization Unlikely," has pointed out the biological obstacles. Inter-species breeding is a virtual impossibility, because each species has different numbers of chromosomes; the numbers range from 2 to 200. There is no record of successful mating between humans (with 23 pairs of chromosomes per cell) and gorillas or chimpanzees (with 24), so the aliens would need to be even closer to us than the apes.

The chemistry of life on Earth is extremely complex, and it is specifically adapted to conditions on our planet. Even if life were to develop on another planet in exactly the same way as it did on Earth—itself an astronomically unlikely chance—all the components would need to be the same. Even if we assume that coincidence, it would still be necessary for those ingredients to be present in the same proportions, and to match in number and arrangement. Even on Earth, there is enormous variability in this respect. The likelihood is almost zero that aliens from another planet, even one very similar to our own, would match us sufficiently for successful mating to take place.

Some of the "ancient astronaut" theories discussed in Chapter Two suppose that the human race originated elsewhere. If we grant that that is what occurred, it is possible that today's alien visitors come from the same planet, and are therefore of the same species as ourselves. In that case, mating would be much less of a problem. But from what we have seen of our alien visitors, this doesn't seem likely. Only a tiny percentage of all the visiting aliens are sufficiently humanlike in appearance for it to be possible that they are of the same species. If we do share a common origin, either they or we have changed so much in the past tens of thousands of years that we could no longer be taken for members of the same family.

However, there are some humans who claim from personal experience that sexual relations with aliens are possible. Elizabeth Klarer was a wife and mother living in the hills of Natal, South Africa, where she had seen UFOs on several occasions. Eventually, in 1956, she met one of their occupants, Akon. He was a scientist from Meton, a planet in the Alpha Centauri constellation and was seeking an Earthwoman as a mate for experimental purposes. "We rarely mate with Earthwomen," he explained. "When we do, we keep the offspring to strengthen our race and infuse new blood."

What began as a clinical experiment turned into a meaningful relationship:

> I surrendered in ecstasy to the magic of his love-making, our bodies merging in magnetic union as the divine essence of our spirits became one ... and I found the true meaning of love in mating with a man from another planet.

She also found motherhood, for she became pregnant and was taken by Akon (together with her beloved MG car) to Meton, to bear her child there. She spent four idyllic months on Meton, where there was no pollution (except that caused by her car, presumably); everyone was vegetarian, and there were horses for her to ride once she had recovered from childbirth. Unfortunately, however, because Meton had a different vibratory rate to that of Earth, she could

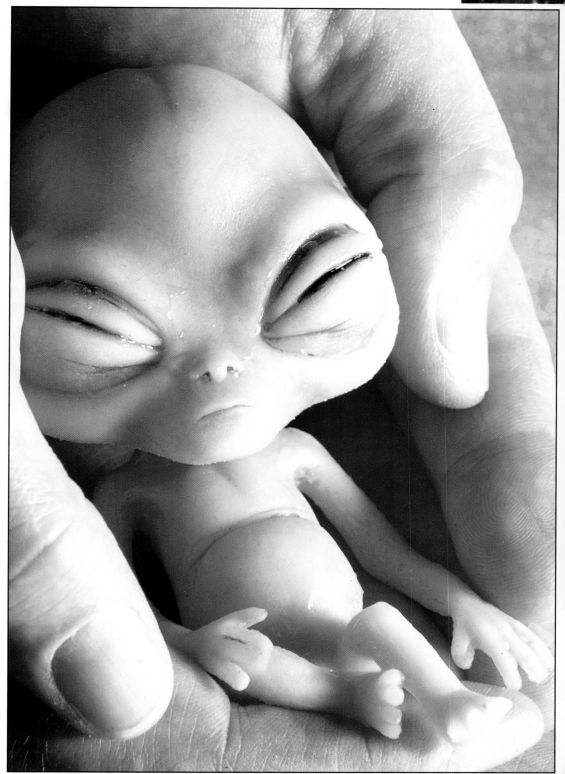

Some who have been abducted claim to have had sexual relationships with aliens. Could such trysts produce alien-human hybrids?

not live there permanently. She had to return (together with her MG) to Africa, leaving her son, Ayling, to be brought up by his father.

The following year, a similar experiment was carried out, this time

between a human male and an alien female. Once again, the location was an isolated rural one, but this time it was a Brazilian farmer, Antonio Villas Boas, who was the selected mate. He was working in his fields late on the night of

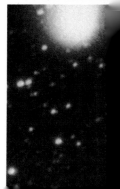

October 15, 1957 when a UFO landed close by. He tried to get away, but his tractor stalled, presumably immobilized by the three short aliens who dragged him into their spacecraft.

There, they undressed him and rubbed a liquid over his body with a wet sponge-like object, led him into another room where a blood sample was taken, and then left him for half an hour. Some kind of gas was pumped into the room, which made him vomit. Then a woman came into the room:

> She came in slowly, unhurriedly, perhaps a little amused at the amazement she saw written on my face. I stared open-mouthed, for the woman was entirely naked, as naked as I was ... She was beautiful, though of a different type of beauty compared with that of the women I have known. Her hair was blond, nearly white ... her body was much more beautiful than any I have ever seen before. She was much shorter than I am, her head only reaching my shoulder. The woman came towards me in silence, looking at me all the while as if she wanted something from me, and suddenly she hugged me and began to rub her head against my face from side to side. At the same time I also felt her body glued to mine ... I became uncontrollably sexually excited ... We ended up on the couch, where we lay together for the first time. It was a normal act, and she reacted as any other woman would. Some of the growls that came from her at certain times nearly

Tommy Lee Jones and Will Smith starred in the Hollywood blockbuster, The Men in Black, *which was based on the idea of a secret organization formed to tackle all forms of alien life.*

> spoiled everything, as they gave me the disagreeable impression of lying with an animal ... Then we had some petting, followed by another act, but by now she had begun to deny herself to me, to end the matter. When I noticed that, I too became frigid, seeing that that was all they wanted, a good stallion to improve their own stock.
>
> Before leaving, she pointed to her belly, and smilingly (as well as she could smile) pointed to the sky. I interpreted the signs as meaning to say that she intended to return and take me with her to wherever it was that she lived.

The female entity that Antonio Villas Boas mated with seems to have been physically compatible with him, and may have been genetically so. This implies that she was of the same species as ourselves. We cannot be sure that she was of the same species as her companions, though Villas Boas supposed this to be so. He never had a clear sight of any of his other captors, though he describes them as "men." They wore close-fitting clothes which covered them entirely, and helmets twice the size of a human head with three tubes coming backwards out of them. This suggests that they had some difficulty adapting to Earth's atmosphere.

It is reasonable to suppose that the purpose of the gas which made Villas Boas vomit when he was put in the second room was to enable the female

to function without a helmet. In other words, apart from a minor difficulty in adapting to our atmosphere, his captors were of the same species as ourselves. This makes the Villas Boas case, consequently, very much the exception. Only very rarely are abductions carried out by beings like ourselves. The case is also exceptional in other ways. For instance, most abductees are beamed up to spacecraft which they never see, whereas Villas Boas was manhandled up an Earth-type ladder into a landed vessel.

There are many questions whose answers would tell us much about our extraterrestrial visitors. Was Villas Boas' lover the same species as the rest of the crew, or could she have been created specially—an android, or whatever? He describes both her and his captors as short, but not so short that he could not copulate with her. She seemed in no doubt how to go about the act. Does this mean that the procedure is the same on her planet, or had the aliens gotten hold of instructional videos?

Other problems arise in another Latin American case, that of Liberato Anibal Quintero, an illiterate farm hand employed on a ranch in Magdalena province, Colombia. One night in November 1976, he returned home tired from work and fell asleep in his hammock. Not even a thunderstorm outside roused him. Then he woke, sweating and feeling strange, and hurried out of the house. In the yard

An artist's impression of Antonio Villas Boas' experience with aliens. He allegedly had sex with, and impregnated, a female alien.

outside, he saw an egg-shaped UFO descend from the sky and land by the cowsheds, and "people" about 5 ft. tall came down a sort of stairway. Three of them had long hair, and looked like women.

They noticed Quintero, and overpowered him. He came to in a room bathed in light; the only other occupants were the three women, who were rubbing his back as though to relieve the pain incurred in his struggle. He responded to the caresses of the nearest woman and this led to sexual intercourse. Afterwards, she seemed to want more, and when he proved exhausted, she made some barking noises which were answered from elsewhere in the craft. A yellowish drink was brought to him, which restored his sexual energies, and something of an orgy followed. Finally, he was given an injection and came to lying on the grass, with no sign of the UFO or its occupants.

In the Villas Boas case, there was a clear indication that breeding was the purpose of the encounter. In the Quintero case, it is less evident, but we must suppose that if this was a carefully planned space mission, it is unlikely that a casual sexual encounter would be permitted. We must suppose that this, too, was intentional; and if intentional, then purposeful.

The real meaning behind this mating with aliens may be disclosed by another sexual encounter, this time from North America. Sightings of UFOs had given Bruce Smith, of Oregon, a strange yearning for a relationship with a space female. His therapist suggested that this was because he was having difficulties with his Earthly sex life—he was currently going through divorce. Smith would have liked to believe this, but one night an alien female appeared in his bedroom, accompanied by two male companions. She was approximately 5½ ft. tall, "not bad looking," and naked, according to Smith. They made love, and some time later he was taken on a mental voyage to a galactic nursery, where between 30 and 40 of the children that he saw were his.

The aliens told him that there were already either 340,000 or 34 million children—he wasn't sure if he'd understood them correctly—born with

Earth fathers like himself. The intention was that when they reached adulthood—somewhere around 2020 to 2030—they would colonize Earth. With Earth fathers, there should be no legal obstacles. Bruce was delighted: "I'm proud they picked me. I've got kids in space."

THE MEN IN BLACK

Even though there is no consensus as to what aliens look like, most witnesses have no problem recognizing the beings they see as otherworldly. Villas Boas, Quintero and Smith may have been having sex in the normal way, but they had no doubt they were coupling with aliens. Naturally, if the being was seen stepping out of a saucer, the presumption would be that it is an extraterrestrial. But even when they are seen independently from their craft, they are recognized. It did not cross American abductee Whitley Strieber's mind—when he was disturbed at night by intruders in his bedroom—that his home was being robbed by terrestrial burglars. Even in the semi-dark, he knew that the 3-ft. tall being was neither a child or a dwarf, but something otherworldly.

However, there is one category of entity which seems to stand at the borderline. They seem to be both part of a continuing folklore tradition and a new species which might have been created specifically for our conspiracy-suspecting age—the so-called "Men in Black."

We have been watching you and your activities. Pleased be advised to discontinue delving into the mysteries of the universe. We will make an appearance if you disobey.

An artist's impression of the sinister Men in Black —aliens masquerading as official investigators into paranormal experiences.

Albert Bender, director of the International Flying Saucer Bureau (IFSB), had been warned, but flying saucers were his life, and he was determined to unearth their secret. So he persisted—and in July, 1953, he became the most famous of all who have been privileged with a visit from the legendary Men in Black.

Despite its grandiose title, the IFSB was an amateur, one-man affair. Its headquarters were in Bender's own home, in an attic den decorated with occult imagery like a schoolboy's bedroom. But this was the height of the flying saucer boom, and his Bureau had been well accepted in the saucer community. A year after founding his organization, Bender felt he was in a position to reveal the truth about the flying saucers to the world. Before Bender finally committed himself, he felt he should report his knowledge to the authorities in Washington. But neither his organization nor the U.S. government were ever to learn his secret. Before he could mail his report, it was stolen from a locked box in his den, even though his family assured him that no one had set foot in his room.

A few days later, he had the explanation. The Men in Black came calling. Bender was lying down in his bedroom after being overtaken by a fit of dizziness when he became aware that three shadowy figures had entered his room. All were dressed in black clothes, like clergymen, but wore Homburg hats which concealed or shaded their faces.

Despite their menacing appearance, the three men were not hostile. All fear left Bender as they started to communicate with him telepathically. After requesting him to address them as Numbers 1, 2 and 3, respectively, they confirmed that, yes, he had indeed stumbled upon a part of the secret of the saucers, but he must not reveal it. Further, he was to disband his organization, cease publication of its journal, and swear not to reveal the truth to anyone. Bender swore to do so on his honor as an American citizen, and in return they told him the rest of the secret. True to his word—though he subsequently wrote a book-length account of the incident—Bender has never revealed the secret of the saucers.

Bender is just one of many individuals

One of the Men in Black who visited Albert K. Bender in August, 1953.

in the UFO world who claim to have been visited by the Men in Black. Typically, they appear in a group of three, generally male. They may arrive by car, which is likely to be a black Cadillac in the United States, or a black Rolls Royce in Britain. In either case, the model will be somewhat out of date, yet immaculate and even new-smelling. When Robert Richardson was visited by two MIB after a UFO sighting in 1967, his visitors arrived in a black 1953 Cadillac. He noted the number and checked it, and found that it had not yet been issued—another characteristic feature.

In appearance, the MIB conform closely to the popular image of the "secret service man"—dark suit, dark hat, dark shoes and socks, but white shirts, all crisp, clean and new-looking. They are frequently described as vaguely foreign or exotic. Often, there are more bizarre features. They walk stiffly, perform even trivial movements awkwardly, or handle familiar objects as if doing so for the first time. The MIB who in 1976 came to silence Dr Herbert Hopkins, a 58-year-old doctor who had been asked to act as consultant on a UFO case, seemed to be wearing lipstick. In other respects the MIB behaved like a poorly-programmed robot. He terminated their talk by saying, very slowly, "My energy is running low— must go now—goodbye," and walking unsteadily to the door.

Their faces are expressionless; not hostile, but slightly sinister. They reveal little about themselves. If they produce evidence of identity, it is invariably found to be false. In March, 1967, the United States Air Force issued a memo entitled "Impersonations of Air Force Officers" that was specifically concerned with impostors claiming to be USAF officers checking up on UFO witnesses. What the impersonators have to say is usually menacing. After George Smyth of Elizabeth, New Jersey, had questioned some boys about a possible alien encounter, he saw two figures watching from a parked car. Later, he received a phone call telling him to give up UFO investigation.

The MIB speak in quaintly formal phrases reminiscent of Hollywood B-movies—"Again, Mr. Stiff, I fear you are not being honest," or "Mr. Veich, it would be unwise of you to mail that report." UFO witness Robert Richardson received a typical threat—"If you want your wife to stay as pretty as she is, then you'd better get the metal back!" In this as in many cases, the Men In Black seem to have astonishing sources of information. Somehow they knew of Richardson's encounter when only four people— himself, his wife and two senior officials of a UFO organization—knew of it.

Men in Black show many signs of unfamiliarity with human ways. Dr. Hopkins' son, John, was visited by a stranger with a female companion who claimed to know them. The female seemed strangely built, with breasts set very low and with something wrong about her hips. They sat on the sofa, pawing and fondling each other. The male asked John if he was doing it correctly, and when John went out of the room for a moment, asked his wife Maureen if she had any nude photos of herself.

Are the Men in Black human beings such as secret service or security officers or agents of an international conspiracy? Could they be aliens masquerading as humans? Are they flesh-and-blood entities, astral entities or hallucinated phantasms? All these and many other hypotheses have been proposed, and profound psychosocial theories have been advanced to account for their origin. They seem in many ways to be creatures of the imagination—direct descendants of the demons and other evil entities who have figured in popular folklore throughout human history. Yet at the same time, those who have encountered them have related the incidents in such matter-of-fact terms that it seems they must be something more than fantasy.

The lone MIB who appeared to Peter Rojcewicz in the library of the University of Pennsylvania seemed human enough. He was dressed in what is standard gear for MIB—black suit, white shirt, black tie and shoes. He suddenly appeared before Rojcewicz, saw that he was reading a book about flying saucers, and asked if he had ever seen one. When Rojcewicz said he hadn't, his visitor asked if he believed in their reality. Rojcewicz said he wasn't sure he was very interested in the phenomena, and the MIB screamed at him, "Flying saucers are the most important fact of the century and you are not interested?" He then rose, put his hand on Rojcewicz's shoulder, said, "Go well on your purpose," and left. Rojcewicz looked to see where the MIB had gone and found the library totally deserted. He returned to his reading, and after a while things returned to normal.

What makes this case exceptional is that Rojcewicz is a psychologist and a professor of folklore. He sees today's UFO-related MIB as part of an ongoing tradition that describes "part of the extraordinary encounter continuum — fairies, monsters, ETs, energy forms, flying saucers, flaming crosses." An encounter with a MIB will frequently change the witness' life. Though some are left frightened and nervous, others report that their lives have changed for the better. We shall see in Chapter Seven that this is true of many types of encounter with otherworldly beings.

What does Rojcewicz make of his own encounter? He doesn't think he was dreaming, but suspects he was in an altered state of consciousness. He describes the MIB as being "somewhere in the crack between real life and fantasy." With their evident association with UFO incidents, the MIB could as well be terrestrial security agents as extraterrestrial beings. But on balance, the evidence points towards the second interpretation. The many reports of their awkwardness and unfamiliarity with human ways and their uncanny access to private information seem unlikely characteristics for agents of the FBI or CIA. What we can say for certain is that,

whatever their nature, the Men in Black are truly a myth of our time. They symbolize man's age-old fear of the unknown in a strikingly contemporary guise. What remains uncertain is what kind of reality underlies the myth.

On the face of it, we would expect the occupants of UFOs to be more easily understood than any of the other categories of visitors we have considered. If they are the equivalent of our own space explorers, we should be able to share their motivations and understand their behavior. In fact, as we have seen, just the reverse is true.

Ten years ago, it was estimated that there had been about 150,000 serious UFO sightings which could not be explained by conventional means. If we accept this, it means that 150,000 crews of extraterrestrials left their home planets, doubtless at considerable trouble and expense, to come visit our planet. Why? Even after a half century of UFO visits, the nature of these visits remains ambiguous, their purpose is obscure, and even their very existence is open to question. Compared with the other beings from other worlds, they seem singularly ineffective.

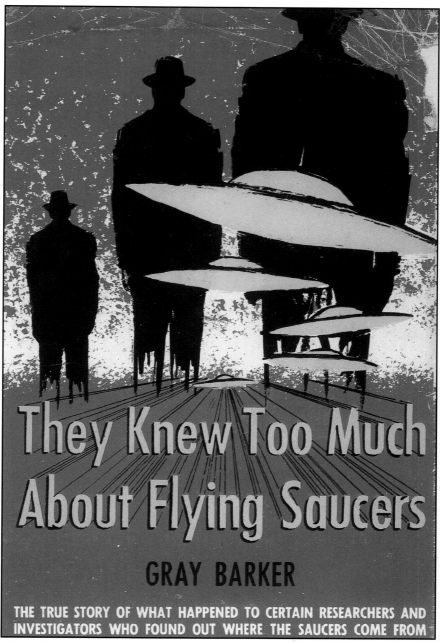

THE TRUE STORY OF WHAT HAPPENED TO CERTAIN RESEARCHERS AND INVESTIGATORS WHO FOUND OUT WHERE THE SAUCERS COME FROM

Gray Barker's 1956 book, They Knew Too Much About Flying Saucers, *which discusses the experiences of those who have been visited by the mysterious Men in Black.*

MAKING CONTACT

Since 1952, Mr Adamski has repeatedly claimed contacts with spacemen. He claims to have ridden in their spaceships, on trips around Venus and the moon. He has published photographs alleged to be pictures of UFO scouts and mother ships. These reports and pictures have been called fakes by several critics. But Adamski's believers insist he is an honest, persecuted man.

When people reported seeing Flying Saucers, their stories were widely accepted; when people reported seeing their occupants, they, too, were generally able to obtain a sympathetic hearing. But when individuals started claiming that they had *met* the occupants, they encountered a barrier of skepticism. Major Donald Keyhoe, writing in the newsletter of his organization NICAP—the National Investigations Committee on Aerial Phenomena—recognized the importance of settling the matter:

> False or true, the sensational nature of his claims has kept many people from seriously considering the verified UFO evidence. For this reason, it is vitally important that Adamski's stories either be proved beyond question or, if false, that they be completely discredited.

Yet, logically, it was inevitable that closer contact would take place sooner or later. If the flying saucers were space ships, they must have had occupants, and distant observations would surely lead to closer encounters. What provoked skepticism was partly the stories themselves, and partly those who told them. The stories were so far-fetched that they would hardly have

been believed even if told by the most believable people, and those who told them were simply not the most believable people.

No two contact stories are exactly alike, but they follow a fairly predictable pattern. Typically, they comprise a series of episodes:

- The contactee often has premonitions that something special is in store or, at least, so we are told after the event.
- Even if the contactee is surprised by

Jodie Foster and Matthew McConaughey in the 1997 film, Contact.

A spacecraft looms over the car of humans who have been lined up for abduction

the contact when it comes, the surprise doesn't last long. He or she rapidly adjusts to the circumstances and is soon on good terms with the alien or aliens. These are generally more or less human in appearance, are able to communicate easily in the contactee's own tongue or by telepathy, and are friendly and well-intentioned.

- Generally, they invite him or her aboard their vessel and give a guided tour of the craft. Often, they treat the contactee to a journey in space, though instead of allowing their guest to enjoy the sights, they tend to deliver a lecture comparing Earth with other civilizations. The comparison is invariably to Earth's disadvantage.
- After returning to Earth, life for a contactee will never be the same. For some, there will be just the one experience, while for others there will be further encounters. But almost always there is a message to be passed on to mankind. Usually, it contains a warning of what dreadful things will happen if Earthpeople go on being so materialist and aggressive. Sometimes a contactee will be given "official" status as the visitors' representative on Earth.
- For a while, the contactee is likely to enjoy a period of notoriety, during

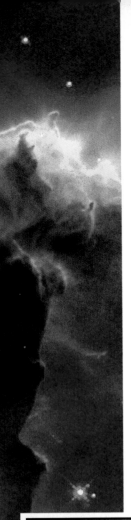

which he or she is a guest on radio talk shows, gives lectures, appears at flying saucer conventions and publishes (often with the help of a ghost writer) an account of the adventure. Sometimes, he or she becomes the center of a cult or the founder of a School of spiritual enlightenment, or may diversify into ecology, free energy machine design, radical politics, or some other New Age activity.

THE CONTACTEES

The contactees are a varied crowd. Consider these:

George Adamski was brought by his parents to the United States from Poland at age two. He claimed to have been educated privately, by extraterrestrials, at "the highest school of Cosmic Law at a monastery in Tibet." After six years study, he graduated, styled himself "Professor," and founded the occult-philosophical "Royal Order of Tibet" in

Orfeo Angelucci's leisure-time interest was scientific experiment, so he was not surprised to be contacted by extraterrestrials.

order to pass his knowledge on to others. During Prohibition, he used the Order as a cover for trading in bootleg liquor. At the time of his encounter, he was working in a friend's restaurant on Mount Palomar, California.

Orfeo Angelucci was a sickly child who spent many of his early years in the hospital for "organic weakness." He authored a thesis on "The Nature of Infinite Entities," which he mailed to eminent scientists, but none of them showed interest. At the time of his encounter, he was working at the Lockheed plant in California. In his leisure time, he conducted "scientific experiments." It was when he sent up materials in balloons that he attracted the attention of a flying saucer that happened to be close by.

Rose C. was described by science fiction writer Jimmy Guieu as "an average Frenchwoman." At the time of her encounter, she was 24, divorced with a 4-year-old child, living with her widowed father in southern France.

Stefan Denaerde was a well-to-do Dutch businessman, living in Den Haag.

Truman Bethurum was a construction engineer, working in the desert.

Woodrow Derenberger was the manager of an appliance store in West Virginia.

Aladino Felix (a.k.a. "Dino Kraspedon") was a former theological student, well educated, living in Sao Paulo, Brazil with his wife and children.

Daniel Fry, though described on the wrapper of his book as "the best-informed scientist in the world on the subject of space and space travel," was an obscure engineer whose achievements were limited to minor developments in missile systems. His Ph.D. was purchased from an English institution in exchange for a 10,000 word thesis and a cash payment.

George King had been concerned with esoteric matters from an early age, so was mentally prepared for his experiences: "When I was fifteen, I knew that one day I would visit other worlds." He practiced yoga for ten years before his contact, and was a faith healer. A colleague reported that "he had successfully and repeatedly demonstrated all psychic powers then commonly known," though it is not stated when, where or to whom he

demonstrated them. In May, 1954, he heard a voice telling him, "Prepare yourself! You are to become the voice of Interplanetary Parliament." A few days later, he said, "an Indian Swami of world renown" unexpectedly materialized in his apartment.

Eduard "Billy" Meier saw his first UFO at age 5, and began receiving telepathic communications shortly after. During the 1960s, he found his way to an ashram in India, where he met Asket, from the DAL Universe. Later, he settled in his native Switzerland.

Frenchman **Pierre Monnet** recalled that as a kindergartner, he sat on a bench and thought deeply about the immensity of the universe. "I looked up at the skies and thought, 'What are the other 'me's' doing on other worlds? Are they playing games, or are they, too, thinking?' That such a young child should think like that may seem impossible, but I assure you I'm not making it up."

CONTACT

This mixed bag of individuals all share one thing in common: They all believed they had met extraterrestrials. Most of them also believed they had been specially chosen for the privilege after being watched by the aliens, sometimes since infancy. Howard Menger, in 1932, at the age of 10, had a meeting with "the most exquisite woman my young eyes had ever beheld," who told him, "I have come a long way to see you, Howard, and to talk with you." Her people (she is a Venusian) had been observing him for a long time and now, she told him, "We are contacting our own." Though from Saturn, at the time of his later experiences he was working as a sign painter. His wife Connie/Marla, who was born on Venus, says:

I had been mentally space traveling since I was a child. I can remember the tingling sensation when I looked up at the stars ... longing, waiting for some ephemeral lover.

French contactee "Rose C." was an ordinary person with an everyday lifestyle who had a brief encounter with aliens, then relapsed again into obscurity.

Rose C...

RENCONTRE AVEC LES EXTRA TERRESTRES

les carrefours de l'étrange

EDITIONS DU ROCHER

Pierre Monnet had speculated about other worlds since early childhood: this photo was taken three years after his contact with aliens.

Her mother used to take her to lectures in New York, "usually on metaphysics and allied subjects." While married to her first, terrestrial husband, she said she had "a strange feeling that I was being observed—that someone was watching, waiting …"

In June, 1946, Menger again met the Venusian lady of his boyhood encounter. She revealed that despite her appearance, she was more than 500 years old. This was followed by frequent meetings with aliens from Venus, Mars and elsewhere:

> The nature of the meetings required that many of them take place at night. Often I would receive such mental impressions between 1:00 and 2:00 a.m., and, while my wife lay sleeping, I would drive away to meet the space people and be given further instructions pertaining to my work.

This work largely consisted of helping the aliens adjust to earth conditions: Menger cut their hair, and one day was instructed to buy several outfits of female clothing.

> The women went into the next room, from which I soon heard a series of giggles and groans. Finally the door opened and the bras were flung out. They apologized, saying they just could not wear them, and they never had. Just why I didn't know, and you may be certain that I felt it wise not to ask!

On July 4, 1950, Daniel Fry discovered that it was a warm evening and his air conditioner was malfunctioning, so he took a walk in the neighborhood of his place of work, White Sands Proving Ground. About 9 p.m., he saw a strange-shaped object descend to ground level; he walked towards it to investigate, and found himself close to what was evidently an alien spacecraft. He was about to touch it when a voice warned, "Better not touch the hull, pal, it's still hot!" Taken by surprise, he stumbled back, tripped and fell, at which the voice added, "Take it easy, pal, you're among friends."

The speaker, A-lan, was actually more than 808 miles away, observing him from a mother craft. He invited Fry to enter the ship, which was conveniently furnished with four earth-style seats. A-lan explained he was from a civilization which had more or less made itself independent of planetary life, and permanently inhabited huge artificial spacecraft.

In July, 1951, 19-year-old Pierre Monnet had been visiting his fiancée who lived in a village a few miles away. He was cycling home to his house in Orange in southeastern France, when he and his bicycle were suddenly teleported to a quarry some 3 miles out of town. He dismounted at the entrance to the quarry, made his way into it "as if directed by an irresistible force." There he saw a domed disc some 49–66 feet in diameter hovering over the ground, giving off a blue-white glow which lit up the surroundings. As he got closer, the sounds of everyday life seemed to fade away.

Four "human beings" wearing close-fitting clothes were standing near the disc. They were beautiful, seemingly sexless, with long, neatly combed blond hair. Their look radiated gentleness, goodness and peacefulness. They imprinted a long message on his memory, which he was later able to transcribe perfectly. They also—though he wasn't aware of it at the time—took him on board their spaceship to perform an operation of "regeneration," which enabled him to live to the age of 120.

He turned away without saying goodbye, and remounted his bike. Then it seems he must have been teleported again, for the next thing he knew, he was arriving at the outskirts of Orange at the same time he had left his girlfriend's village, 1:30 a.m.

On March 23, 1952, which was his thirty-third birthday, Sicilian Eugenio Siragusa was waiting at a bus stop to go to his job, as a customs official, when he saw a strange object in the sky. This was followed by telepathic communications instructing him in his role as "Messenger." Ten years later, on October 30, 1962, he received a sudden impulse to drive up onto nearby Mount Etna. He had the feeling that he was not driving the car, but that it was controlled by a superior force. Once at his destination, he met two beings in spaceman-like costumes, who gave him a message before returning to their disc.

It was May 3, 1952, Orfeo Angelucci felt odd while working at the Lockheed plant. Driving home, he saw a strange disc-shaped object in the sky. Thinking it was "one of those flying saucers I had read about," he pulled off the highway to observe it. Two smaller objects separated from the disc, descended and hovered near his car. A voice told him, in perfect English, not to be afraid. The entity—still unseen—informed him that they had been observing him ever since his balloon experiment. He was the most important of three who had been chosen for contact; another lived in Rome, a third in India.

Angelucci was given information about flying saucers and the visitors' mission: "With deep compassion and understanding, we have watched your world going through its 'growing pains.' We ask that you look upon us simply as older brothers; we will aid Earth's people insofar as they, through free will, will permit us to do so." They then said that they would contact him again.

On July 27 and 28, 1952, Truman

Bethurum was out in the Nevada desert in his truck. He had been taking "a little snooze" in the truck's cabin, and he woke around midnight to find himself surrounded by small, strange-looking uniformed men. He began conversing with them, then saw the Saucer hovering nearby. He was taken to its Captain, who turned out to be a very attractive and friendly lady named Aura Rhanes. She invited him to sit down, and they talked for quite a long time.

On November 20, 1952, George Adamski and a group of friends drove out into the desert, hoping to see saucers. At Desert Center, after seeing a "mother ship," Adamski asked a friend to drive him away from the others and leave him alone. He then met a Venusian from a small flying saucer; they talked for some time, chiefly by telepathy. The Venusian left footprints in the sand with enigmatic markings. One of Adamski's companions, ancient astronaut theorist George Hunt Williamson, had thoughtfully brought along some Plaster of Paris, so was able to take a mold. His companions, though at a distance of a mile or more, later signed sworn affidavits that they witnessed the encounter.

Buck Nelson, an Ozark farmer, saw his first flying saucer on July 30, 1954. It shot a ray at him which permanently cured his lumbago and neuritis. On February 1, 1955, a saucer hovered over his farm, and a voice called down to ask if he was friendly. He replied that he was. On March 5, Nelson was again visited by the Saucer. This time it landed, and three aliens emerged, one of them an Earthman who has been living on Venus for the previous couple of years. The aliens had their dog with them. They chatted for an hour or so, until it was time to be getting along, but they promised to return.

One day in May, 1957, sisters Helen and Betty Mitchell stopped off for a soda in a downtown St. Louis coffee shop, where they met Elen and Zelas, crewmen from a huge mother craft that was orbiting Earth. Their visitors told them the Space People had been watching them for the past eight years, and had been noting their progress since birth. The sisters suspected a leg pull, but at a second meeting, they were shown how to construct a simple device that enabled them to communicate with the Space People.

In July, 1967, Stefan Denaerde was sailing with his family in the Oosterscheldt, on the Dutch coast, when his boat hit a submerged object. While investigating the cause, he rescued a body, which turned out to be that of an alien being. The submerged object was in fact an alien spacecraft. In return for rescuing their colleague, the occupants invited him aboard their craft. He was treated to an 8-hour instruction session, while his family remained in the boat nearby. Initially, they conversed in English, but subsequently used a form of universal pre-Babel language which seemed to him to be Dutch, but was in fact "the language of all living species in this universe: Even a plant or an animal will understand it." They gave a detailed account of life on their planet, Iarga, which is largely covered with water; the population density is 3728/ miles^2 – 18 times as high as that of the densely populated Netherlands! This did present problems, but the Iargans resolved them with admirable ingenuity.

On August 11, 1969, Frenchman Jean Miguères was driving his ambulance, carrying a patient—who in fact had died during the trip—from Perpignan to Rouen. Nearing the end of his journey, at 5:30 a.m., he

The aliens preferred to make contacts in out-of-the-way locations: no one beside engineer Truman Bethurum saw this huge "scow" when it landed in the Nevada desert.

Unlike today's abductors, the aliens encountered by the contactees were mostly of the type classified as "Blond Nordic", human-like and often indistinguishable from Earth people.

feel any pain and won't suffer at all as a result of this accident. From now on, you will be much stronger than before. I am going to "regenerate" you by a process not yet known on your planet.

Miguères later learned that the whole event had been monitored by the extraterrestrials.

We did not provoke anything, Earthman; all we did was orchestrate an event which was going to happen in any case ... Thanks to our detector, we saw the crazy car long before you did ... a rapid inquiry to our computer, whose sophistication is beyond your knowledge, told us the accident could not be avoided ... thanks to a magnetic field of a power surpassing your imagination, we were able to control the danger of fire and thus save the lives of the occupants of your vehicle.

Miguères asked, "In fact, then, you were using me as a sort of guinea-pig?" The alien admitted, "Yes, in a way." The alien then reminded him that without their intervention, he would have been killed ...

During April, 1975, John H. Womack was driving down a lonely country road in the Tennessee Valley in northern Alabama, when a ball of fire dropped through the sky onto the road. While he was watching it, a 164-foot disc appeared and hovered over a nearby meadow, humming gently. A beam of light deprived him of consciousness. The next thing he knew, he was sitting inside the vessel with a helmet on his head in a room full of gadgetry, surrounded by a variety of non-human entities. By means of a box connected to his helmet, the leader explained their good intentions, and gave Womack information about them.

Womack was surprised by how happy and relaxed he felt; the extraterrestrial explained that this was thanks to a pill he had just swallowed, an "anti-demon pill."

You are experiencing life completely free of demons for the first time. Demons exist throughout the universe. Demons are real, not just states of mind as most people

experienced unfamiliar physical sensations, and "felt" that someone was speaking to him, saying:

Don't be afraid—let yourself be guided, no harm will come to you, we are here to protect you and it will all be like a story for you. You will feel nothing; we order you to be calm ...

He noticed a strange cloud ahead of him, hovering over the road halfway between his ambulance and an approaching car. The dials on his dashboard immediately went haywire.

The approaching car was in the middle of the road, but when Miguères tried to avoid it, it seemed to direct itself at him, and there was no way he could avoid a collision. He was traveling at 87 mph, the other vehicle at 99 mph, and the accident was appalling. The other driver was killed, and he himself was trapped inside the wreckage and very badly injured. It seemed to him as though a being materialized in the seat beside him, and said (in French):

Don't worry, you only seem to be injured; in reality, you're not hurt at all. You won't

Helen and Betty Mitchell, two contactees from St Louis, tell of their exciting meeting with two handsome Space Brothers.

WE MET THE SPACE PEOPLE

THE STORY OF THE MITCHELL SISTERS

BY HELEN and BETTY MITCHELL

$1.00

SAUCERIAN PUBLICATIONS, CLARKSBURG, W.VA.

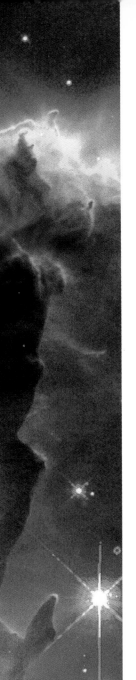

think. They are not visible to the eye, but they do exist on a higher plane of living. Demons are able to invade our minds and cause us to be evil, greedy, selfish, and unhappy. The pill I gave you has driven all demons and their influences from your mind, leaving you with nothing but pure joy in your soul. The anti-demon pill is our greatest discovery. It eliminates all forms of hate, jealousy, greed, misery and wars. It causes a person to be completely happy with just being alive. A person who is demon-free has no need for material possessions to give him a false feeling of security. When the mind is free of demons, only love and joy is left inside …

Womack saw much more, including a video of life on the aliens' (unidentified) planet; then he was returned to where he left his car. Regrettably, he did not think to bring a packet of those Anti-Demon Pills back with him.

THE ENTITIES

As a rule, the beings encountered by contactees are more or less humanoid, but with slight distinctive differences. All adjust without much difficulty to Earth's atmosphere, though Rose C.'s visitors found it exhausting, and Schmidt's contact took three cautious breaths before removing her mask. Derenberger's Indrid Cold from Lanulos was entirely human in appearance and behavior; the two of them communicated telepathically. Many of the visitors can, and often do,

George Adamski's meeting with Orthon from Venus, witnessed by his companions at a distance, may qualify as the first recorded alien encounter.

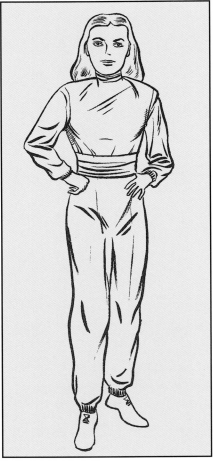

Orthon found no difficulty in adapting to Earth temperature, atmosphere and gravity, though our conditions differ vastly from his home planet, Venus.

pass for human when circumstances require: Brazilian Aladino Felix's visitors were so human-like that his wife took one to be a visiting priest.

Adamski's Venusian, Orthon, was entirely human in appearance, except that "the beauty of his form surpassed anything I had ever seen" and "from him was radiating a feeling of infinite understanding and kindness." The sketch by Alice Wells, made while watching the interview through binoculars, showed a figure of indeterminate sex. Adamski commented that it fell far short of doing justice to the Venusian.

Angelucci didn't see his Luciferan entities during his first contact, but they spoke to him in perfect English. When he met "Neptune," the being was totally human in appearance, "but just to be in his presence was to sense a tremendous uplifting wave of strength, harmony, joy and serenity." When he subsequently met the "dazzlingly beautiful" Lyra,

Angelucci's response was more earthy—this was reflected for all to see as "an ugly mottled red and black cloud" in his aura, to the embarrassment of all present. Later, though, he was privileged to enjoy a more spiritual relationship with her.

Bethurum's people from Clarion were small humanoids, not much over 5 ft. tall. Despite her small stature, he described Aura Rhanes, the captain of the alien spacecraft, as a "queen of women." She wore a black velvet bodice with red ribbons and matching beret. Denaerde's Iargans were basically human, but with dog-like faces and grey skin. In view of the cramped living conditions on Iarga, it was just as well that they were shorter and more compact than humans. The greatest difference between them and us was that they "think collectively," rather than as individuals.

George King, probably the most intelligent of all the contactees, was exceptional also in that his contacts were mostly with disembodied beings more evolved than ourselves and existing on a higher plane of existence. However, in the course of his 1956 Mars escapade, he traveled in a space ship whose Venusian operator, he said:

looked like an incandescent egg suspended about a foot from the floor, for he had discarded his physical body as soon as the action began. His physical body, in a state of semi-dematerialization, looked like a little grey cloud. It was fastened in a locker by a system of magnets.

Communication here was extra-sensory. In fact, language never seems to be a problem. Often, of course, communication is telepathic, but when actual speech is involved, the aliens have generally acquired the language of the contactee in advance, though they often speak it in a somewhat stilted fashion. Adamski and Orthon communicated by sign and telepathy at their first encounter, but by their next meeting, the clever Venusian had mastered English.

Siragusa's "Cosmic Brothers" spoke to him in Italian; Vorilhon's humanoid contacts spoke French perfectly; Felix's spoke fluent Portuguese, and Elizabeth Klarer's lover spoke perfect English.

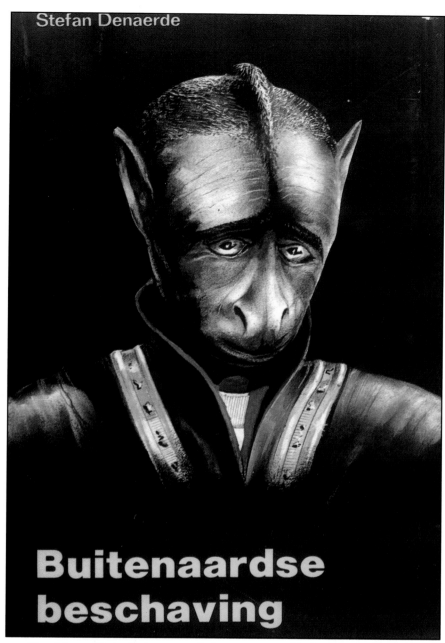

Stefan Denaerde

Buitenaardse beschaving

Though human-like in all other respects, the Iargans encountered by Dutch businessman Stefan Denaerde had dog-like faces and thought collectively rather than as individuals.

which enters Earth's atmosphere is disc-shaped—often, though, these are no more than scouts, associated with an interstellar "mother ship" which does not enter the atmosphere. Dan Martin, for example, was levitated into a scout ship which ferried him to a larger interplanetary craft, equipped much like an ocean liner here on Earth.

No two space ships are exactly alike, but this is only to be expected since it is rare for two sets of visitors to come from the same place of origin. Rose C.'s visitor's vessel was "shaped like one of Maurice Chevalier's hats" but was the size of a bus. Menger's spacecraft were saucer, disc, bell and other shapes—their appearance could vary according to the magnetic fields surrounding them. In the atmosphere, they could "travel in excess of 32,000 kilometres per hour; outside the earth's atmosphere, they can exceed the speed of light."

Most witnesses display a natural curiosity about the technology of the craft, and generally their hosts are happy to show off their vessels—often in tedious detail. It is noteworthy that the equipment is invariably designed with the expectation that the user will have hands to pull handles and fingers to push buttons. All have a force of gravity, whether natural or artificial, and such factors as temperature, air pressure, humidity and so on are at levels similar to Earth. No contactee has ever complained of being too hot or too cold, just as the alien visitors adapt readily to conditions on Earth.

One of Bethurum's companions told him, "We have no difficulty with any language." However, they showed themselves to be more at home with English than French, which was only at schoolboy level. German-speaking Reinhold Schmidt said of his Saturnians that "any one of them could have walked unnoticed among our people." However, they spoke English with a German accent, and among themselves they talked in German—that is, when they talked at all. Mostly, they communicated by telepathy.

THE SPACECRAFT

Since most contactees enter the visitor's spacecraft, and the majority take flights in them, it goes without saying that the craft are "nuts-and-bolts" structures made on a human scale. There are no reports of craft of either Lilliputian or Brobdingnagian proportions, with the exception of George King, who described "mother ships" over 497 miles long. Virtually every alien spacecraft

George Adamski was able to secure fine photos of alien spacecraft because his contacts notified him in advance when they would be flying overhead.

JOURNEYS IN SPACE

If the contactees are somewhat vague about the method of propulsion of the alien spacecraft, this is presumably because the technology is beyond the comprehension of an average Earthperson. Canadian contactee Oscar Magocsi travelled in a "scout disc" which was able to draw up power from the Egyptian Pyramids, Inca citadels and similar places, and discharge it again in order to "charge up" sites such as Mount Shasta. George Van Tassel's contact, Singba—regional fleet authority for the entire forty-fifth projection—told him:

> Our propulsion is the transmutation of hard light particles into soft light particles. Let your scientists figure that one out.

Since contactees have been handpicked by the extraterrestrials, they are treated with some favour. One of their privileges is to be taken for a flight in the spacecraft, usually a brief tour in space. The especially lucky ones get to visit the aliens' own planet.

Conditions vary from one spacecraft to another. Attractive space hostesses serving delicious drinks are a recurring feature corresponding to our own practices on Earth. These always arrive without a demonstration of emergency procedures, however, presumably because the idea of an emergency occurring on an extraterrestrial spacecraft is unthinkable. On the other hand, the craft are often thoughtfully equipped with elaborate equipment, enabling the passenger to receive inflight briefing on his destination.

Adamski had several flights, including a notable one which passed the Moon on the far side, enabling him to see its fauna and flora. This took place before our own first Moon landing; it is a pity our astronauts landed on the near side, which is so much less interesting.

Angelucci was taken to see his Luciferian friends' home planetoid, where Lyra and Orion explained that he too, during a previous existence, was one

Descriptions by contactees of the otherworldly places they visit tend to resemble the fantasies of fiction illustrators, but they are not confirmed by our own explorations of space.

Regrettably, contactees never carry cameras, nor are souvenir postcards available at the places they visit. As a result, we have only their verbal descriptions to tell us how other worlds compare with the conceptions of fantasy illustrators, as shown here.

of them. At that time an arrogant prince —also named Lucifer—almost totally destroyed the planet while rebelling against the "etheric hosts." The planetoid they were now on was all that remained, while "the Luciferian hosts fell into the dream of mind in matter upon the dark planet of the sorrows"

(i.e. Earth). Life on the planetoid was, of course, exquisitely beautiful, and he was reluctant to return to Earth, though to comfort him, they played the Bach-Gounod "Ave Maria" on the audio system.

Lee Crandall accepted the Venusians' invitation to visit their planet on

August 31, 1954. The flight was not too comfortable—he was airsick, which rather spoiled what would otherwise have been an enjoyable and memorable experience, particularly as he was the first Earthperson to set foot there. However, he was welcomed at a formal ceremony and invited to cooperate in the Great Universal Endeavor of Understanding. After shaking hands all around, he returned to the spacecraft and left Venus after a stay of only 46 minutes. He developed a nasty nosebleed on the way back, but the Venusian cared for him and helped him to his mother's home. On a second visit, he saw "hundreds of beautiful feminine creatures, all blondes, all clothed in white trailing garments, floating in a swimming position." He spent seven hours there, sightseeing and enjoying a concert given by five gorgeously beautiful Venusian ladies, who looked to be around 35 years old.

Woodrow Derenberger was taken on several space journeys during the spring of 1966, including a journey past Saturn to his hosts' home planet, Lanulos. He was given an injection which enabled him to land without risk of

the White Sands Incident

By Daniel W. Fry

A TECHNICIAN TALKS WITH A SPACEMAN AND RIDES IN A FLYING SAUCER

As an engineer, Daniel Fry appreciated the extraterrestrials' achievement when he was taken for a flight in a remote-controlled "scout ship."

contamination by or of the locals. During his visit he went into shops, but was not allowed to take anything away with him. He saw that most people go nude in warm weather, and was persuaded to do likewise, despite being "a little bit overweight." Otherwise, he found that life on Lanulos wasn't so very different from that on Earth: "One group of people that I met and talked to were working on a lawn. They were raking the lawn, straightening a paling fence and painting it, the same as we do here on earth." He met John and Carolyn Peterson, from Acapulco, Mexico, who emigrated to Lanulos forty years before; they told him how much they liked the life there. Derenberger himself was invited to move there with his family. "I do really want to go, but I know I can be of so much more use here on Earth."

Daniel Fry was taken for a quick half-hour flight from White Sands to New York and back at a speed averaging more than 7457 miles per hour. During the flight, the distant A-lan gave him technical details, and explained that Fry was chosen for contact because he was

> one of those rare individuals whose brain receives well … We have carefully examined the minds of many of your top scientists. In every case, we found that their minds had hardened into a mold based on their present conceptions

George King's space experiences were among the most dramatic of all, for in 1956 he traveled in a material space ship while participating in a cosmic battle against a hostile planetoid whose robot inhabitants, programmed by evil forces, were scheming to wreak appalling destruction in the solar system. He was thus privileged to witness the saving of Earth from would-be destroyers.

Howard Menger was taken to the Moon, where his hosts maintained a base. This was tastefully decorated with potted plants; refreshments were served by "attractive ladies in flowing pastel gowns." A few weeks later, he flew over Venus, which he described as fantastically beautiful. "I did not get the impression of cities; instead,

I was reminded of beautiful suburban areas I have seen on our own planet, though, of course, different … Vehicles moved on the surface, apparently without wheels, for they seemed to float slightly above the ground."

Could the Venusians have invented the hovercraft before us?

Hillbilly farmer Buck Nelson's extraterrestrial voyages were notable in that he was permitted to take his dog Teddy with him to Mars, the Moon and Venus. Teddy can therefore claim to be the first earthdog in space, predating Laika, the Russian canine cosmonaut, by three years.

Reinhold Schmidt, in February and April, 1958, had some interesting terrestrial trips. On one of them, he visited the Great Pyramid, entering it by a secret way. This led to a hidden room housing a 65.5 ft. circular spacecraft.

Claude Vorilhon, in 1975—two years after his first encounter—was taken to visit the aliens' planet, "relatively close to Earth." It was a beautiful, paradise-like place, where the shell-like houses blended harmoniously with the natural surroundings. He attended a party, where the guests were waited on by robot servants and entertained by female robot dancers. The food, unusually, was not vegetarian. His host, Iahve, President of the Council of the Eternals, told him there were 8400 Earthpeople on their planet, who during their earthly lives reached a sufficiently high level of development.

AFTERMATH

Subsequent to their experiences, the careers of the contactees diverge considerably. Some return to their previous obscurity, while others follow up on their contact adventure in various ways.

Adamski published his account of his contact in 1953. It aroused world-wide interest, bringing fame—though probably only a modest revenue—to its author. It led to lecture tours around the globe. In Switzerland, he was harassed by disbelievers, but most audiences were fascinated by his story.

Angelucci felt himself a "dweller in two worlds," and decided to devote his life to his mission, against his wife's urgings: "I'm sorry, Mae. Believe me, there is no other way out for me. I've got to live with myself." He gave Sunday afternoon talks in a California hotel, and published his story. He and his children were mocked as a result, but he didn't care because he had not failed his space visitors.

Though Bethurum had eleven meetings with lovely spacewoman Aura Rhanes, his workmates were skeptical, and his wife even more so. His daughters did back him up, however. With Adamski's support, he became a star of the contactee lecture circuit and appeared frequently on the radio. Mrs Bethurum, her doubts somewhat assuaged by his celebrity, allowed herself to be photographed smiling alongside him.

Denaerde's publisher refused to issue his account except as science fiction, and as such it was presented to the Dutch public in 1969 (it ran through eleven editions) and later as a paperback in the United States. The editor's introduction to the Dutch edition opened with the words, "Dit is geen science-fiction. Het is een utopisch boek." This translates to, "This is not science fiction. It is a utopian book." For American readers, the word "exactly" is added before "science." In 1982, the story was republished in the U.S. as fact, though the author in his foreword remained oddly evasive:

> Though I shall continue to avoid giving a direct answer to the question of the veracity of this story, the immensity of Earth-alien knowledge contained in this book will serve to prove beyond a doubt that the planet Iarga is not fiction, but fact.

Flying Saucers Have Landed

Desmond Leslie & George Adamski

Desmond Leslie's 1953 book, arguing that flying saucers have existed throughout history, concluded with Adamski's account of his encounter, destined to provide a model for all subsequent contact stories.

The new edition contained additional material, more than twice the bulk of the original text. Most of this was philosophy—lucid, explicit and ingenious—received in the form of telepathic communications every afternoon when the author got home from the office. Curiously, during this period, NATO employees in Den Haag reported being bothered by an untraceable incoming radio frequency electronic signal, which was at its strongest in the near vicinity of Denaerde's home, and which began about 4 p.m. and continued for an hour or more several days each week—precisely when Denaerde received his messages.

When Woodrow Derenberger's story became known, he was considerably harassed by an inquisitive public, and his children were tormented at school.

In August 1967 two men, dressed entirely in black, visited his store and warned him to stop talking so much about flying saucers.

> They would not identify themselves, but just said they had authority to stop me. My personal opinion is that these, and all the "Men in Black," are from the Mafia.

Eventually Derenberger moved to

Aura Rhanes, captain of the alien "scow" which Truman Bethurum encountered in the Nevada desert, resembled an Earthwoman in appearance.

Woodrow Derenberger was told by two "men in black" to keep his experiences secret, but when he published his story, he suffered no consequences.

another town, but he published his story and gave lectures about his experience. While he was participating in a "phone-in" radio program in Washington, a young man named Ed Bailey called the studio to say that he, too, had been to Lanulos. Later the two met, in the presence of author John Keel and journalist Harold Salkin. Bailey's account confirmed Derenberger's, even including certain details which Derenberger had never publicly revealed.

Aladino Felix appeared on Brazilian TV in August, 1968, and stated publicly that his book, which had been enormously successful, was outright invention. At the end of the month, he was arrested for terrorist activities. He threatened the authorities that his friends on Venus would liberate him and his comrades. Undeterred, they sentenced him to 5 years imprisonment, but with the recommendation that he be transferred to an institution for mental treatment. Gordon Creighton, subsequently editor of *Flying Saucer Review*, suggested that Felix was being used as a tool by unnamed evil forces.

George King's life was changed by his encounter only in that it provided him with a specific direction for his existing interests. He gave his first public meeting in January, 1955, at Caxton Hall, London. He was kept busy by his duties as representative on Earth of the Interplanetary Parliament, which was far from being a sinecure: In 1963, King was involved in Operation Bluewater, which saved the western seaboard of the United States from catastrophe. Since that was where King made his home, it must have been comforting to know his property was under extraterrestrial protection.

Menger's knowledge that he himself was a Saturnian gave him a purpose in life—"to complete a mission which had been outlined from my day of birth." In 1956, he met Marla, the sister of his childhood contact, whom he had met previously when he—then a Saturnian—had stopped over on Venus. She, too, was on a mission to Earth, and was conveniently living in the next state. They resumed their interrupted love affair, marrying in 1958. He was a regular guest on radio shows, notably that of Long John Nebel, on which he made a remarkable final appearance.

Howard said nothing, and un-said most of what he had originally claimed. Where he had once sworn that he had seen flying saucers, he now felt that he had some vague impression that he might have on some half-remembered occasion possibly viewed some airborne object – maybe. Where he had once insisted that he had teleported himself, he now speculated that strange things did happen to people and if it hadn't actually occurred to him, well, that's the way the story crumbles. Where he had formerly stated that he had been to the moon, he now suggested that this had most likely been a mental impression of the other side of his consciousness. In other words, Howard Menger backed up and backed up until he fell into a pit of utter confusion and finally sank forever into the waters of obscurity.

But Nebel was mistaken. In 1991, Howard and Connie Menger reemerged, republished their account with additions, and reaffirmed their original claims to have participated in contact with the aliens. But Menger changed his story in one respect:

Years ago, on a TV program, when I first voiced my opinion that the people I met and talked with from the craft might not be extraterrestrial, it was thought that I had recanted. However, they (the aliens) said they had just come from the planet we call Venus (or Mars). It is my opinion that these space travelers may have by-passed or visited other planets, but were not native to those planets any more than our astronauts are native to the Moon.

Several contactees formed groups or cults. Former truck driver Kelvin Rowe published an account of his encounter in 1958. He urged a spiritual awakening of Earthfolk, which he suggested could best be accomplished via The Brotherhood. In addition to conducting regular lectures and classes at its headquarters high in the Rocky Mountains, his organization "teaches by correspondence all the Secret Wisdom of the Ancients" and "gives the Degree of Doctor of Metaphysics on completion of the course."

Another contactee who became a successful cult leader was Claude Vorilhon, who changed his name to "Raël." Following the publication of Raël's first book in 1974, thousands attended his conferences, leading to the

foundation of the Raëlian movement. The movement has enjoyed considerable success, largely because of its popular summer gatherings, at which the master's easygoing philosophy is put into practice.

THE MESSAGES

Almost without exception, contactees believe they were chosen for their individual qualities—they are in one way or another "special." In return, they believe they have been entrusted with a mission to help Earth in very much the same way as the Star People we met in Chapter Two. The message given by the Great Master whom Adamski met on his February, 1953 trip stands as the archetype for subsequent messages given to other contactees:

> My son, our main purpose in coming to you at this time is to warn you of the grave danger which threatens men of Earth today. Knowing more than any amongst you can yet realize, we feel it our duty to enlighten you if we can. Your people may accept the knowledge we hope to give them through you and through others, or they can turn deaf ears and destroy themselves. The choice is with the Earth's inhabitants. We cannot dictate …

Crandall's Venusians were working for peace, and with that in mind, they not only asked him to transmit their warnings to mankind, but had plans to send 1000 Venusian men to land in the California desert some time in 1954, as peaceful and friendly neighbors. Venusian women lived separately from the men and there was no marriage and, seemingly, no children. "I queried if any of these women would ever come down to visit Earth. I got a negative answer."

Denaerde learned of "chosen ones" who, by the purity of their lives, would combat the evil of Satan. Intelligent races on other worlds had their equivalent to our belief systems, but what distinguished Earthfolk was that ours was an "own boss" culture, as opposed to the collective mind culture of the Iargans and others.

On July 27, 1958, at Holdston Down in Devon, England, George King, who was heading the Aetherius Society, met the Master Venusian, who gave him "the twelve blessings" which Aetherians regard as "the Bible for the Aquarian Age." Most of the doctrines were dictated by Saint Goo-Ling, a member of The Brotherhood still living on Earth. The Aetherius Society flourished to become one of the most successful of all extraterrestrial cults, with headquarters in California and branches throughout the world.

French contactee Jean Miguères was told:

> People of Earth, we have no intention of invading your world; if we wanted to, we could have done it ages ago … Our intentions are entirely peaceful; our only aim is to help you. We warn you that you will soon need that help, for we foresee the necessity of a massive and peaceful intervention on your earth in 1996, that is, unless your stupidity doesn't make it necessary for us to step in earlier than that... You, Earthpeople, are on the point of making great discoveries, and our "Supreme Computer" warns that, thanks to them, you run the risk of destroying the entire Solar System before destroying yourself. This we cannot permit, on behalf of your galactic brothers …

Buck Nelson's Venusian visitors warned him that

> the next war, if fought, will be on American soil. America will be destroyed, then civilization all over the world will be destroyed. We have stood by and seen other planets destroy themselves. Is this world next? We wonder, and watch and wait.

Siragusa learned that each of us visits Earth for seven lifetimes. He himself had formerly lived on Atlantis as Barath, a scholar; in ancient Egypt as Hermes Trismegistus; in Renaissance Italy as Giordano Bruno; in Europe during the Enlightenment as Cagliostro, and in Twentieth Century Russia as Rasputin. It was his duty to pass this heritage of wisdom, combined with ongoing teachings, to mankind. He duly formed a Study Center of Cosmic

Brotherhood, which would eventually be housed in a college on the slopes of Mount Etna—the site of his first contact. In 1978, he claimed 50,000 affiliated members, but his success was somewhat marred by scandal, mainly linked to his over-friendly relationships with young female disciples.

The public warmed to the contactees, most of whom seem to have been amiable, likeable people of disarming sincerity. They were popular on radio and TV talk shows, and were star speakers at conferences. One such regular conference was staged by George Van Tassel—himself a contactee—at Giant Rock, California. In its heyday, it attracted more than 10,000 visitors to the dramatic desert location. Did those who attended these legendary events believe what they heard? On the whole, it seems likely. A homely honesty comes through the foreword, which Fanny Lowery wrote in

Buck Nelson claimed to learn from his Venusian hosts that another war would mean the destruction of civilization on Earth.

December, 1956, for her friend Buck Nelson's account of his trip to Mars, the Moon and Venus:

> Ancient and modern history record the visits of Space People to our planet. But now, folks, the most wonderful thing is that one of our own neighbors, Buck Nelson, has actually made a trip to other planets and will tell you about it.

Author John Keel, not easily fooled, concluded his foreword to Woodrow Derenberger's book by asking:

> Are all of these people insane? I have talked to contactee claimants who are doctors, lawyers, newspapermen, police officers and pilots. Woody has a lot of company—sane, reputable people. Perhaps we are the ones who are insane for ignoring them for so long. Strange, unbelievable things are now happening to people all over the world.

Stranger things still were to happen.

FROM CONTACT TO ABDUCTION

During the 1960s, there was a dramatic change in the nature of contact between Us and Them, between humans and extraterrestrials. From being *voluntary*, the encounters switched to being *involuntary*. The Contactees had been treated as honored guests, invited on board the visiting space ships, and given nice things to eat and drink. The Abductees were given no choice. They were beamed aboard spacecraft and forced to participate in medical procedures, with no word of explanation, no friendly welcome, no in-flight refreshment, and no thanks afterwards. The Contactees felt privileged: the Abductees felt used.

The contrast is in some respects so marked that those who accept abduction claims at face value—and they number a great many highly educated and intelligent people—are at pains to set them totally apart from the contact cases we have been considering so far.

However, the difference is by no means as clear-cut as this contrast

A human is shown being abducted. During the 1960s, there was a change in the nature of reported contacts between humans and extraterrestrials, with more people claiming to be forcibly taken.

suggests. The line of distinction between contact and abduction is a blurred one. There are many features common to both kinds of experience, which encourage us to see them as variations on one basic theme. Both involve, in the great majority of cases, solitary individuals. Both occur during the night more often than the day. Both tend to take place in isolated locations, at times when corroborative evidence would be hard to find. Both happen more frequently to Americans than to anyone else, more to North Americans than to Latin Americans, and more to

Caucasians than to others. Finally, both categories rest entirely on witness testimony, unsupported by any convincing evidence.

Significantly, though, the role of the UFO itself is very different. In the contactees' stories, it figures largely in the experience. The contactee is taken on board, often treated to a conducted tour of the spacecraft, even making a journey in space. With the abductees, on the other hand, the UFO's relevance is minimal. The majority of abductees never see the spacecraft from the outside. Even the way they enter it is blurred and ambiguous. Most of them see no more of the interior than the "room" where they are examined.

The contactees prepared the way for the abductees, by attracting the world's attention to the possibility of extraterrestrial visitation. Even if they did not achieve widespread credibility, they won widespread publicity. Consequently, when the more credible abductees appeared, the public was halfway prepared to give them a serious hearing. Many wanted to believe the contactees, but found their claims too hard to swallow. When the abductees started to make their less bizarre claims, the public turned to them in relief as being not as unbelievable.

In one other respect, abduction cases do seem to be objectively different from contact cases—they seem simpler. The abduction of Betty and Barney Hill, for instance, was to all intents and purposes a one-night stand, over and done with in a few hours. This is a far cry from the complex and drawn-out affair of, say, Elizabeth Klarer's contact experience. On the other hand, abduction cases possess a complexity of their own, derived from the response of the individual involved. Like the Star People, abductees often claim a previous history of otherworldly interaction. The experience seems to affect them at a deeper level than that of contactees. To read an account by an abductee is very different from reading the old contactee books: They are more thoughtful, and the experience is more profound. Does this just represent a change in the cultural climate, or is there really an essential difference between the two kinds of experience?

Abductions have split the UFO community as no other events have done. For a great many thoughtful and dedicated persons, they represent the positive event which will carry humanity from one era of history—the era when we seemed alone in the cosmos—to another era, when our destiny will merge with that of otherworldly civilizations. For psychologist Leo Sprinkle, they are part of a learning process involving the human race; for information scientist Jacques Vallee, they are part of the master plan of a cosmic control system.

If this is true, the most important thing that has ever happened to the human

race is happening right now. Why aren't governments, authorities—our leaders—taking any notice? Furthermore, why do others in the UFO community—no less thoughtful and dedicated than the believers—reject the abduction phenomenon as a collective delusion?

The fact is that though the abductees often impress listeners with their sincerity and their thoughtful response, the stories they tell are bizarre, contradictory, inconsistent and fly in the face of common sense. Moreover, though circumstantial and detailed, they are no more than personal statements—they offer no objective, material evidence, and no convincing independent confirmation.

1951: THE SALZBURG ABDUCTION

As if to emphasize the blurred distinction between contact and abduction, the event with the best

claim of being the first true abduction case is tantalizingly vague. In December, 1957, a Canadian local newspaper, the *Prince George Citizen*, reported a story told personally to the editor by an unnamed man who, in 1951, had been working for the U.S. occupation army in Salzburg, Austria. About 11 p.m. on May 15, he was walking home from duty, when he was accosted by a figure in the darkness. The figure pointed a device at him which paralyzed him, then strapped some kind of "plate" on his chest. The entity pulled him, almost as if floating, to a nearby field, where a round object about 164 ft. in diameter was standing:

> My thought was that a spy had captured me for some reason ... I was plenty scared.

They floated up to the top of the object, and entered through a hole. The soldier found himself in a kind of room. He was released from his paralysis, and sank to the floor:

> There was a sort of shaking sensation, and

A model alien is shown with cylindrical head, large elliptical eyes, a small slit for a mouth and two holes in the nose. Many abductees have described their alien kidnappers as having such features.

If Earthpeople sought to colonize Mars, we would have to construct suitable habitats for ourselves. However, aliens visiting our planet seem to experience no trouble adapting to Earth conditions.

I knew the door to the room had been shut. The next sensation I had was of riding up into the air. I had never flown before in my life ... I was so scared, but I figured I was dreaming.

Suddenly, they were—unaccountably —in sunlight, and the soldier could at last see his kidnapper. The alien's head was cylindrical, with large round eyes more like a fly's than a human's, with two holes instead of a nose, and a very small slit for a mouth. Otherwise, the being was more or less human in appearance, though somewhat shorter than the average.

The spacecraft seemed to be constructed of a translucent glass-like material. It carried them silently close to the Moon, and the soldier could see Earth far away. They approached another planet with red fields, blue rivers, roads and bridges. They landed in a field full of other saucers like their own. The entity left him alone in the vessel and went into another ship:

I got to thinking I must be on Mars. I remembered what I had learned in school about it being red with canals, and it seemed to me that this must be Mars, although I wasn't 100 percent sure ...

The entity then returned, and they took off again. The witness was returned to Earth, where the entity pulled him out the same way as he was pulled in, left him seemingly paralyzed, and flew off. Throughout, there was no

communication or contact between them. The witness ran home:

My wife was still up, and she saw me all excited. She asked me what happened and I told her, "Nothing, I'm just sick." I couldn't tell her about the experience because she would have thought I was completely crazy.

By the clock, he saw that the journey had lasted about an hour. He explained to the editor that he was telling the story because he had a heart condition and didn't expect to live much longer, and felt people should know what was going on.

Those people are much ahead of us ... this creature treated me only as an animal.

Unsatisfactory though it is in almost every respect, the Salzburg case is of interest because it predates any other abduction story. The account of being floated through the air occurs again in later reports, but for earlier instances we would have to turn to fairytales. Similarly, the immobilizing device resembles that used in the Valensole case discussed in chapter four. But the Valensole case took place eight years after the Salzburg incident was printed; for earlier instances, we would need to turn to science fiction.

Where the aliens come from, and how they travel to Earth, is hard to determine. In this illustration, the abductors of Barney and Betty Hill show them a "star map" depicting their journey.

1961:
BARNEY AND BETTY HILL

The case which for many years set the pattern for abductions was that of Barney and Betty Hill, which presented virtually every feature—and raised virtually every question—of the entire abduction phenomenon.

In 1961, Barney and Betty Hill were living in Portsmouth, New Hampshire. Barney, a 39-year-old man, worked as a post office sorter, a job rather below his intellectual capacity. He was also an active campaigner for civil rights. His wife, Betty, 41, was a child welfare worker. Both had been married previously; they were popular and had many friends.

On the night of September 19, 1961, the couple were returning home after a short spur-of-the-moment vacation in Canada, driving through the night because their funds were running low. They stopped for a snack at a roadside restaurant, leaving a little after 10 p.m. What happened then is recounted in a letter Betty wrote six days later to Donald Keyhoe—a prominent UFO investigator whose book, *The Flying Saucer Conspiracy,* she found in a local library:

> My husband and I have become immensely interested in this topic, as we recently had quite a frightening experience, which does seem to differ from others of which we are aware. About midnight on September 20th, we were driving in a National Forest area in the White Mountains. This is a desolate, uninhabited area. We noticed a bright object in the sky which seemed to be moving rapidly. We stopped our car and got out to observe it more closely with our binoculars. Suddenly, it reversed its flight path and appeared to be flying in a very erratic pattern. We continued driving. As it approached our car, we stopped again. As it hovered in the air in front of us, it appeared to be pancake in shape, ringed with windows in the front through which we could see bright blue-white lights. My husband was standing in the road, watching closely. He saw

> wings on each side and red lights on the wing tips.
>
> As it glided closer, he was able to see inside this object, but not too closely. He did see several figures scurrying about as though they were making some hurried type of preparation. One figure was observing us from the windows. At this point, my husband became shocked and got back in the car in a hysterical condition, laughing and repeating that they were going to capture us. As we started to move, we heard several buzzing or beeping sounds which seemed to be striking the trunk of our car.

At that stage, there was no more to the case than a fairly dramatic UFO sighting—alarming enough to the witnesses, but nothing more. Then, for five successive nights, starting on September 30, Betty experienced disturbing dreams in which their sighting, instead of ending when they got back into the car, continued with a series of dramatic events. In Betty's dream, the Hills unaccountably found themselves on a different road from the one on which they had been traveling. They came across a group of figures standing in the middle of the road. Barney slowed down and the motor died. The figures surrounded the car, opened the car doors, took Barney and Betty by the arms and led them along a path through the woods to where a spaceship was parked. They were taken inside and led to separate rooms, where they were stripped and subjected to what seemed to be a medical examination. The entities were not unfriendly, and the experience was not especially unpleasant. The leader apologized to Betty for frightening her. She was then reunited with Barney, and they were led back through the woods to their car. Betty by now was talking with the leader, saying she was happy to meet him and begging him to return.

On October 21, Walter Webb—an investigator for NICAP, Keyhoe's UFO organization—visited the Hills and heard about the sighting, though not the dreams. He reported:

> It is the opinion of this investigator, after questioning these people for over six hours and studying their reactions and

The abduction of Betty and Barney Hill allegedly took place after they had stopped their car to observe a low-flying UFO.

personalities during that time, that they were telling the truth, and the incident occurred exactly as reported except for some minor uncertainties.

Significantly, he added:

> Mr Hill believes he saw something he doesn't want to remember. He claimed he was not close enough to see any facial characteristics on the figures [the ones seen in the UFO, not those encountered in the dreams], although at another time he referred to one of them grinning ... It is my view that the observer's blackout is not of any great significance. I think the whole experience was so improbable and fantastic to witness – along with the very real fear of being captured added to imagined fears – that his mind finally refused to believe what his eyes were perceiving and a mental block resulted.

On November 25, during the course of a second meeting with NICAP investigators, a curious anomaly emerged. Barney reported:

They [the investigators] were mentally reconstructing the trip. One of them said, "What took you so long to get home? You went this distance and it took you these hours: where were you?" I thought I was really going to crack up ... I realized for the first time that at the rate of speed I always travel, we should have arrived home at least two hours earlier than we did.

Accounts of the event often give the impression that the Hills noted their "missing time" as soon as they got home. This was not the case. Another feature which has often been misinterpreted in the interest of heightened drama is the allegation that they "unaccountably" turned onto a side road—the implication being that the aliens somehow brainwashed them into leaving the highway onto a totally wrong road. But the map shows that Route 175—the one they took—runs almost parallel to Route 3, the one they wanted. Traveling at night, it would be easy to take the other road which, as it happens, was a perfectly reasonable alternative.

Such details as these—unimportant in themselves—warn us that a mythmaking process may be at work.

During February, 1962, and the following months, the Hills made a series of "pilgrimages" to the scene of their experience. Then on March 12, on NICAP's suggestion, Betty inquired about the possibility of using hypnosis to help clarify what happened to them:

> The moment they suggested hypnosis, I thought of my dreams, and this was the first time I began to wonder if they were more than just dreams. I thought, if I have hypnosis, I'll know one way or the other, because I thought, well, maybe my dreams are something that really happened.

A doctor listened sympathetically, but discouraged them from doing anything at the time. During the summer of 1962, Barney developed physical and psychological symptoms that forced him to seek medical help. As his condition deteriorated, they decide to try hypnosis after all, and were recommended to approach Dr. Benjamin Simon, an experienced and open-minded practitioner. On January 4, 1964, seven months of hypnosis sessions commenced. It is important to realize that the purpose of the hypnosis was to see what relevance the alleged UFO sighting might have had to Barney's health, both physical and mental. Moreover, the sessions were carried out entirely at the Hills' instigation, at what must have been very considerable expense for a couple in their modest circumstances. Their motivation was evidently strong.

Each was hypnotized separately, with the other out of the room. Neither heard the recordings of either his or her own session or the other's, until the whole series of sessions was completed.

The record revealed that each, independently, had told a story which matched Betty's troubling dreams in

Dr. Simon emphasized that the events "'recalled" under hypnosis by Betty and Barney Hill were only the truth as they felt and understood it, and not necessarily objective truth.

detail, except that each described the events as seen from his or her own viewpoint. It was not surprising that many jumped to the obvious conclusion—that the Hills had undergone an experience so alarming that they couldn't face it. Instead, observers reasoned, they had repressed the memory of it, and it then emerged subconsciously in Betty's dreams and Barney's psychogenic troubles. The hypnosis had brought the repressed memories to light.

Attractive as this scenario is, it is invalidated by the fact that apparent memories that emerge during hypnosis cannot be taken at face value. Dr. Simon himself pointed out:

> The charisma of hypnosis has tended to foster the belief that hypnosis is the magical and royal road to *truth*. In one sense this is so, but it must be understood that hypnosis is a pathway to the truth as it is felt and understood by the patient … this may or may not be consonant with the ultimate nonpersonal truth.

It is often assumed that Barney's sickness was due to anxiety caused by their experience. Apart from the fact that at that point the experience was thought to be only a UFO sighting—dramatic enough, no doubt, but less dramatic by a long way than the abduction encounter of which they were at that stage unaware—Barney was ill before the incident. What happened in 1962 was not that he developed an ulcer, but that the ulcer from which he was already suffering grew worse. The UFO experience could more plausibly have been a consequence of his state than the cause of it.

Betty, too, may have been preconditioned. Her sister Janet and many other members of the family had experienced UFO sightings. Moreover, she had a history of psychic experiences in her family, including poltergeist phenomena and precognitive dreams.

Perhaps the most serious question, though, is that raised by the similarity of the hypnotically revealed story to the dream story. As we all know, dreams rarely present a literal playback of real life events. When such events occur, they are generally reworked, distorted, and combined with other kinds of material.

The fact that the Hills' hypnosis recall exactly matched Betty's dream story suggests that what they recalled under hypnosis was not the event itself, but the dreams.

So how did Barney's hypnosis-story come to match Betty's? Because he was recalling the dreams she had narrated to him, not his own personal experiences. Dr. Simon himself, though he was discreet enough to never commit himself to a specific assessment, evidently favoured some such version as this:

> I was ultimately left with the conclusion that the most tenable explanation was that the series of dreams experienced by Mrs. Hill, as the aftermath of some type of experience with an Unidentified Flying Object or some similar phenomenon, assumed the quality of a fantasized experience.

The Hill case is important not only in its own right, but because it served as the yardstick by which other abduction experiences would be judged. In particular, the idea of recall under hypnosis—previously regarded with some hesitation as a tool which occasionally produced useful therapeutic results—became the treatment of choice for abduction witnesses. Not until the 1990s would the shortcomings and dangers of reliance on hypnosis be recognized, and even then not by all.

1967: BETTY ANDREASSON

If abduction stories are accurate narrations of what actually took place, then what Betty Andreasson experienced on January 25, 1967 was bizarre, indeed.

That evening, Betty was with her seven children and her parents at their family home in South Ashburnham, Massachusetts. Her husband had been in the hospital for more than a month due to injuries suffered in a car accident.

Around 6:30 p.m., the house lights flickered and went out. Soon after, a pulsating pink light appeared outside the kitchen window. Her father went to investigate, and saw strange creatures he likened to "Halloween freaks." Betty sent all her family into the living room, while she remained in the kitchen. She was thus the only one to see four creatures enter the house, passing through the closed kitchen door; they moved "in a jerky motion, leaving a vapory image behind."

Unfortunately, how much of the experience Betty was able to remember consciously is not clear from the accounts we have. Clearly, though, she remembered enough to believe she had experienced an encounter with UFO occupants, because in 1974 she responded to an invitation from the *National Enquirer* for UFO stories. The fact that she was a reader of this particular paper—known more for its enthusiasm than for an unshakeable

Betty Andreasson believed she was entertaining angels when extraterrestrials appeared to her after having passed through a solid door.

attachment to literal truth—is in itself an indication of possible preconditioning. However, the *Enquirer* was not interested in her story.

Betty later contacted UFO organizations and, after some delay, her case was passed to veteran investigator Raymond Fowler. It was decided that hypnosis was needed to release Betty's hidden memories. She agreed, and under hypnosis was able to tell a richer and more dramatic story.

It started with an odd but revealing assumption. Because she was a devout Christian, Betty jumped to the conclusion that because her visitors were able to pass through a solid door, they must have been angels. They didn't look like traditional angels, though, any more than they looked like people: They had huge pear-shaped heads, slanting eyes and three-fingered hands.

However, she was reassured by their air of friendliness, and was no longer frightened. The lights came back on. Recalling the Biblical phrase about "entertaining angels," she asked with characteristic American hospitality if they were hungry, and when they nodded, she started to prepare food for them. But there was evidently some misunderstanding, for they rejected what she offered.

Everyone else, apart from Betty, had been put into a state of suspended animation, though 9-year-old Becky was momentarily revived, to reassure Betty that the others were alright. Under

During this typical incident from an abduction, aliens are shown implanting an object in the victim's nose.

hypnosis, Becky was able to recall seeing her mother speaking with the visitors. When Betty questioned her visitors, a bizarre but revealing conversation followed.

Betty asked, "What are you doing here?" Their leader, who told her he was named Quazgaa, replied:

> "We have come to help. Will you help us?"
> "How can I help?" asked Betty.
> "Would you follow us?"
> "Are you of God? You keep saying you have come to help the world. Why?"
> "Because the world is trying to destroy itself."
> "How can I help the world?"

The visitors repeatedly asked Betty, "Would you follow us?" Eventually, she agreed to go with them.

The visitors floated her out through the door to where their spacecraft was parked outside. As they looked at it, the bottom became transparent. Inside the spacecraft, she was given a complex and painful medical examination. This involved removing a small buckshot-like object from her nose and inserting probes through her navel. Some of the things they did to her indicated concern for her comfort, but the overall experience was distinctly unpleasant.

After the examination, Betty was taken to "a higher place" with tunnels and huge rooms, where she had what seemed to be some kind of mystical experience. She was then returned home.

This bald summary gives no more than a sampling of Betty's story, which— with its complexities and sequels—fills five volumes of meticulous narration and analysis by Fowler. There is, for instance, the ever-present religious aspect. Betty herself was a strong fundamentalist Christian, and spent much time reading the Bible. The phrase "Follow me" certainly sounds like an echo of Jesus gathering his disciples. Fowler, who himself converted to Christianity in 1952, asked the hypnotized Betty:

> "Have they anything to do with what we call the second coming of Christ?"
> "They definitely do."
> "When is this going to occur?"

> "It is not for them to tell you."
> "Do they know?"
> "They know the Master is getting ready, and very close."

Hypnosis also revealed a considerable history of previous events, going back to when, at the age of seven, Betty seems to have had her first contact. She suffered a "sting," which may have been the implanting of some monitoring device between her eyes— perhaps the one which was removed during her 1967 experience. She also heard a voice telling her, "They have been watching me, and I'm coming along fine," and that they would be back in five years' time.

She had another encounter at age 12 with a being who emerged, like the White Rabbit, from a hole in the ground while she was out in the woods. The being resembled her 1967 visitors. Again she heard voices discussing her, and one said, "She's got another year."

A year later, they were back, and this time they took her somewhere (in fact, the same "higher place" that she was taken to in 1967) and gave her a medical examination. Further contacts were reported at age 18 and age 24, seeming to confirm Fowler's suggestion that "a race or races of aliens have a long-term interest in certain members of our species, for some unknown purpose." There was a clear inference that they selected Betty Aho (as she then was) as a child, and monitored her throughout her life, checking up on her at intervals, notably at puberty and shortly after the birth of her first child.

The sexual connotations of the case, too, are inescapable. Much of the imagery of her abduction is susceptible to a sexual interpretation. The probing of her navel was read by psychoanalyst Ernest Taves as a "displacement" for the sex act. Taves rightly pointed out that a satisfactory investigation would have elicited much more about the sexual and religious aspects of Betty's personality and situation. At the same time, we can understand that whereas a psychoanalyst such as Taves might feel it essential to explore such avenues, a hard-headed UFO investigator like Fowler might feel diffident about treading on such delicate ground.

Taves posed the question:

Which is the simpler, more reasonable, more rational explanation of this exotic adventure: (1) Betty was taken aboard an extragalactic spacecraft by aliens who have been visiting Earth since the beginning of time but haven't been able to effect meaningful communication with man. (2) Betty recalled, or relived, in hypnosis, a dream or fantasy (or a number of them) that had meaning and utility in terms of her life history and her emotional needs.

For Taves, sitting at home reviewing Fowler's book, the answer was self-evident. Fowler, who lived through the sessions leading to the writing of the books and who, in the course of his investigation, came to realize that he was himself an abductee, came to the opposite conclusion: "The witnesses believed it happened. And so, for that matter, do I."

1973:
CHARLES HICKSON AND CALVIN PARKER

Charles Hickson (age 42) and Calvin Parker (age 19) were fishing on a riverbank at Pascagoula, Mississippi, on October 11, 1973. Around 7 p.m. (or 9 p.m. in later versions), they saw a bright object descend behind them, about 65.5 ft. away. It became a craft about 10 ft. in diameter (or 23 to 33 ft. in later versions), which landed. Three creatures emerged from the craft. They were classic alien entities—shorter than humans, pale grey color, wrinkled skin, two-fingered hands, small ears. The eyes—usually a prominent feature—were almost invisible in the folds of their wrinkled skin, if they possessed eyes at all.

The two men sat unable to move as the beings approached them. Hickson

had the impression that Parker fainted with fright, and this was Parker's own impression. Under subsequent hypnosis however, Parker was able to recall being carried into the ship. Hickson had a conscious memory of being seized by two of the creatures,

and together they floated towards the UFO.

Hickson found himself in a brightly-lit room. He couldn't see Parker, and assumed he had been taken elsewhere. Alone, he was given some kind of physical examination. Then the two

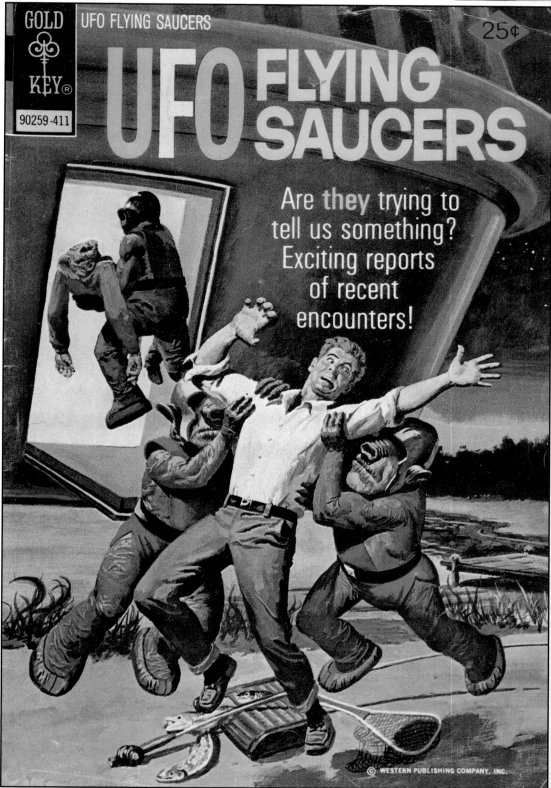

The Pascagoula incident was sufficiently dramatic to justify this illustration. The men were not invited, but were forcibly taken on board the spacecraft.

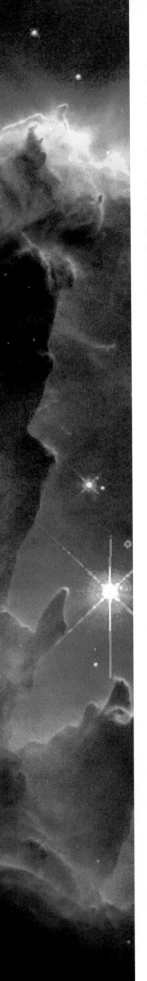

men were floated out of the spacecraft and left on the riverbank, Parker still unconscious. The creatures floated back to their craft, which took off and disappeared, leaving an unspoken, seemingly telepathic message: "We are peaceful, we meant you no harm."

The two men went that very evening to tell their story to the local sheriff, who recorded it. They hoped to avoid publicity, but the media learned of it somehow, and by the next day their story had spread far and wide. Their account was wildly and irresponsibly sensationalized. When the men successfully underwent a lie detector test, there was a widespread impression that the event really happened as told, and that it had been scientifically validated.

Hickson reported additional contacts and psychic experiences subsequent to their experience. Later investigation included hypnosis sessions which added fresh material. but also opened up new questions.

1975:
TRAVIS WALTON

On November 5, 1975 seven men spent the day cutting wood in the Apache-Sitgreaves National Forest in Arizona. They were preparing to go home at 6:10 p.m., when their truck rounded a bend in the forest track and they saw a glowing structured object about 98 ft. ahead of them, hovering some 16 ft. above the ground.

Travis Walton (age 22) shouted to the driver to stop, jumped out, hurried towards the object, and stood looking at it. It was a classic "one shallow bowl inverted on another" UFO, seemingly some 16 ft. in diameter. His companions shouted to him to be careful, and to come back. He stepped back two paces and a blue-green beam shot out from the bottom of the craft. It struck him, lifted him into the air and threw him back onto the ground.

Believing that they were all in danger, the driver headed away rapidly with the five others. After traveling some 1300 ft., they stopped. Looking back, they saw a light rise from the

ground, which they assumed to be the object. Somewhat ashamed of running away, they drove back to the clearing, but there was no sign of Walton. After searching in vain, they drove to the nearest town, Heber, and informed the Sheriff.

Next, they informed Walton's family. When his mother heard the news, according to one of the men, "She did not act very surprised, and said, 'Well, that's the way these things happen.' " His sister, too, took the news surprisingly calmly.

The following morning, some fifty persons took part in a thorough but fruitless search. There were no signs of

the UFO at the alleged site. Late in the afternoon, Walton's mother said, "I don't think there is any use of looking any further. He's not around here. I don't think he's on this earth." His brother, Duane, in an interview, expressed no fear for Walton's well-being. because he was convinced Walton was alive and well in a flying saucer. The brothers had discussed the subject many times, and had agreed that if the opportunity presented itself, "We would immediately get as directly under the object as physically possible" in hope of being taken up. Duane's only regret was that it was Travis, not he, who was "having the

"Well, that's the way these things happen," was Travis Walton's mother's philosophical comment when she heard that her son had been abducted by aliens in a scenario like the one shown here.

experience of a lifetime."

Because the police had to consider the possibility of foul play, Walton's co-workers took polygraph tests that seemed to confirm that they were telling the truth. Five days after his disappearance, at around midnight, Walton called the only member of the family with a phone, his brother-in-law, from a pay phone in a gas station in Heber. The brother-in-law picked up Duane and drove to Heber. There, they found Walton slumped in the phone booth, unshaven and looking thin.

Under hypnosis, Walton recalled a more-or-less stereotypical abduction experience, including a physical examination in what he took to be a hospital, conducted by short, pale, thin aliens with oversize heads, large eyes and seamless clothing. When he resisted them, his examiners left the room. He went wandering around the premises, visiting other rooms and meeting other aliens who forced him onto a table, where he lost consciousness. These memories seemed to cover only a period of about an hour. When Walton recovered consciousness, he was lying on the ground near a highway. He saw the spacecraft, in which he had presumably been for five days, flying away.

The Walton case is unique in that there were six witnesses who saw the spacecraft and the beam of light. Unless they were conspiring with him to deceive, it seems that the mysterious object (though not necessarily an alien spacecraft) and his five-day absence (though not necessarily on board the craft) are matters of fact.

Grounds for doubting the physical reality of the abduction have been demonstrated by Philip Klass, who has unearthed a mass of circumstantial detail which other investigators had either failed to find, or chosen to disregard. Klass established that not only Walton but all his family were obsessed with the idea of going aboard a UFO. He also pointed out discrepancies, contradictions and outright lies in the testimony.

Yet we consider the fact that today, even after more than 20 years, Walton and his companions are still sticking firmly to their story. In 1996, Walton reissued his original account, replying at length to Klass' criticisms. In some ways, Walton is as believable as his story is unbelievable.

1976: LOUISE SMITH, MONA STAFFORD AND ELAINE THOMAS

Though multiple abductions have been reported at other times, in most cases smaller numbers of people are involved—couples like the Hills, parents with children like Betty Andreasson, or two close friends like Hickson and Parker. In this case, however, the abductees were three women, aged 44, 35 and 48. Each lived independently of the others, though they enjoyed a close friendship based on shared artistic interests.

On January 6, 1976, they were driving home after a late dinner when all three women saw a strange object in the sky, seemingly a domed-disc UFO. This seemed to affect their control of the car. They also saw luminous phenomena which, when they got home, had affected their eyes

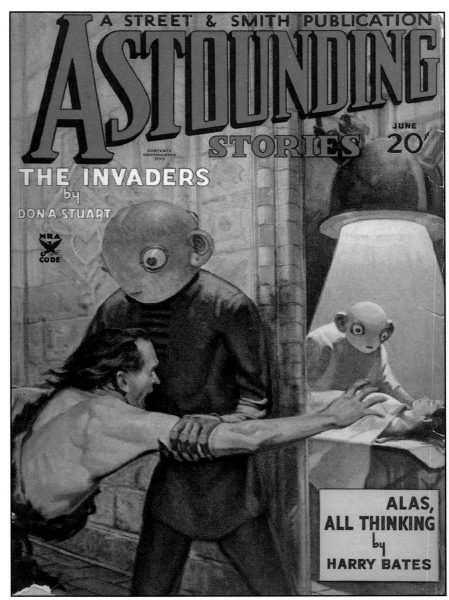

The physical examination of humans by aliens—a standard feature of abduction stories—was anticipated by the creators of science fiction as early as 1935, when this tale was written.

A portrait of an alien kidnapper with the image of the hysterically screaming abductee mirrored in his eyes.

and skin. They also noted that their journey seemed to have taken some 90 minutes longer than they would have expected.

They reported their experience to UFO investigators. Under hypnosis, each woman had an abduction tale. The space ship took the car—with its three occupants—up into itself. The aliens separated the three women, and took Stafford onto a different spaceship, which gave her the feeling of being "in a cave or volcano—underground somewhere." Both she and Smith described being subjected to a painful physical examination by grey, hooded aliens, about 5 ft. tall, with large eyes slanting towards the temples.

Dr. Leo Sprinkle, who examined them, favored a literal interpretation:

Although it is not possible to claim absolutely that a physical examination and abduction have taken place, I believe that this is the best hypothesis to explain the apparent "loss of time" experience and the apparent physical and emotional reactions.

Those who investigated the case were all impressed by the testimony, and shared Sprinkle's view. However, some details do warrant notice:

There were long-term personality changes in the witnesses, and mystical overtones. Both Stafford and Thomas had subsequent experiences. A few weeks before her death—which occurred shortly after the incident, though there is no reason to suppose a connection—Thomas noticed that her home was being "watched" by a UFO, which sometimes slowly approached the house. One evening, Stafford found an alien in her trailer kitchen. The alien spoke to her enigmatically, then left.

Louise Thomas had purchased the car in which the three had their experience that very day. People buy cars all the time, but it is still a curious coincidence that a car which seemed to go out of control should be an unfamiliar vehicle which its new owner was driving at night for the very first time.

As chance would have it, it was Mona Stafford's birthday. On average, 1 in 365 abductees has a birthday abduction. This causes us to wonder whether—as seemed likely in the case of contactee Eugenio Siragusa—the occasion may have had a special significance.

Smith was a widow and Stafford a divorcee. Thomas was married. All three were notably devout churchgoers. This is significant in indicating that all subscribed to a belief system which may have had a part in shaping their experience.

These are trivial points, no doubt, and if the circumstances of their experience were more solidly rooted, it would seem trivial to raise them. But in fact, their experience was far from being solidly rooted. Their stories were more like dream impressions than detailed memories. They did not seem to share the same experience, and there were subjective aspects to their stories which are hard to account for if it was an objective reality. A curious feature was noted, though without comment, by the Lorenzens in their account:

Certain similarities were observed: a feeling of anxiety on the part of each witness regarding a specific aspect of the experience. For Ms. Smith, it was the "wall" and the "gate" beyond which she was afraid to "move" psychologically; for Ms. Stafford, it was the "eye" which she had observed and the impression that something evil or bad would happen if she allowed the eye to "control" her; for Ms. Thomas, it was the "blackness" which seemed to be the feared condition or cause for anxiety.

Just what this means—and what may have been significant about any of the various features—we can only guess. However, it all adds a further dimension of mystery to a very mysterious incident.

1978 AND OTHER TIMES: DEBBIE JORDAN

New York artist Budd Hopkins has been investigating abduction experiences since 1975, and the three books he has written about his work make an impressive case for the physical reality and extraterrestrial origin of these experiences. It is a case made all the stronger by the fact that Hopkins is well aware of the objections to this viewpoint. He insists that he has come to espouse it only because his first-hand work with scores of witnesses has convinced him that abductions are real.

Between 1976 and 1981, when Hopkins' first book, *Missing Time,* was published, the author says he was:

involved to varying degrees with the investigation of 19 similar abduction cases involving 37 people. These 19 cases have yielded clear patterns … it seems to me as if these quite similar abductions constitute some kind of systematic "research" program, with the human species as

American artist Budd Hopkins has become the leading investigator of abduction cases and is a staunch believer in the literal truth of the accounts.

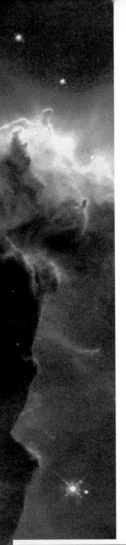

subject. Individuals or small groups of people are involuntarily "borrowed" and most often the memory of such an encounter is effectively erased from the individual's consciousness … What the purposes of these temporary abductions are, and what part of the experience may be purely psychic, we can only guess, but that they have a physical dimension seems to me beyond doubt …Several abductees bear scars on their bodies from incisions made years earlier when the subjects had been children … I have heard these witnesses, under hypnosis, describe in almost exactly the same words the equipment used to make these incisions.

From the seven cases that Hopkins narrates, such similarities emerge clearly and forcefully, and it would be easy to share his conclusion that "extraterrestrials have been observing us in our innocence for many years; they are already here." This conclusion was reinforced by the Debbie Jordan ("Kathie Davis") case, an account which Hopkins published in 1987.

The story was immensely complicated, and made more so—as Hopkins himself acknowledges—because he narrated the details in the order he learned them. What was distinctive about the Jordan case was the ongoing nature of the events, giving the impression that Debbie was living two lives at once—her conscious Earthly existence, and one which emerged only under hypnosis, but whose events intertwined with her consciously-lived life. In the following brief summary, the bracketed events are those recalled only subsequently, under hypnosis, during Hopkins' investigation.

In 1947, Debbie's sister Kathy was born; when she was two years old, her mother had a strange dream in which she hid Kathy from two men who were in the house to take her away. Later, the family came to believe that this prevented an abduction.

Debbie was born in 1958, and almost from birth suffered from ill health. She was treated for high blood pressure. During childhood she suffered from hepatitis, pneumonia, hypoglycemia, hyperadrenalism and various allergies. Also, her appendix was removed, along with cysts on her ovaries. She had traction for two extra vertebrae which became fused. She was chronically overweight, seemingly due to hormonal imbalance. Debbie also suffered from chronic anxiety and had strange dreams. Around the age of 8, she had a dreamlike experience of visiting a strange house where a strange child plays a strange game, which gave Debbie a permanent scar. At one point, he seemed to turn into a small, large-headed, grey-skinned entity.

In July, 1975, visiting a state park, Debbie saw strange lights and had a weird encounter with three strange men. In December, she was driving around the countryside with friends and they saw UFOs and stopped to look. (Years later, under hypnosis, Debbie recalled being taken into a landed UFO and subjected to a gynecological operation.)

Debbie was "sexually active" but, though ignorant of contraception, had been lucky enough not to become pregnant. About this time she met and fell in love with her husband-to-be. They planned to marry in mid-1978. When she found herself pregnant, they planned to marry sooner. In March, Debbie was shattered—and her doctor surprised —to find she was no longer pregnant. (In subsequent hypnotic recall, she remembered being abducted and having her unborn child surgically removed.)

In April, Debbie married. That summer, living in a suburb of Indianapolis, she had an extremely vivid "dream" of seeing two strange figures in her bedroom. One was holding a small black box which he handed to her, telling her that "when the time is right, you will see it again, you will remember and you'll know how to use it." Her family remembers her talking about the dream. In July, Debbie's son was born two months prematurely due to kidney failure.

In 1980, pregnant with her second son, Debbie received strange phone calls at around the same time each Wednesday afternoon over a period of several months until her baby was born. No words were uttered, just weird sounds. Debbie changed her phone number to an unlisted number; a few minutes after getting the new number, the mysterious being called on the new number, sounding angry. Debbie's mother and a friend each took one such call and confirmed this. In September, her second child was born; he grew up with a speech

A swirling gateway is shown separating the Earth and Moon in their parallel universes.
A reversed clock face highlights their time differences.

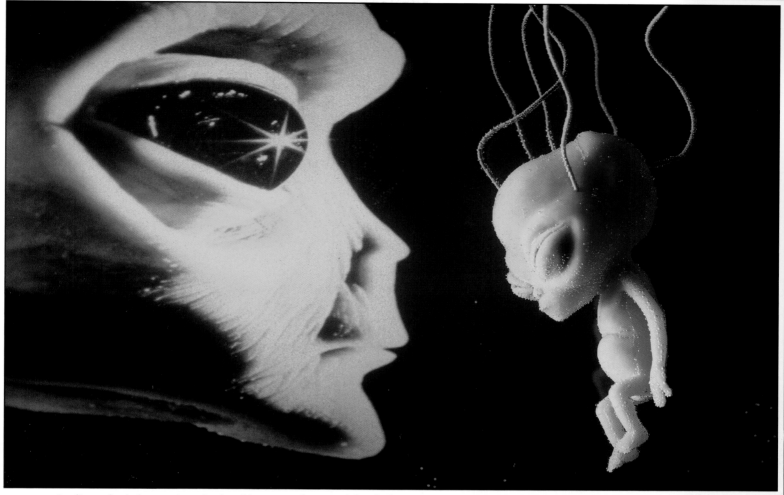

An alien mother is shown gazing at her fetus. Many woman have revealed, under hypnosis, memories of having had their unborn babies surgically removed, while being held prisoner by alien beings.

problem, and made sounds closely resembling the mysterious telephone caller.

In 1981, Debbie divorced and went to live with her parents. One night in 1983, her mother saw a ball of light around their property. There was quite a lot of coming and going, but overall, it seemed there was an hour unaccounted for in Debbie's time. The next morning, they found mysterious traces on the lawn, which were still visible two years later.

Debbie read Hopkins' recently published book, *Missing Time,* and recognized similarities between the cases he described and her own experiences. In August, she wrote to him, and eventually met and was investigated by him. On October 3, as subsequently recalled under hypnosis, she encountered an alien entity while driving to the store. (Later, she was taken from her bedroom to a UFO where she was shown a small child. She recalled that an entity visited the

Jordan home, paralyzed the older child and seemingly placed a nasal implant in the younger child; she herself was abducted again.)

In 1984–85, Debbie had dreams of being pregnant. In 1986, she was wakened by her older child who had been frightened by a strange light: Debbie then saw an entity walk past her door from the younger child's room. In April, she had a dream—perhaps concealing an abduction—in which she was shown a tiny baby, and told that it, and the small girl she saw in 1983, are two of nine children born from ova removed from her in 1978.

Assembled in this way, the incidents in Debbie's life seem to form a consistent and plausible story in which she is used as breeding stock by visiting extraterrestrials. But if this is true, it is a story unlike that of any other abductee or contactee. There is virtually nothing to her experience except matters

involving pregnancy and childbirth.

We are asked to believe, however, that —having the entire human race at their disposal—the aliens chose Debbie Jordan, with her obvious ill health, anxieties and other problems, to be the parent of their experimental offspring. Alternatively, if they had some special reason for using her, why didn't they give her the benefit of their scientific expertise and cure some of her ailments, as we have seen aliens do in other cases?

In 1994, Debbie Jordan and her sister Kathy Mitchell published their own account of their experiences. It continued the saga of extraordinary incidents: opening the book at random, we read that Debbie was in her current (third) husband's bathroom when the toilet paper roll suddenly unwound spontaneously, almost to the end. This is not the sort of way we would generally expect otherworldly visitors to indicate their presence.

1985:
WHITLEY STRIEBER

The most blatant difference between Whitley Strieber's abduction experience and everyone else's is that where the others received little except anxiety and wretchedness, Strieber received an advance of $1 million for telling his story, not to mention film and translation rights. He told a Washington audience in 1987:

> I have explained myself 225 times in public since January, and had the experience of being laughed at in front of an audience of seven hundred people and eight million viewers on the Phil Donahue show. I have cried all the way to the bank because it's no secret that I made a million dollars from *Communion*. However, up until now it's been a secret that I found out I deserved every penny.

Doubtless, there are many who would willingly undergo his experiences for such a financial reward, yet there is a sense in which Strieber is justified. For if the events he described did not physically take place—and there are grounds for supposing they didn't—then he is spiritually and mentally disturbed to a degree for which no possible financial gain would be adequate compensation.

There are other important differences, stemming from the fact that Strieber was already a well-known author in his own country. Literary criticism would only make this study even more complicated than it is, but it is disturbing that Strieber seems to combine a breezy intimacy, as follows:

> When they held me in their arms, I had been as helpless as a baby, crying like a baby, as frightened as a baby ...

... with a pretentious solemnity:

> In all of us there is an unaddressed urgency which we cannot really name, which seems to lie at the heart of our hope for ourselves. It is the flight of the eagle that we seek, the walk of the monk down the nirvana road, the faith of the old priest whose Mass in his humble little church last Sunday was really said between the worlds of body and soul ...

This leaves the reader wondering where the reporting of an agonizing personal experience ends and fictional literature begins.

Certainly, it is hard to assess what part reality played in his story. To do Strieber justice, he says so himself, frequently. But he doesn't help by embedding his narrative in a mess of words which may have been intended to give us a precise description of what was going on, but have the effect of being far less explicit than, say, the direct simplicity of Hickson and Parker.

The primary event of his story occurred on December 26, 1985, when he was spending a white Christmas with his wife and son in their isolated log cabin in upstate New York. At 8:30 p.m., he set the burglar alarm, which included movement-sensitive pads outside the house, and carried out his customary practice of going round the house "peering in closets and even looking under the guest room bed for hidden intruders." This is behavior that might cause a reader to ask, "What kind of a man is this?" By 10 p.m., he was in bed, and by 11 p.m., asleep.

In the middle of the night, according to Strieber, he was awakened by a peculiar noise from the living room downstairs, "as if a large number of people were moving rapidly around in the room." He checked the burglar alarm panel beside the bed—the row of glowing lights showed no sign of entry.

Shortly after, the bedroom door opened and an entity entered—a short figure wearing a hat (one of the very few aliens to do so) and what seemed to be some kind of breastplate. This,

Actor Christopher Walken played the part of Whitley Strieber in the film adaptation of "Communion."

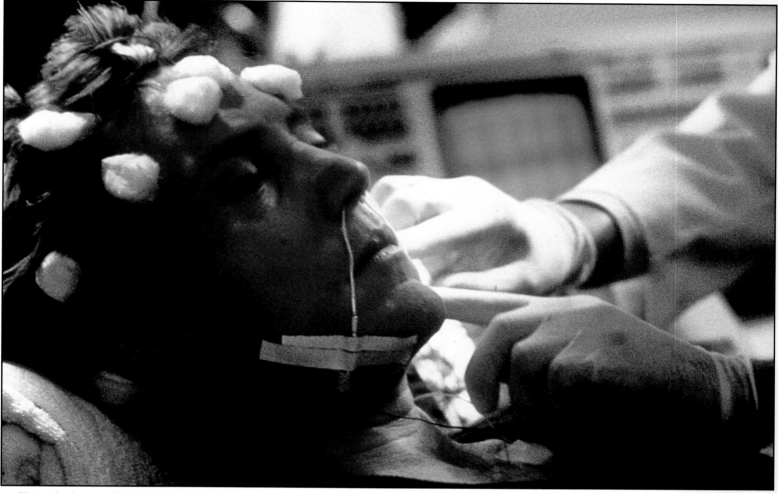

Playing the character of Whitley Strieber in the movie version of Communion, *Christopher Walken is shown being thoroughly examined and put through hypnotic regression to reveal the horrific events that occurred during his alien abduction.*

Strieber speculated, may be meant as protection against the shotgun the entity knew was kept in the bedroom as the ultimate deterrent in case intruders penetrated the outer defenses of Fort Strieber, as indeed this intruder seemed to have done. But the entity gave Strieber no chance to reach his gun.

There followed a succession of scenes, separated by intervals during which Strieber blacked out. First, he was taken—he doesn't know how—out of the house. Then he found himself in a depression in the woods, surrounded by little beings. Then he was in a "messy round room," again surrounded by the creatures. He was very, very afraid, and described his fear in rather vague language:

> Whitley ceased to exist. What was left was a body in a state of raw fear so great that it swept about me like a thick, suffocating curtain, turning paralysis into a condition that seemed close to death. I do not think that my ordinary humanity survived the transition to this little room. I died, and a wild animal appeared in my place.

In the "messy room"—a unique instance, I believe, of an abductee being taken to an untidy location for his experience, as they are usually clean and orderly—Strieber had some kind of needle thrust into his brain, an incision made in a finger, and a large object shoved up his rectum.

Then he was returned to the house. The next morning he didn't remember any of it, but memories gradually returned, triggered by soreness and the discovery of a mysterious cut on his finger. This had a very bad effect on his personality. A few months earlier, he had gone through "personal hell" with his wife, who had been on the brink of leaving him; the same thing threatened to recur, and he realized he had to do something about it.

By a fortunate coincidence, Strieber's brother had given him as a Christmas present a book called *Science and the UFOs*, by British authors Randles and Warrington. About a fortnight after his experience, he glanced over the book, but it frightened him, so he read no more than 5 or 6 pages. Later, however, Strieber read it through, and was "shocked" when he read an account of an "archetypal abduction experience." He says that his "first reaction was to slam the book closed as if it contained a coiled snake," but it named Budd Hopkins as a leading investigator in the abduction field, and since Hopkins also lived in New York, Strieber made a date to meet him. This led to a course of hypnotic regression, and the revelation of the events in greater detail.

As Strieber tells his story, the complexities of the witness' personality

reveal themselves. We learn that

for half of my life I have been engaged in a rigorous and detailed search for a finer state of consciousness

And now Strieber wonders if his "years of eager study of everything from Zen to quantum physics" are leading him "into some strange and tragic byway of the soul."

Compared with the bald, hesitant narratives of other abduction witnesses, it is hard to know how to evaluate an account in which the story is garnished with quotations from Meister Eckhart and Blake, and which has references to Aztec imagery and Japanese haiku. If such things are, indeed, a true representation of a person's everyday thinking, then they can no more be seen as a sign of insincerity than when a Bethurum or a Menger rhapsodizes over the physical charms of his female contact.

But even if we confine our attention to factual matters, Strieber's story raises unsettling questions. During 1967–68, Strieber experienced a series of bizarre incidents in Austin and San Antonio, Texas; in London, England; and in Italy, Austria, France and Spain. In all of these places, he had, if not an amnesiac spell, then a dissociation of personality—at the very least, a time when he manifestly ceased to be his habitual self. How do these earlier experiences relate to the later one? Do they make it more or less likely that his story is true on a physical level?

In addition, what are we to make of the naiveté with which Strieber can say, "I do not recall thinking or talking at all about extraterrestrials." Can he really have forgotten that, at the age of 13, he informed a friend that "spacemen" had taught him how to build an antigravity machine?

Such memory lapses occur more than once in his story, and hardly encourage confidence in the rest of the facts—for which, let us not forget, he is the only source. There is not a scrap of worthwhile external confirmation of any of this from, say, any neighbors or patrolling policemen.

Finally, if Strieber's experience was so profoundly shattering on a personal level, why the precipitate rush into print? We may accept that for a professional writer, setting his thoughts down on paper is the most effective way of ordering them and coming to terms with his experience. Setting thoughts down on paper is one thing, however; publication is another. Wouldn't it have been more prudent, from every point of view, to allow a reasonable time for a balanced evaluation? Yet Strieber got his manuscript off to his publisher *even while the events he is writing about were still proceeding.*

With so many causes for doubt—and his books contain many more—there seems little reason to take this seriously, and indeed I do not propose that we do so. What we *should* take seriously, however, are the social circumstances of the book's publication—the fact that such a man wrote such a book in such a way, and that so many people responded to it strongly enough to keep the book high on the best-seller list for weeks on end. No doubt, the second part follows from the first— never before had a person in Strieber's position claimed the kind of experience usually reserved for "nobodies" like Debbie Jordan.

That the general public should yield to the publisher's promotion efforts is understandable, but that investigators abandoned their normal critical standards is more strange and more disturbing. That such standards have been abandoned is shown by this statement from Donald F. Klein, M.D., Director of Research at New York State Psychiatric Institute, in the press release for the book:

I see no evidence of an anxiety state, mind disorder or personality disorder.

By strict clinical standards, this may, for all I know, be a valid assessment. But no one can read Strieber's account of his safety precautions at his house and not feel that he is displaying more anxiety than most of us. No one can read about his recurrent amnesia without feeling that his mind has been periodically disordered. Furthermore, no one can read of his ability to "forget" about his childhood preoccupation with extraterrestrials and not feel that his personality is somewhat less than ordered.

1989: LINDA NAPOLITANO

At 3:15 a.m. on November 30, 1989, a convoy of cars—3 or even 5—carrying some of the most important political figures in America was mysteriously brought to a halt beside the Hudson River in New York City while their occupants watched an event taking place near the river. They saw a female figure floated out of a high apartment building into a UFO hovering overhead. Once the show was over, the Secretary-General of the United Nations and his two security officers—but none of the other occupants of the motorcade— were teleported out of their vehicle to a seaside location on Long Island, to watch the abducted female and some alien beings take part in some kind of ecological activity.

When they got back from the beach, the other cars had gone. Supposedly, the other drivers and passengers, having witnessed the abduction of a top-ranking political VIP and his two minders, had driven off into the night, not even putting a note under the windscreen wipers, leaving the ill-fated trio to their fate.

The abduction of Linda Napolitano ("Cortile" in the earliest accounts) by aliens on November 30, 1989, and its consequences, unquestionably constitutes one of the most bizarre episodes in the history of otherworldly visitation. If the events occurred as claimed, the implications are almost immeasurably profound and far-reaching.

The story, which has been narrated by investigator Budd Hopkins in a book-length account, is extremely complex. However, the crucial incident occurred when the New York housewife was abducted from her Manhattan apartment in the dead of night. She was floated through a closed window and then through the air to a hovering spaceship, which then dove into the

The abduction of Linda Napolitano from her apartment was allegedly witnessed by others, but their testimony raises questions, as does Linda's.

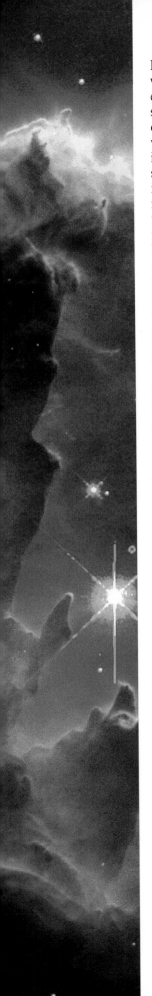

Hudson river. She then took part in what appeared to be some kind of an ecologically-directed "show," after which she was returned to her home. Much of this was seen by up to a score of witnesses, of whom six have been identified to some degree. The sight so worried three of them—one an international statesman of the highest rank who (it is an open secret) is alleged to be Javier Perez de Cuellar, at the time Secretary-General of the United Nations—that they became emotionally disturbed for years to follow, setting in motion a series of bizarre incidents involving Napolitano. All this was in addition to a succession of experiences earlier in her life, including incidents involving her children, relatives and friends.

The episode of the distinguished spectators, above all, defies belief. Let's say we accept that those members of the party who were not abducted, on finding themselves de-immobilized, decided their best course was to hustle the other VIPs to safety. Surely, they would have left a police presence at the site so that the abducted three, on their return from their seaside excursion, would find their car surrounded by NYPD's finest, flashing lights and armed guards galore! Instead, they returned to an empty car which—though left unattended in New York at 3 in the morning—had escaped vandalism or theft. Did the abducted security officers have time to set the alarm before being whisked away? Maybe their alien abductors kept a watchful eye on the vehicle …

Apart from its intrinsic implausibility, Linda's story is full of contradictions and unanswered questions. The chief investigator, Budd Hopkins, has never met the principal witnesses apart from Linda herself; he has only spoken with them on the telephone or received letters from them. The two principal witnesses, the security guards who were teleported along with the Secretary-General, waited 15 months after witnessing the abduction before telling anyone about their experience. It also seems odd that though they were security officers working at the highest political level, they chose artist/author Hopkins as their confidant, rather than going to their own superiors to report a

situation which was tantamount to an alien invasion.

It is so completely improbable that a series of events with such strong social, political and military implications could take place in a sophisticated city like New York without attracting any official notice that we might reasonably deem it a waste of time to give it serious attention. If it should turn out to be true, the story would be of immeasurable consequence to the U.S. Government. There have been no front-page headlines, however, no official inquiries (that we know of) and certainly no official statements. Instead, the public learns of these events—if at all—in the form of a commercial book purchased over the counter. It is as though we were to learn of the discovery of life on Mars from a popular paperback.

Such incongruities present the abductionists with a formidable challenge. Hopkins does his best with the story, and fellow abductionist Professor David Jacobs has supported him as best he can. In this excerpt, the Professor explains how Linda was able to fly through the window of her apartment:

> In spite of hundreds of accounts of people flying through closed windows, it is exceedingly rare to find an outside witness who has observed it. Therefore, although it sounds impossible, the physical mechanism that allows people to pass through solid objects probably renders them invisible, at least for this part of the abduction experience.

Ingenious, but a mystery isn't explained by theorizing another mystery! If the aliens know how to pass a physical object—Linda—through another object—her apartment window —then float her unharmed through the air, their power is virtually limitless: they could seize our Earth whenever they wish. In the face of such absurdity, how is it that any serious people are taking the abduction claims seriously? The answer is that the witnesses make those claims seriously—and it is evident that they do so sincerely, genuinely believing they have lived through these experiences. One thing is certain; they have been through an experience of some kind.

THE ABDUCTION SNOWBALL

Linda Napolitano and Whitley Strieber are just two among hundreds who have claimed experiences similar to those of Barney and Betty Hill. Each summer, Professor Leo Sprinkle of the University of Wyoming at Laramie holds a "Rocky Mountain Conference," at which people who seem to have had contact with extraterrestrials gather to share their experiences. To spend a week at Laramie, surrounded by people who are alleging these otherworldly adventures, is extraordinarily impressive.

Sprinkle feels that a vital function of his reunions—perhaps the most vital—is to provide moral support for the witnesses, who more often than not have received negative responses from friends, colleagues and relatives. Here is one of his speakers telling how her story was received:

> Family reaction? Horrendous! They threatened to send me to an institution, so I quit telling them of my UFO contact. I now realize that you can't awaken anyone until they are emotionally, spiritually, and mentally ready to handle this.

Many others have testified to the lack of comprehension and consequent lack of support that they receive from the rest of us. However, while the witnesses certainly need sympathy and support, and while Sprinkle and Hopkins are certainly performing a valuable service in providing them, this cannot be much more than a temporary fix. Long-term help must be based on understanding, and understanding can come only from finding out what is really happening. The therapist is required to be an investigator just as much as the investigator has a duty to be a therapist.

According to criteria adopted by Mark Rodeghier and his colleagues at the Center for UFO Studies, the abduction experience includes the following agenda:

- The witness is taken against his or her will from normal terrestrial surroundings by non-human beings.

- These beings take the witness to another enclosed place, that is assumed or known to be a spacecraft.

- In this place, the witness is subjected to examination and/or engages in communication with the beings.

This summary by no means covers the entire range of abduction scenarios. There are countless variants. For example, there is "independent *hybrid* activity," in which the place of the alien is taken by a hybrid. A hybrid is the offspring of mixed Earth and alien parenting, obtained via egg- or sperm-collecting, or by impregnation and fetus-removal. According to Professor Jacobs, "reports suggest that they (the hybrids) can exist in human society for about twelve hours." During this time, looking as human as a "Star Person," they make contact with their victims and bring about sexual contact, carrying the alien agenda into a new phase.

Whatever form it takes, however, it is abundantly clear that the abduction experience is essentially a *physical* experience, in which something real and tangible happens. This is particularly the case if we accept Jacobs' view that the purpose of abductions is essentially reproductive—this cannot be anything other than real in the most hands-on, here-and-now human sense.

Those who support the "abductions-are-real" interpretation point to the high degree of correlation between the stories told by the witnesses. Among the recurring features are:

- "missing" periods of time, suggesting that memories have been blocked out by the aliens for some reason

- "black boxes" used by the aliens or given by them to witnesses to hold

- details of the "spacecraft" such as doors which seem to "disappear" when closed, tunnel-like corridors, light sources which can't be discerned, and so on

- medical examinations, generally involving probes and scanners

- marks on the skin which are supposed to be the implant of some subcutaneous monitoring device

The fact that such features turn up in story after story is impressive, but it is still no more than the duplication of one subjective story by another. It does not constitute proof that those stories relate to real-life events.

If abductions are really taking place, it should not be difficult to prove. All it needs is for just one abductee to take his camera with him and shoot a roll of film, or bring us back an artifact; or make drawings containing convincing details, or show surgical or other marks which are unquestionably non-human, or for just one independent witness to see an abduction taking place, and take photos or otherwise give convincing testimony.

Until one or other of these things happens, it will remain an open question whether Betty Hill and the others really were abducted by beings from other worlds.

The mating of aliens and humans raises questions about the biological and genetic factors involved.

WATCHERS OF THE SKY

"Egregors are astral entities, formed from invisible vital forces, grouped in collectives, oriented towards a single order of ideas. In nature, they are colossal forces, giant and terrible creatures, capable of generating whirlwinds and convulsions which can shake entire countries. These are the genii of the ancients, the Watchers of the Sky of occultists, the Titans of Fable ... When they are angered, they unleash catastrophes. But they also direct the stars and protect just nations and men. They include the nine powers: angels, archangels, thrones, dominions, principalities, virtues, powers, cherubim and seraphim. They are the knights of the holy grail."

Paul Carton, a twentieth-century occultist, is one of many thoughtful scholars convinced of the existence of otherworldly beings, somehow intermediate between the gods and ourselves. These, though they are among our most frequent visitors, are the ones which make us most uneasy. The gods today are seen either as imminent beings in whom we have absolute trust, or as remote and inaccessible. We are relatively "comfortable" with the extraterrestrials because, however alien, they seem to exist on the same plane of reality as ourselves. But these other intermediate categories of visitor, neither gods nor physical beings, disturb us more profoundly. Although they evidently inhabit some other level of reality, they are not far removed from our everyday reality, and they intrude upon our lives in disconcerting and often horrifying ways ...

GHOSTS

Sightings of ghosts have been reported throughout recorded history. Millions of "ghost stories" have been told, some

Füssli's depiction of the nightmare transforms a psychological experience into a visitation from a physical entity whose intentions are not benevolent.

with a shiver by the fireside on wintry evenings, others with morning-after puzzlement at the breakfast table. Although they are continually dismissed by skeptics, they persist. While fairies, leprechauns, witches, mermaids, and other such beings have largely faded into folklore, ghosts continue to be reported in all sorts of contexts. They are the most varied and the most persistent of paranormal phenomena.

Most ghosts are phantoms of the

Humans are shown being abducted by demons. Traditionally, artists have depicted benevolent entities with birdwings, and the malevolent as winged bats.

living, and it may seem inappropriate to be considering them in a book about visitors from other worlds. But there are a minority of ghosts who do, indeed, seem to come from the beyond. It may be that we should think in terms of another dimension of reality rather than of another place in the physical universe, but the spirits of the dead certainly do not inhabit our here-and-now world.

Every culture has its own ideas about what happens to us when we die. For some, it is simple extinction; for others, flesh-and-blood resuscitation. Some believe that we are reincarnated in a continuing spiral until we have earned sufficient credit as humans to qualify for admission to a higher level of existence. Some believe that at death we lose our individual identity, and are absorbed into some communal "greater being."

In this book, we are not concerned with any of these possibilities. Many cultures, however—perhaps most—believe that death is not the end of personal existence, but a transition from one form of existence to another. They suppose that we move on to another stage of development, as an infant moves from childhood to adulthood. The difference is that the next stage takes place elsewhere than on Earth.

If this is so, then perhaps the dead have the power to revisit Earth, and

During a séance at the Paris home of researcher Delanne, a misty figure is shown detaching itself from the medium and approaching the sitters.

for witnesses to see, hear and sometimes even smell and touch.

The fact that apparitions are occasionally seen by some of those present but not by others suggests that some extrasensory process is at work. Technically, this amounts to hallucination. However, hallucination takes so many forms that it serves more as a handy label than a precise definition. Ghosts are sometimes photographed. If we could be confident that they are what they seem to be, this would establish that they have some degree of material presence. Unfortunately, there are only a handful of ghost photographs that merit serious attention, and even these fall short of being entirely convincing.

But even if ghosts are no more than hallucinations, something is needed to trigger the process, and if the dead survive, they may be the ones responsible. We may reasonably suppose that whatever form our future existence takes, it allows for at least a partial return to Earthly life, in something resembling Earthly form. Moreover, the dead retain their Earthly appearance and attributes, or else they resume it for the purpose of revisiting Earth, for otherwise they would not be identified.

One reason why the nature of ghosts remains unresolved even though they have been around for more than 2000 years is because—as in the case of UFOs—there has been a tendency to lump all paranormal apparitions together. Despite superficial similarities, they are not all alike. It is only recently that poltergeists have been separated as a category; perhaps we shall soon make the necessary distinction between the other three categories—phantasms, hauntings and revenants. We are not concerned here with the first two of these, because they do not come from other worlds in any sense of the word. Phantasms of the living are by definition Earthly events, and though hauntings seem to involve the dead, they appear to be spirits which are for some reason earthbound. There is an abundance of

even intervene in Earthly affairs. This possibility has been a source of controversy among Christian theologians. Some religious denominations say they can, while others say they can't. Many native cultures have formulated their own ideas as to how and under what circumstances the dead will return. For example, there is a widespread belief around the world that if the dead are not buried in the correct manner and with the appropriate rituals, they will be sad or angry, and return to Earth to reproach or harass their negligent relatives.

Where are they returning *from*? We Earthpeople cannot conceive of anything existing outside space and time, and so those who accept survival as a fact necessarily assume that the dead exist *somewhere*. The more sophisticated theorists have stopped thinking in terms of Valhallas and Heavens, and accept that any future existence may take place on some level beyond our imagining. Be that as it may, when the dead return to Earth, they do so in a more or less physical form. There is something seemingly material

Edward Kelley and Paul Waring, Sixteenth Century magicians, summon a spirit from the grave, hoping it will tell them where to find buried treasure.

Italian scholar Marsilio Ficino added posthumous fame to his living reputation when he appeared to his friend, Mercati, to tell him about the afterworld.

testimony that both these categories of ghost exist, but on what level they exist, and how they function, remain subjects for speculation.

The third category is that of "revenants." The French word, meaning returners, or "those who come again," has no equivalent in English. These are, ostensibly, the dead returning to visit the Earth, where they once lived. As such, they qualify for inclusion in our survey of visitors from other worlds. The clearest examples of this type of case are "compact" cases—when an agreement has been made between two people that whichever should die first will return and tell the other. Here is a classic instance from the Fifteenth Century:

The scholar Marsilio Ficino, after a discussion on the nature of the soul with his friend and pupil Michele Mercati, agreed that whichever died first would try to revisit the other. Early one morning in the year 1491, while Mercati was studying at his San Miniato home, he heard a horse galloping in the street and stopping at his door, and Ficino's voice exclaiming, "Oh, Michele, what we said about the other world is true!" Mercati hastily opened his window, and saw Ficino on a white horse. He called after him, but he galloped away out of his sight. The servant whom he sent to Florence to enquire about Ficino learnt that he had died about that hour.

Clearly, though Ficino is only recently dead, he has had time—assuming "time" has any meaning there—to see enough of the "next world" to know that it does exist. His visit to his friend does, indeed, constitute a return from another world.

In other cases, the dead person has definitely been "gone" for a considerable period. A British climber at 16,000 ft. in the Himalayas found himself suddenly confronted by the figures of two school friends, both of whom had been killed in a car crash several years earlier. The physical circumstances—extreme cold, oxygen shortage, fatigue—combined with the psychological stress, are sufficient for us to assume a hallucination. But that doesn't answer the question of why these particular people were chosen to play the part of the "ghosts." The climber was not consciously thinking of them. Did his subconscious mind create the hallucination, or did his dead friends make the decision to "return" to give him moral support?

These particular ghosts seem to have done nothing positive, but perhaps their mere presence was a comfort to the climber. The publisher of one of my books, Peter Dawnay, told me how once—driving alone across Spain through the night, in a great hurry to catch the

ferry to North Africa—he felt certain there was someone in the passenger seat who "took control," and seemed to be protecting him from danger.

More specific were the experiences of Edith Foltz-Stearns, an American aviator whose life was repeatedly saved thanks to warnings from invisible co-pilots. At the age of twenty-six, taking part in an air race between Los Angeles and Cleveland, she was off-course and low on fuel. A forced landing was her only option. She looked for a possible place, and thought she'd found one—a stretch of railroad track. She started the descent when a girl's voice said, "No, Edie, don't!" She leveled off and flew on, and minutes later she found herself approaching the runway of Phoenix airport. The voice had been that of a school friend who had been killed in a car crash years before, when she was only fourteen years old.

Most career pilots, however skillful, suffer an accident sooner or later, but Edith's professional life was accident-free. (Ironically, she died as a result of injuries sustained when stepping off a bus.) She was convinced she knew why—she never flew alone. When danger threatened, a deceased friend or a relative would actively help her to safety. During World War Two, she was ferrying a Mosquito over the English

Extreme conditions, such as mountaineering or polar exploration, are notorious as generators of hallucinations in which otherworldly beings appear as guides, companions, even protectors.

Midlands in dense cloud when her dead father's voice suddenly cried, "Edie, look out!" Without even thinking, she shot upwards—and narrowly missed a jagged mountain peak.

It is common for widows and widowers to have the illusion that their lost spouse has returned. Sometimes this is with some kind of message or even an explicit purpose. For others, they are simply a "felt" presence which, nevertheless, gives comfort to the bereaved one. Here is a typical instance: Three members of an English family—a brother and a sister living together, and a sister married and living further down the same street—all reported being visited, separately, by apparitions of their mother, who had recently died. None of the family was regarded as mentally ill, but the brother had a history of paranormal experiences, and twice saved his family from death during World War Two by predicting bomb hits.

After his mother's death, he reported seeing her:

Her apparition comes usually twice a week through the closed door of my bedroom and stops at the foot of my bed. She stands there for a while and stares at me. I have the impression she wants to tell me something but can't.

He found the experience so frightening that he would hide his head under the blanket until she disappeared. Both he and his sister, at breakfast, would hear their mother's footsteps on the upstairs landing, and hear her calling them—but while the brother heard her call his name, the sister heard her call hers! The sister also saw her mother on several occasions, when going to sleep or waking. Like her brother, she didn't welcome the visits.

Always I have tried to keep her out of my room, trying to push her away. But I have not felt anything to touch.

Once she asked her mother if she was happy; her mother nodded and said, "Yes."

The other, married, sister also said she'd seen her mother very often, coming into the bedroom and stopping at the bed and gazing. Like her brother,

she hid under the bedclothes, but she could still see her with her eyes closed.

Twice I woke up my husband, but Frank never could see her, though she was there, just at the foot of the bed, staring at me. He said I was just as mad as my poor mother was, and the next minute he was back asleep.

The others did not know of her experiences till some time later.

In the view of Dr. Lucianowicz, who reported the case, the apparitions were hallucinations, created by the witnesses as a way of expressing feelings of which they were not consciously aware. This may be so, but it does not rule out the chance that the dead mother actively participated in the event, a possibility supported by the fact that all three saw her independently.

There is less room for doubt when something is actually *achieved* as the result of the ghostly visitation. Around 1830, a German priest, Johann Weber of Mittelberg, Bavaria, was called out one winter's night to a sickbed about an hour's walk away. On his way home, he lost his way in the snow and darkness, and strayed onto a frozen lake, whose ice broke beneath his weight. Suddenly, he saw a bright light coming towards him from the atmosphere. The light materialized into the shape of a young orphan boy who Weber had helped and taught, but who had died earlier that year. The apparition stretched out its hand and—with much more than a boy's strength—pulled the priest out of the water. Without speaking, he indicated the way home, then vanished.

The next morning, the priest revisited the scene of his accident. The broken ice and his footsteps in the snow confirmed that the event had really happened. But what of the rescuing boy? Was it the boy himself, returned to Earth to help the man who had previously helped him? Was it his guardian angel, taking the likeness of the boy? Was the apparition a hallucination produced by his subconscious mind?

Whichever explanation we find least implausible, one thing has still to be accounted for—the fact that Father Weber was really and truly rescued. That, at least, took place on the here-and-now physical plane.

In Shakespeare's play, Hamlet, *the ghost of Hamlet's father returns to Earth because he has "unfinished business" that he wants his son to perform.*

SPIRITS OF THE DEAD

Visiting the theater today, we would be surprised if the hero of a modern drama were to receive a visit from his father's ghost. But when Shakespeare's audiences watched Hamlet speak with his father, returning from the grave in quest of revenge, they accepted it as part of the familiar order of things. It was only a short step from the "natural" to the "supernatural"—a distinction which they would not have recognized. It is only our age of science which has hung a curtain to separate this world from the next.

If interaction between the dead and the living has been taking place throughout history, so have claims by individuals that they possess a special power to facilitate such interaction. When Saul, in the Old Testament, asks the Witch of Endor to help him contact the spirit of Samuel, it is clear that he is making use of a socially established

institution. In the mid-Nineteenth Century, though, what had been a service provided by isolated individuals became a widespread movement involving neither marginal folk making a dubious living on the fringes of society nor a priestly elite performing esoteric rituals, but a collective activity in which all could take part. What happened in Hydesville, New York, in 1848, made otherworldly communication a democratic phenomenon.

The breakthrough could hardly have taken place in more humdrum circumstances. When the home of the Fox family was disturbed by strange rapping sounds, 12-year-old Catherine Fox called out, "Do as I do, Mr Splitfoot!" She soon found that the raps echoed her hand clapping. This was hardly more than a childish game. But when the two-way exchange developed into a rudimentary form of what seemed to be communication with the dead, the implications were recognized. As news of the event spread, so did enthusiasm. American society, impatient with authoritative religion, welcomed the indication that two-way communication with the dead was not the exclusive privilege of saints, mystics or magicians, but a right available to one and all.

However, just as older religions had found that professional priests were a convenient interface between the populace and their gods, so spiritualism developed its professionals—individuals who seemed specially gifted when it came to contacting the dead. Though they humbly insisted they were little more than a telephone exchange, the most proficient practitioners could expect to win fame and, if not a fortune, at least a comfortable living in return for their labors.

Inevitably, a spirit of competition entered the business. Mediums vied with one another as to who could produce the "best" phenomena—that is to say, demonstrations which provided the strongest evidence that the spirits were responsible. They improved their techniques. From laboriously rapped out

Saul, King of Israel, asks the Witch of Endor to help him contact the spirit of Samuel. Today, we would call her a Spirit Medium rather than a Witch.

The spirits levitate a table to impress a visitor to the Fox sisters. Such "parlor tricks" were used as evidence of mediums' supposed spiritual powers.

messages, mediums moved on to direct voice. It was found that if a medium let herself lapse into a trance state, her body might be temporarily possessed by a "control" from the Other Side. Often, this was the spirit of a Native American —such as Grace Cook's "White Eagle" or Gladys Leonard's "Feda"—with whom the medium would get on intimate, everyday terms. Speaking through the medium, the control would act as stage manager, requesting music, arranging the seating, introducing the spirits to the sitters and generally ordering everyone about.

Are "White Eagle," "Feda" and their kind really visitors from other worlds? Though some controls display considerable individual personality, many of them reveal disconcerting lapses of memory. Leonora Piper's "Dr Phinuit" mysteriously lost his ability to speak his native French, and Professor Broad records:

> I have been asked for "the key of my wigwam" by a control who professed to be a child, and I have heard an entranced medium suggest that the sitters should sing to encourage a control who claimed to be an Indian chief.

Eileen Garrett, probably the most perceptive and intelligent of all mediums, acknowledged that she very much doubted whether her control

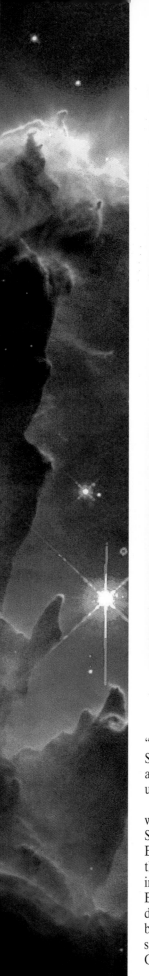

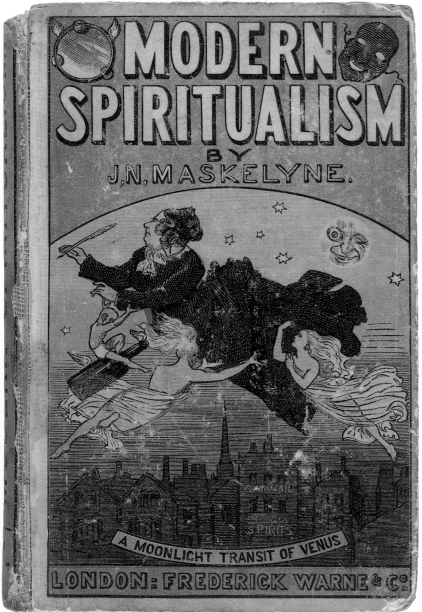

The American medium Mrs. Guppy is shown flying through the night sky over London, borne by spirits at the bidding of sitters gathered in a distant séance-room.

objects of all kinds were appearing in unexpected places—including, on one memorable night in June, 1871, the stout American medium, Mrs. Guppy, who was teleported through the London skies half-clothed.

The American medium D. D. Home caused tables—and sometimes himself—to rise in the air. He would handle hot coals, and pass them on for others to hold, in full light and in the presence of many observers. Never once was he caught cheating. Unless we are prepared to dismiss a mass of eyewitness testimony—often made reluctantly by people who would have liked to catch him out—we must conclude that much if not all of Home's performance was genuine.

But genuine *what?* Home claimed that his ability to do these things was a gift from the spirits. There is no obvious connection between a flying table and an otherworldly spirit, though, apart from the medium's say-so. Do the dead return to perform these crude parlor tricks? Can they not devise some more effective way to prove they have survived? The trumpet-blowing, table-rapping séances were more like noisy children's parties than solemn reunions between the living and the dead. They were degrading to the spirits, and disgusted many of those who might have made a serious study of phenomena which presented a genuine challenge to science. As a result, spiritualism acquired a "marginal" label. Even the involvement of a few eminent sympathizers, such as scientist Sir William Crookes and British Prime Minister Arthur Balfour, was insufficient to restore respectability.

Many believers, too, were dissatisfied with the evidence. The conviction gradually grew that, to be totally sure the dead were really implicated, they should be seen. Some mediums found they had the ability to cause spirits to appear, visibly, in the séance room. At first, it was supposed that the dead were actually reappearing in their own bodies, but gradually investigators came up with a theory about the actual process. The medium exuded from body cavities—mouth, navel, or elsewhere—a psychic substance which Nobel laureate Charles Richet named "ectoplasm." This useful stuff could be shaped into

"Uvani" had any independent existence. She considered he was more probably a convenient creation of her own unconscious mind.

But if that is true of the controls, what about the spirits themselves? Spoken messages are easy to fabricate. Even if they contain personal details, the medium might herself acquire the information by chance or by design. Equally ambiguous were the descriptions of the next world supplied by the dead. In the 1880s, a band of spirits gave Miss M. T. Shelhamer, of Cleveland, Ohio, a book-length account

of the blissful "Summer Land" to which those of us who behave ourselves can expect to go when we die—but can we trust her spirits to tell the truth?

For those who doubted, some more tangible proof was needed. This took the form of asking the spirits to prove they were "superhuman" by doing things we humans can't do. By the 1860s, in séances such as those conducted by Herne and Williams in London, tables were being raised from the floor, music was being broadcast through trumpets floating in mid-air, messages were being written on slates inside sealed boxes and

A demonstration of levitation by the American medium D. D. Home, about 1868. On several occasions, Home was seen rising to ceiling height.

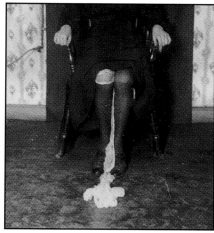

Medium Kathleen Goligher is shown exuding ectoplasm, around 1917. Sometimes, it was reported to become sufficiently rigid to support a table.

Via Florence Cook, the spirit of "Marie" appears at Hyde, around 1902. The concealing draperies are typical of séance room appearances.

any form, so the spirits used it to make likenesses of their living selves, according to the theory. To all intents and purposes, the old dream of summoning the dead from their graves had become reality.

Unfortunately, there were problems. First, while ectoplasm was being produced, the medium seemed to be exceedingly light-sensitive, so all manifestations had to take place in very reduced light. Second, the ectoplasm itself was sensitive to touch, so only rarely were observers permitted to feel it, and then only very gently. Third, the medium needed to be isolated for the process to be carried out, usually behind a screen or within a "cabinet," unwatched by others. Finally, when the materialized spirit emerged from the cabinet, it was invariably wearing long white drapery, usually with a massive turban. While it is possible that this is the normal dress in the next world—setting aside the question of why the dead feel any need to be dressed at all—it was an unfortunate coincidence that by wrapping the body so completely, only an absolute minimum of flesh was visible for identification purposes. However, it seemed to be enough, for the voluminous draperies rarely prevented sitters from identifying their deceased friends and relatives.

Clearly, such conditions lent themselves to trickery. From the first, it had been suspected that some mediums were cheating, but so long as communication was limited to spoken messages, this could be little more than suspicion. But when walking, talking, materialized spirits made their appearance in the séance rooms, it was relatively easy for a skeptic to establish whether the alleged spirit was what it was claiming to be, or the medium (or an accomplice), suitably disguised.

One of England's most successful mediums in the 1870s was a young girl named Florence Cook, who convinced the eminent scientist Sir William Crookes that her powers were genuine. Her séances were often enlivened by the appearance of Marie, the spirit of a girl who had died at the age of twelve. Two sitters, Sir George Sitwell and his friend, Carl von Buch, noted that beneath her customary long white robes, Marie was wearing a corset. If it was surprising that a spirit should wear a corset, it was particularly so for a

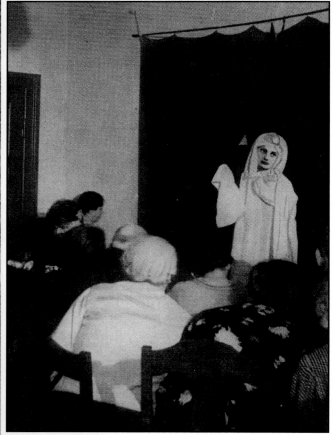

Princess Astrid of Belgium, killed in a car crash in 1935, allegedly reappears three years later at a séance with Einer Nielsen at Copenhagen.

12-year-old spirit. One of them grabbed the materialized adolescent, while the other drew the curtain of the cabinet where the medium herself should have been sitting entranced. Not surprisingly, Florence Cook and the spirit of "Marie" turned out to be one and the same.

Had Cook been cheating when she materialized "Katie King" at Crookes' home? We can't be sure. But the fact is that one medium after another was found cheating in this way. Understandably, sitters demanded more rigorous tests, and the spirits reluctantly agreed to be photographed. Once again, the results were ambiguous. The cameras showed extraordinary phenomena taking place—but close-ups of ectoplasm often revealed a woven substance, very similar to cheesecloth, a fabric which coincidentally happens to be the kind most easily concealed in body cavities.

Furthermore, the materialized forms were often ludicrous in appearance. On May 31, 1938, the Danish medium Einer Nielsen produced a materialized form purporting to be Princess Astrid of Belgium, who had been killed in a motor accident three years earlier. Apart from the face, the entire figure was draped in robes. Not even the hands were visible. In past times, when the dead were coffined in their winding sheets, it was understandable that on their reappearance they should be wrapped in long white drapery. But by Princess Astrid's time, the practice had long been abandoned, so why didn't she appear in the clothes she was buried in?

Moreover, since all mediums agreed that ectoplasm was produced only with great fatigue and suffering, it seems wasteful that they used it to manufacture clothing when it could have been used to show us more of the figure beneath. If one of the purposes of materialization was to convince us of their identity, the spirits might have managed something better than these unconvincing performances.

There is no doubt that curious things happen at séances; but the evidence that they happen as the result of otherworldly intervention is only circumstantial. Alleged materializations such as that of Princess Astrid of Belgium are as much an insult to the dead as to the living.

OTHERWORLDLY PHOTOGRAPHS

No actual photographs of gods exist. Quite a number of Star People—Brad Steiger, Howard Menger and others—have been photographed, but because they are incarnate in human bodies, they look pretty much like anyone else. Ghosts have shown themselves to be remarkably camera-shy. Even extraterrestrials—who as real beings should present no problems to the photographer—have yielded remarkably few photographs. Elizabeth Klarer successfully photographed her lover's flying saucer, but when she wanted to show us what Akon himself looked like, she provided her own drawing of him. For her half-breed son, we did not even get a drawing.

But only a dozen years after the dead began to communicate with the living, they allowed themselves to be photographed. Around 1860, a photographer in Roxbury, Mass, found a second figure on some of his plates. There seemed no other explanation than that the camera had caught what the human eye could not detect—the presence of a spirit. Soon, many others confirmed that when a medium sat in on a photographic session, spirits might manifest on the finished photo, even though they had not been visible to the eye when it was taken.

Unfortunately, faking such photographs is child's play for a photographer, and in 1874 French spirit photographer Edouard Buguet was taken to court for defrauding his clients. His guilt was manifest. However, even when he had been proved a charlatan, many of his former sitters remained convinced he had been genuine, and accused the authorities of a conspiracy.

With so much trickery and fraud going on—not to mention unconscious self-deception—few scientists were willing to take the trouble to see whether spiritualism contained anything of value. Only a handful of people braved the ridicule and investigated the claims, forming the *Society for Psychical Research* in London in 1882, and similar organizations in France, the United

This photograph by Buguet allegedly shows the spirit of the poet Gerard de Nerval beside the sitter, a M. Dumont. About a year after this picture was taken, Buguet was convicted of faking his photos.

spirits of the dead, or any other otherworldly source. Two of the most perceptive and intelligent mediums—Eileen Garrett and Geraldine Cummins—both cherished doubts as to the origin of their gifts. While both clearly possessed remarkable powers of *some* kind, it is misleading to label them "spiritualist."

Today, while spiritualism is still very much alive, with millions of enthusiastic followers throughout the world, it has become a belief system that appeals to some and not to others. It has not proved to be what the first starry-eyed table rappers of the 1850s expected it would be—the rift in the veil which separates this world from the next.

ON THE EDGE OF THE UNKNOWN

If Spiritualism is genuine, it ought to be a vital factor in the lives of us all: if false, then it and its high priests should be ruthlessly exposed, and believers in it disillusioned of a faith that is altogether vain.

The editor of *Pearson's Magazine* did not conceal his private opinion, "that every séance at which physical 'phenomena' occur is simply an exaggerated conjuring entertainment." Nevertheless, when, in his March, 1910 issue, he introduced the first of four articles by William Marriott under the heading, "On the Edge of the Unknown," he issued an open challenge to the champions of spiritualism to "come forward with absolutely unimpeachable evidence of genuine Spiritualistic phenomena."

Marriott, a professional magician and illusionist, had been examining the claims of spiritualism for many years, but had yet to receive any indication that they were what they claimed to be.

A hundred mediums have conjured before me, filling me more and more with amazement at the credulity of human nature, and only the most accomplished of them giving a performance that would have mystified an intelligent child.

States and elsewhere.

What these investigators established is that, while spiritualism was riddled with trickery on the one hand and self-delusion on the other, it has also produced some truly puzzling phenomena. If we can believe the investigators and their cameras, the French psychic Marthe Béraud—though she was suspected of cheating on other occasions—successfully produced white materializations even when her mouth

was full of red fruit juice. Engineer W. J. Crawford photographed Belfast medium Kate Goligher's ectoplasmic extrusions in the act of raising a table. The Polish poet Franek Kluski caused monstrous animal forms—including a large bird—to materialize in a small locked room.

But even though these and other phenomena remain unexplained, the fact remains that there is no direct evidence that they originate with the

William Marriott with the "spirit forms" he used in his demonstrations of spiritualist fraud. In a darkened room, these absurd figures deceived many.

He had attended many séances, and on several occasions successfully exposed the deceivers. But he did not stop there.

> I have gone farther than merely establishing, to my own satisfaction at any rate, the fact that materializations at séances are produced by fraud. I myself have produced the same effects—also by fraud, or perhaps I should say, by purely physical means.

Whereupon he found—as many debunkers have found—that he was thought to have medium-like powers himself.

> Avowed Spiritualists who have seen these spirits of my own production have frequently refused to believe that I was not a medium. Only by displaying the apparatus by which the materializations were brought about have I convinced them that my spirits were merely due to exaggerated conjuring tricks.

At one séance, the medium retired into a curtained cabinet, from which a luminous spirit form emerged. With the aid of a luminous globe, the being was identified by the sitters as "King Draco." Meanwhile, the mischievous Marriott surreptitiously slipped into the cabinet where, of course, the medium should have been sitting entranced. For obvious reasons, the medium was *not* in the cabinet. In a short while, however, the spirit form returned:

> As the form entered the cabinet, he sat down on what he thought was the settee. It happened to be my knees. As my arms went round him, he gave a yell followed by language which I will not repeat. My friend had the light up in a moment. And there for the faithful was the edifying sight of the medium, clothed in flimsy white draperies, struggling in the arms of myself! His wife shrieked out that we had murdered her husband, and came to his rescue. Fortunately, she was restrained by some of the others present.
>
> Our money was hastily returned to us, and the party broke up in an excitement that bordered on hysteria on the part of some of the believers. On visiting the house next day, I found that the birds had flown. Mr. and Mrs. X had vanished into thin air; though, as I afterwards found, they contrived to keep in touch with some of the circle, who still maintained their faith in these incapable charlatans.

Marriott was particularly astonished that such eminent and otherwise intelligent persons as Sir William Crookes and Sir Oliver Lodge found the evidence convincing. The most brilliant of the founders of the Society for Psychical Research, F. W. H. Myers, had died in 1901. It was not long before a number of mediums claimed to receive messages from his surviving spirit. One of them was Rosina Thompson, who had known and worked with Myers during his lifetime. She gave two sittings to Lodge, at which communications ostensibly from Myers came through. But when Lodge asked, "Do you want to say anything about the Society?" Myers, its most prominent member, replied, "Do not think I have forgotten. But I have. I have forgotten just now." Later, he remarked that he had also forgotten his mother's name. Marriott commented:

> To Sir Oliver Lodge, this sitting was "as convincing as anything that could be imagined of that kind." To me, and surely to all unbiased persons, it is as unconvincing as any alleged phenomena could possibly be.

But Marriott kindly lets them off the hook by adding:

> The great point is this: they did not know how the "phenomena" could have been caused by trickery—in other words, they did not know what to look for ... Scientists, however eminent, are emphatically not the people to investigate these matters ... The scientist who sits where he is told to sit and looks where he is told to look is the ideal subject for the wiles of the conjuror or the medium, and before him effects can be brought off that would be impossible before an audience of schoolboys.

His comments on Crookes were particularly perceptive, when he wrote:

> Brilliant as he is in investigations where chemical precision and insight only are required, he proved himself totally unable to make any allowance for the human equation. His experiments with Florence Cook illustrate this fact. They took the form of materializing séances, at which a spirit called Katie King appeared. She was photographed on several occasions, and Sir William wrote: "Katie never appeared to greater perfection, and for nearly two hours she walked about the room, conversing familiarly with those present. On several occasions she took my arm, and the impression conveyed to my mind that it was a living woman by my side, instead of a visitor from another world, was so strong that I asked her permission to clasp her in my arms. Permission was graciously given, and I accordingly did— well, as any gentleman would do under the circumstances."

Marriott commented:

"Spirit hands" are credited with many séance-room phenomena. Here, Marriott shows how a clever "medium" can provide himself with as many helping hands as he needs to perform his wonders.

Exclamation marks, italics, and all the stereotyped forms of wonder would be wasted on this amazing revelation. Sir William, after walking and talking with a young woman for two hours; after holding her in his arms and presumably kissing her; after emphasizing the strength of his impression that she was a living woman, still prefers to believe not that she was a mundane being in collusion with the medium, but that she was—a spirit!

He concluded his investigations more in sorrow than in anger:

If I am one of the "scoffers," it is not because of any original bias, but because of the humbug, cheap trickery and pathetic self-delusion that I have encountered at every point of my investigations of Spiritualism, and I combat its teachings because I believe them to be in defiance of the soundest of all laws—those of common sense and human experience.

Such exposés throw doubt on the validity of much ostensible communication with the dead, but it was

a 1972 experiment which demonstrated the mechanism by which plausible spirits might be created. The "Philip" experiment was carried out by a group of Toronto researchers, who deliberately created a fictitious historical personage who gradually took on a semblance of a life of his own. The imaginary Philip not only produced physical phenomena like those produced by "real" spirits but provided a good deal of information about himself!

While the success of the Toronto experiment does not prove that *all* ostensible spirits of the dead are in fact constructed by the subconscious minds of the living, it does demonstrate that it is a viable alternative to the idea that they are coming to us from other worlds.

CHANNELING

Many who have been fortunate or unfortunate enough not to have face-to-face encounters with extraterrestrials have, nonetheless, enjoyed contact of a different kind in the form of "channeling," by which they receive messages from extraterrestrial beings, generally when in a trance state.

Again, this is nothing new. From the Old Testament prophets onwards, there have been people claiming to receive communications from otherworldly sources. The coming of the saucers gave a new impetus to the channelers simply by suggesting a new category of communicators. Scores of people— virtually all of them American— began to receive messages from extraterrestrial entities. These are much the same as the messages given to those who have personal encounters with alien visitors, but since the channeler is sitting in his own cozy home instead of being out at night on a lonely mountainside, his messages tend to be wordier—much, much wordier.

For example, in the 1950s, a young lady named Pauline Sharpe began to receive messages from an entity named Nada Yolanda, who in turn was able to pass on messages from Christopher Columbus, among others. Pauline

The vision of an angel appears before Abraham to bring him the news that he will become the Father of Sons.

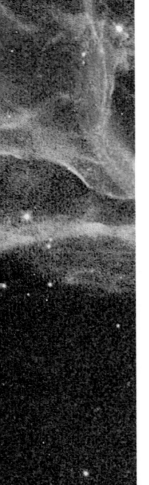

learned that in a previous incarnation, she had agreed to carry out a mission on Earth, in which she would act as a "female polarity." During the early years, she employed automatic writing; since 1960, she

> speaks the words aloud as she receives them through mental telepathic impression or electro-magnetic beam from higher dimensions and from interdimensional and interplanetary spacecraft.

These are generally tape-recorded and subsequently transcribed. Volume after volume of these messages have been published. In *Visitors from Other Planets*, we learn how a crew of 2353 extraterrestrials have come to Earth in a city-size spaceship to stimulate and train us for the New Age of Aquarius, scheduled to commence around the end of the Twentieth Century.

Most of these books consist of "teachings," but occasionally the Yolanda experience comprises deeds

as well as words. She is sometimes able to visit the spacecraft above the Earth. What happens is that her Etheric Self conveys her physical body up into the ship "like an envelope, from which the real Self could slip in and out."

Though it is possible that channels like Yolanda gained financially from the groups they set up in connection with their messages, it is the new generation of channelers who have made it big business. In 1987 Jach Persel, who acts as channel for an entity named "Lazaris," charged $275 for a weekend course which attracted 400 to the Los Angeles Hilton. Even after deducting hotel expenses, there must have been a tidy sum left over from the total take of more than $100,000.

Currently, the most popular channeler is J. Z. Knight, through whom an entity named Ramtha is able to share his wisdom with us. She was joking with her husband one Sunday afternoon in 1977, in their home near Tacoma, Washington, when a "being of

light" appeared in the doorway of her living room and spoke to her. He revealed himself to be Ramtha, a former Earthperson—originally from Mu, but living in Atlantis—now residing in another dimension. Knight was a child of his long, long ago (actually 35,000 years ago, give or take a year or two). He made contact with her by coming around her body in the auric field, and working through the seals or chakras—though what this meant in biological terms was not explained. He revealed that we ourselves are God, and offered such timeless wisdom as, "You are rich if you are happy in your soul, for gold cannot buy happiness." In the 1980s, he announced that

> President Reagan will lead the American government till it's like Solon's in ancient Greece and in so doing give the country back to the people.

Not all communicating entities are so far removed from us in time. Bernie King is an electrical engineer, formerly of Mojave, California, who since his earthly death in 1974 has been:

> residing on a Space Ship, along with several hundred other Beings who are dedicated to the preservation and, if you will, the salvation, of the Planet Earth.

Fortunately King's wife, Beti, is a psychic, and through her, he sends informative messages and answers questions about other planes of reality. Eisenhower, Robert Kennedy and Gandhi are allegedly with him, as are many showbiz people, including Louis Armstrong, Tommy Dorsey and Nat King Cole. King reports that thanks to the purer environment, his fingernails grow less fast, and he does not need to shave at all, since "whiskers on your planet are an environmental result."

Generally speaking, the question of whether these channeled communications are what they seem to be is not a vital one to society at large. If that's how people choose to spend their weekends—and their dollars— that's their business. From time to time, however, they lead to social consequences which make it a matter of importance that we establish what's really going on.

In 1975, a couple naming themselves "The Two" announced that they were "about to leave the human level and literally (physically) enter the next evolutionary level in a spacecraft," and invited others to share the undertaking, which was named Human Individual Metamorphosis. When some 20 people were reported missing, the police investigated and identified the couple as former music teacher Marshall Herff Applewhite (then aged 44) and one-time nurse Bonnie Lu Trusdale Nettles (48). Other names they took were "Nincom" and "Poop," "Tiddly" and "Wink," "Winnie" and "Pooh," but it was as "Bo" and "Peep" that they captured the headlines.

Without going into too much tiresome detail, they gave the impression that though they appeared in the likeness of Earthpeople, they had graduated from other planets—Bo from one planet, Peep from another. At the height of their popularity, they may have attracted a thousand people to share their experience. Many gave up all their possessions and abandoned their families; there were angry confrontations with distressed relatives. Some of the followers, too, were dissatisfied. One made the revealingly naive comment, "I have to blow the whistle on these two. I'm not saying I don't believe in people from outer space, but these two are spacy. They have to be stopped."

In the end, they stopped themselves. In the summer of 1997, a comet passed within visible distance of Earth, and, for some inscrutable reason, many came to believe that it carried within its tail a mighty spaceship. Applewhite and his followers—Nettles had died in the meantime—claimed they had obtained instructions to board the spaceship; this they were to do by relinquishing this Earthly life. Their mass suicide made headline news.

Another recipient of channeled messages was Marion Dorothy Martin, who in 1949 was told by her extraterrestrial contacts that the destruction of the world was imminent, but that those who "believed" would be rescued. Several people were convinced. Dr. Charles Laughead gave up his post at Michigan State University and dedicated himself to

For more than 20 years, Applewhite and Nettles—"The Two"—and their followers awaited a summons from their alien contacts. In 1997, Applewhite claimed a comet was the signal, with tragic results.

spreading the warning, issuing press releases about the forthcoming event, and inviting would-be evacuees to join their group. Others left jobs and homes, broke family ties, and joined Mrs. Martin in waiting hopefully for rescue.

Among those who did not respond to the invitation were sociologists from the University of Minnesota, who took the opportunity to observe the motivation of those who don't merely receive channeled messages, but positively act on them. They were able to see what happened "when prophecy fails"—when the promised flying saucers failed to show up on the appointed day to ferry the believers to safety on some other world, for example. Since the announced catastrophe never took place, either, the non-appearance of the rescue-ships did not matter too much—that is, apart from the effects on the lives of those concerned, their relatives and friends.

Channeling is significant for our study, because it shows clearly how a well-established practice—of people serving as mediums or channels for otherworldly messages—can be adapted to suit the prevailing myth. Once, such messages came from the gods; later, from the spirits of the dead; today, from extraterrestrials.

Following Marshall Applewhite, 39 members of the "Heaven's Gate" cult committed suicide in 1997 in the belief that they would be taken aboard the spaceship.

ANGELS

Originally, angels were perceived as the agents of God, entrusted with such missions as counseling Noah and Abraham, expelling Adam and Eve from Eden, and so on. Following Biblical times, the importance of angels as ambassadors from Heaven to Earth seemed diminished. However, they have never ceased to perform their two more mundane functions, ministering and guarding.

One who was lucky to often see ministering angels at work was Joy Snell, an English hospital nurse. She worked among the sick during World War One, some of whom were destined to die, others to recover:

By the light of a shaded lamp I was writing one night at a table in the middle of the ward. The few other lights that were burning were turned low. Glancing up, I saw a figure moving about at one end of the long and dimly lighted room. I thought that it was some patient who had got out of her bed, but when I approached near I perceived that it was not a patient, but an angel. The figure was tall and slender, the features were those of a woman of middle age.

I had become too familiar by this time with the sudden appearance of these radiant visitors from another world to be alarmed or startled by it, however unexpected, and I stood still and watched her. She went to three or four beds, pausing for a brief space at each one of them and laying her right hand on the heads of the patients occupying them.

As long as I remained at the hospital, scarcely a day passed that I did not see this angel ministering to the sick. That this

On the wings of an angel: News and counseling were given to the earthly recipients by these trusted messengers of God.

angel was endowed with some power by means of which she could at times materially benefit the sick was so abundantly evident that I came to call her the healing angel.

Her healing powers were not exercised on patients only when they were asleep. I have seen her more than once lay her hand on the forehead of a patient who was suffering... a little later, relieved of the pain, the patient would sink into a calm sleep, to awaken greatly improved.

Often, the healing angel helped me when I was attending a patient, sometimes guiding my hand; at other times, incredible as this may seem, she actually assisted me to raise or shift some heavy and helpless victim of disease or accident.

Snell had no doubt that her healing angel was female, and that others were male. Unlike many of our visitors from other worlds, there seems never to have been any doubt that angels are human-like in appearance. Swedenborg, the Eighteenth Century Swedish mystic, tells us that this is because they *are* human—or rather *were*, for some of us become angels after death. This would explain, too, why angels often look distinctly male or female—they really are so! Snell also saw other angels:

I often saw the dark, veiled form standing at the foot of a bed in which lay some patient whose condition was critical. I came in time to recognize that it portended the speedy death of the patient at the foot of whose bed it appeared.

But she also learnt to recognize a bright, joyous angel:

I came to regard the latter as the harbinger of renewed life ... In all my experience as a nurse I never knew a patient to die with whom I had seen the radiant figure.

The other function with which angels are even more associated is that of protecting. Many believe that each of us has a "Guardian Angel" assigned to us, to guide our actions and occasionally intervene to show us the right way, to discourage us from the wrong way and, sometimes, to actually take direct action. In a book written in 1919, two

years after Joy Snell's, Maurice and Irene Elliott quote a friend's account:

It was on Easter Monday. My friend and I had left our picnic party, and strolled over to the rocks. Having found a rock higher than the rest, we both sat down and my friend began to paint, while I busied myself with squeezing out the salt water from my dress. Presently I raised my head and found to my horror that we were surrounded by the sea. Of the rocky beach we had lately crossed, no trace remained. There was no escape. We called in vain for help. What could we do? The cliffs in front of us were almost straight as a wall, yet, with the rising tide behind us, there was nothing for it but to attempt the seemingly impossible task of climbing these cliffs.

We prayed for help, and attempted the ascent. My friend went first, and I followed. Never to my dying day shall I forget that climb ... With our faces close against those cruel cliffs, we had to dig out with our fingers tiny notches in which to place our feet, and so rise step by step while the angry sea was rising, too. With heroic effort, my friend, an expert gymnast, reached the top. Slowly, I managed to reach a point about 6.5 ft. from the top, and came to solid rock, which nothing but a tool could have pierced ... breathless, in a fainting condition, I gazed impotently at the rock above me.

My friend was looking down upon me, and I cried "Go back!" for I did not want her to see me slip. "No," she cried, "I am praying for you." And I prayed, too ... And then, as if in direct answer to our prayers, there came to the center of my back a sudden support, as it were, of a hand, pressing my body tightly against the cliff. To my amazement, I found myself suspended in the air and lifted up bodily towards my friend's outstretched hand ...

Although there exists a stereotype picture of what angels should look like, the real ones do not necessarily conform to their stereotype. Joy Snell's ministering angels did not, for instance, have wings. The case of Frau Elsa Schmidt-Falk, narrated in Chapter Three, has obvious similarity with the "guardian angel" concept, yet her "Chinese-looking gentleman" was certainly not the traditional form.

One dark night in 1986, 5-year-old Starlitt Arrance was sitting in the back of a van while her mother Susan drove up a steep gravel country road near Lebanon, Oregon. Unsure of her way in the darkness, the woman lost her sense of direction and made a wrong turn. The van went off the side of the road and fell into a ravine 100 ft. below. Halfway down the slope, Starlitt was thrown free.

Down in the ravine, her mother lay badly injured and unconscious. Starlitt, though bruised and bleeding, began to climb the cliff despite the pitch darkness. Her father had taught her that if you find yourself in a ravine, there's sure to be a road at the top of it. At one point during the night, exhausted, the girl found a hole in the face of the cliff and went to sleep in it before continuing her climb.

The barefoot girl had reached the road and was walking painfully along it when she was found by Ellen Walker, a vet. Ellen took her home and questioned her about what had happened. When they had heard her story, Ellen's husband drove back and searched the area. Only because he knew what to look for did he spot the van, all but hidden in the depths of the ravine.

So steep was the cliff, it took the rescuers three hours, using rock-climbing gear, to get to the unconscious Susan and bring her up onto the road in a rescue basket. She was rushed to the hospital by helicopter. Critically injured, she would have died if help had not come when it did.

Her rescuers asked Starlitt how she had managed to climb the cliff in the dark on her own? Well, she had not been alone, she explained. During her climb a young boy, holding a puppy, had come to her and comforted her.

Hallucination? Technically, very likely, and probably investigation would have found that the image of the boy with the puppy was a figure from school or the neighborhood, chosen because he was someone Starlitt would trust, someone whose presence would give her the encouragement she needed. But "chosen" by who? Was it her own unconscious mind, or was this the form in which her guardian angel prudently manifested, so as to reassure rather than frighten her?

A Guardian Angel watches over a child as she crosses a dangerous bridge. Many believe that each of us has a personal protecting entity like this one.

The angel-or-ghost question applies equally to the case of the sailor Arne Nicolaysen. On Christmas Eve, 1955, after celebrating the festive season rather too well, Arne fell from the deck of his ship into the waters of the Gulf of Mexico. No one saw him fall, and his ship steamed away into the dark without him. For hours he kept himself afloat, but could not attract attention from any of the ships he saw passing. The following night, he saw two fellow sailors walking across the water towards him. They told him that if he swam towards the moon, he would reach safety. He did as they directed, and a few hours later, he was picked up by a tanker after surviving more than thirty hours in the water.

Once we allow that guardian angels can take any shape they choose, there are no limits. Who should get the credit in the next case? Around 1951, a woman was lying ill with a viral infection. Her doctor had prescribed medication, but the drugs seemed to be making her worse rather than better. Suddenly she saw *herself*, sitting on a chair beside the bed, wearing a dress which she had thrown away more than a year before. The patient didn't speak, but the "me" in the chair told her that if she went on taking the pills she'd been prescribed, they could finish her off. If she wanted to recover, she should stop taking them at once. Though she still said nothing, she thought, "So what if they do finish me off?" The other "me" seemed to read her thoughts, for she said that would be a stupid thing to do, and finally persuaded the woman to stop

Berbiguier, the dedicated "Scourge of the Farfadets," was plagued by demons in his bedroom. When he caught small demons, he imprisoned them in bottles.

taking the pills, and tell the doctor. She then disappeared. The patient stopped taking them, and immediately started to get better.

In this case, we seem to have a doppelgänger performing the same kind of guardian angel role as did the sailors walking on the sea. We have two alternative ways of explaining this whole class of phenomena. On the one hand, they could all be manifestations of the "guardian angel" phenomenon—that is to say, beings from another plane of reality who intervene in human affairs to heal, comfort and aid. Alternatively, they could all be individual examples of a process in which the subconscious minds of people who find themselves in trouble create fantasy figures who come to their rescue. This would be a scientist's explanation, no doubt—that is, assuming that the scientist granted the existence of a subconscious mind in the first place. But it leaves some

unanswered questions. How did the subconscious mind know how to heal Mrs. Hight, how to guide Frau Schmidt-Falk safely down the mountain, how to help Starlitt Arrance to the top of the cliff, and how the sick woman could be cured?

The only way out of the paradox, it seems to me, is to allow that under certain circumstances, such as a personal crisis, the subconscious mind can obtain access to information normally inaccessible. Subconscious knowledge or guardian angel—either way, the explanation lies beyond the frontiers of reality as we know it.

DEMONS

I am acting in the interests of the human race, I wish that all the demons shall be restrained, then my aim will be achieved. The Earth will no longer be peopled with these abominable vampires, households will be happy, girls will not be exposed to the criminal visits of these monsters, all men and all women will become virtuous …

Alexis-Vincent-Charles Berbiguier, born at Carpentras in southeastern France about 1774, was a sickly child who became obsessed with the idea that his ailments were the work of demons. Attending magic sessions only confirmed this notion, and gradually he came to believe himself the victim of a persecution directed particularly at himself. Priests and doctors tried to convince him otherwise, but he had a visionary visit from a mystical being, who told him he had been selected for the task of fighting the farfadets and farfadettes (for some of the demons

were female). Styling himself "The Scourge of the Farfadets," he devoted his life to the work, while the demons devoted themselves to making his life disagreeable. He caught thousands of them invading his room in the form of fleas and lice, and sealed them in bottles …

Few people have been so single-mindedly resolute in opposing demons, but throughout history, demonic forces have been recognized as the source of most of the evils of the world, even by intelligent and enlightened people. The eccentric Austrian physician, Paracelsus, alongside his brilliant medical ideas, believed that menstrual blood and sperm emissions peopled the air with phantoms. According to the French occultist Constant ("Eliphas Lévi"), this clearly accounts for the origin of *larvae*, which possess an aerial body formed from the vapor of blood. This is why they are attracted by spilt blood, and used in former days to feed on the smoke from sacrificial altars. They are the monstrous offspring of those impure nightmares that used to be known as incubi and succubi.

The incubus was a demon who came into women's beds by night and lay on them, while the succubus visited males and lay beneath them. The Thirteenth Century theologian Thomas Aquinas stated that a demon could transform itself into either, so that as a succubus it could gather semen from a man and then, as an incubus, inject it into a woman. In either form, they made themselves very attractive, provoking the male to produce the emissions needed for effective magic.

This colorful belief has been given a Twentieth Century form by alien

A succubus attacks a sleeping man, enticing him to have sex with her so she can recycle his semen for her magical practices.

abductions. Taking sperm from male victims and forcibly impregnating females is part of the recognized pattern.

> A final variation is an alleged sexual encounter between an abductee and an alien or a hybrid. Sexual imagery is often an important part of this event. In an envisioning procedure, the abductee is made to believe that either her husband or loved one is with her. Abductees sometimes say that the face of the husband, for instance, tends to "phase" in and out of the face of the alien. Intercourse takes place ...

Interestingly, this account—from David Jacobs' definitive study of the abduction experience, *Secret Life*—echoes the stories told by witches of the Sixteenth and Seventeenth Centuries, who described sexual relations by the devil as more painful than pleasant.

A catalog of the marginal creatures held to exist by different cultures at different times would be encyclopedic. Gordon Creighton, editor of *Flying Saucer Review*, holds demonic beings, known in Islamic culture as *jinns,* responsible for many negative manifestations in the world of UFOs. Just as angels are composed of light, jinns are composed of flame. They are equally removed from humankind. But just as we have seen that angels can interact with humans, so can jinns. If only temporarily, they can assume physical form, for how else could they interact with us to the point of enjoying sexual relations with us? This would also explain the otherwise puzzling fact that they need nuts-and-bolts spacecraft to fly about in.

Creighton is by no means the only serious UFO investigator to believe that jinns—or some such demonic entities—are the real UFO occupants, responsible for abductions and other alien manifestations.

The Spanish author Salvador Freixedo once lectured me in a Madrid café for hours on end about the intermediate spirits he believed existed midway between humankind and the gods:

> I believe these entities exist in their

Demons and their victims are depicted in this Fifteenth Century Flemish school representation of Hell, which is similar to the inferno detail of 1055.

own right, not simply in the mind.

I believe their real form is not that which we see.

I believe they are not purely "spiritual," but come from a physical world whose nature is unknown to us.

I believe that *duendes* such as fairies, monsters, etc. have existed and still exist in this form.

I believe that the pagan gods—Jupiter, Vishnu, Osiris, etc.—were manifestations of these entity-energies.

He explained that these creatures derive their energy from human passions and emotions. This can be individual—anger or sexual excitement —but is better when it is collective, as at a football match or a political rally. Far and away the majority of

intermediate beings are evil. Man's fears are stronger than his hopes, and every human culture includes in its pantheon one or more destructor-demons. These can be blamed for everything negative that happens, from crop failures to earthquakes. Spirits of evil in all sizes and shapes (often not their true shapes) proliferate, seeking people to devour, dangling temptations before us. In old popular prints they would often be depicted in opposition to angels—the individual would be shown with, on one side, an angel pointing upwards and exhorting him to think of his heavenly salvation, while on the other hand a devil offered sex, fame and an abundance of consumer goods.

Just as angels are generally supposed to come from Heaven, so Satan and his evil henchmen are supposed to come from Hell, where they were consigned after rebelling against God. In popular iconography the Devil has distinctive features: he dresses in black; wears a pointed hat; one or more of his feet are cloven like that of a goat; he has pointed ears, and—above all—a tail which is, with difficulty, concealed beneath his clothing when he visits Earth. Since he can take whatever form he chooses, it is hard to understand why he does not discard such distinctive appendages.

For many of us today, demons are a phenomenon we can safely relegate to the category of folklore—beings that no longer have relevance for us. But even among the most sophisticated religions, there are people who continue to believe in real forces of evil. In 1974, Pope Paul VI, in his Christmas Message, declared:

> We know that this obscure and disturbing Being really exists, and that he still operates with treacherous cunning; he is the occult enemy who sows error and disgrace in human history ... a perfidious and astute charmer ...

He recommended that demonology should be more fully studied as part of Catholic theology. Many Christian theologians go further, insisting that *all* spirits are evil. When flying saucers first appeared, they were perceived by fundamentalists as the vehicles of the devil. In 1961, writer Stuart Campbell, today a ruthless skeptic, was a firm believer in a very material devil:

> The appearance of UFOs in our skies means the devil is intensifying his satanic campaign against good and against God ... all our space traveling friends are liars and they are *all* evil ... there is one mind behind the whole business and that mind is NOT God but the DEVIL.

Throughout history, tales have been

When flying saucers first appeared, they were hailed by some as divine, by others as demonic. One contactee said he was taken on "a round-trip to Hell" aboard a flying saucer.

told in which Satan seeks to lure religious people from their vows—saints, nuns and others were continually having to withstand the wiles of the devil. The seductions seem never to have been successful—or is it just that we don't hear about the monks who allowed themselves to be tempted? For the most part these attacks were so naive that they wouldn't deceive anyone, and we might think that over 2000 years the demons would either improve their techniques or try a different strategy. But as recently as the Nineteenth Century, we find Vianney, the celebrated curé d'Ars in eastern France, continually harassed by what most of us would classify as poltergeist phenomena. He insisted they were *grappins*—imp-like demons who were sent by Satan to discourage him from his religion. Needless to say, their childish efforts didn't succeed.

In the twentieth century, Padre Pio, the celebrated Italian stigmatic, wrote to his confessor:

January 1911: I lack courage to tell you what has happened to me during these last few days. Who could believe that even in my hours of repose I am tormented? The Demon wishes to destroy me at all costs. If I was less of a Christian, I would believe myself possessed …

1912: He comes with his henchmen, armed with sticks and metal implements, and, what is worse, in their own likeness. Who knows how many times he has thrown me out of my bed?… I was still in bed when I received a visit from these brutes, who beat me so roughly that it was an immense grace that I did not die …

May 20, 1912: This wretched individual, from the moment I went to bed at 10 o'clock through till morning, spent his time hitting me … I thought it was the last night of my existence.

Frequently Satan would manifest to him in physical form and inflict ill-treatment on him; he retained the marks on his face and body and his lacerated clothing. As with Freixedo's demons, these are no creatures of the mind—we are up against material manifestations by physical beings. Often, the furniture in his cell would be overturned, his books and papers torn, his ink-well thrown against the wall; at Pietelcina,

La Domenica del Corriere

The Capucin friar Francesco Forgione, known as "Padre Pio," was plagued by demons who sought to discourage his devotion to the Church.

he was thrown out of bed and severely thrashed. His mother found his sheets covered with blood.

Nor was Satan always so crude in his methods. Sometimes he would manifest in the shape of holy people, who would discourage Pio more subtly. Once, he even appeared as Pio's own confessor, gently seeking to persuade him that he wasn't suited for the religious life, and even that all these stories he was telling about the Devil were attributed by his colleagues to an overheated imagination. Pio was astonished to hear his own confessor talk to him in such a way, and became suspicious. When he asked him to write the words "Viva Gesù!"—"Long live Jesus"—his visitor vanished in a cloud of smoke, leaving behind a disgusting smell as a souvenir.

His biographer Boniface wrote: "Those who don't believe in marvels will consider as purely legendary the episode that I have just reported," and indeed many of us will have difficulty in believing it. Yet Padre Pio has an immense following, and reports of demonic attack remain very common even in our time.

The most durable of satanic beliefs is the belief in demonic possession. Supposedly, this takes place when the Devil actually enters an individual, enabling him to do whatever he pleases with his host. If it seems

improbable that the Devil would go to so much trouble to make life a misery for a single Italian monk, it seems even more unlikely that he would leave his home, however hellish, to take up residence inside a troubled adolescent girl in order to turn her towards a life of sin rather than piety. This, nevertheless, is what thoughtful theologians have for centuries held to be the Devil's favorite occupation. Many witches confessed that they were possessed by Satan. This was also the preferred explanation for the many outbreaks of convent hysteria which occurred in Seventeenth Century Europe, when nuns would roll on the ground in convulsions. Even today, the belief in demonic possession is flourishing, along with the belief that it can be cured by exorcism. A sensationalized version of the possession-exorcism process has become familiar to all, as a consequence of being a popular theme

Medieval monks were continually harassed by demons, who tempted them in all kinds of ways, though they rarely succumbed.

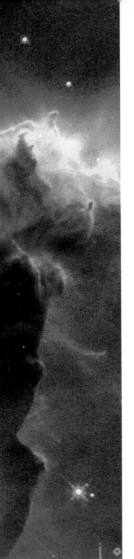

of horror books and movies.

An influential contemporary believer in possession is W. Scott Peck, who has himself taken part in exorcism procedures. He wrote:

> Possession is no accident. I very much doubt that somebody can go walking down the street one day and have a demon jump out from behind a bush and possess him.

But after treating other cases with more conventional methods, he was:

> ... left with a critical five percent I cannot explain in such ways. I am left with the supernatural or, better yet, subnatural ... Almost all the [exorcism] team members were convinced they were in the presence of something absolutely alien and inhuman.

The rise of "New Age" beliefs in America has, in many cases, taken the form of an extreme religion, typified by various cults. For many of these, Satan is a reality. Twenty-six-year-old Craig Skinner, who joined such a group, told of his experience:

> I came to a point where I had a definite choice—Satan and die, or the Lord and live. I was awakened one night at three a.m. Something came in human form,

floating in. I was like mesmerized ... The thing came over next to me and knelt down. It had an iridescent smile. A spirit, but not one of the Lord's. It jumped in me as I blacked out. Satan made me feel I would die that night. I was possessed. Rockets attacking and blowing up are not as scary or as deep as this terror. I told the people at the house to call the morgue ...

Luckily for him, the moment he called for a Bible, the possessing devil left him. Hiley H. Ward, from whose account the story is taken, told of meeting Mr. and Mrs. Robert Cornforth, who report that they have cast out demons from some 70 youths.

One whom they had helped save was 17-year-old David, who said he had been possessed by a demon while looking at snakes in a zoo. The Cornforths delivered him successfully, but subsequently, the same demons returned in the night, woke him up, turned on lights and harassed him.

There seems no indication that belief in demonic possession is dying out. In 1993, in Victoria, Australia, 49-year-old Joan Vollmer died at the farm she ran with her husband, Ralph. The *Australian Parapsychological Review* noted that Ralph was obsessed with the belief that his wife had been "dedicated to Satan by baptism." His

bizarre beliefs affected his wife, to the point where she developed different personalities of animals and people, became paranoid that people wanted to rape her, and believed that her stomach was full of cancer.

One January morning at 4 a.m., Ralph found her dancing wildly in a paddock. He phoned the leaders of the charismatic religious group he belonged to: evil spirits were duly diagnosed. Though Joan refused to acknowledge that she was possessed, a form of exorcism was commenced, consisting of seven days of "deliverance," prayers and exorcisms. Joan was tied to a chair and deprived of food, water and sleep. Not surprisingly, she became agitated and violent.

Other group members joined the team. On January 30, one of them grabbed a roll of cling-wrap and ran around the house seven times to create a seven-fold sheath of protection, though it is hard to believe that a demon from Hell would be thwarted by seven thicknesses of plastic film. Joan's collection of figurines, jewelry and ornaments was smashed and her flowerbeds uprooted because evil spirits might be concealed there. When none of this had any effect, Joan was tied down on a table, her eyes and jaw were pried open, and her stomach was pumped, in hope of squeezing the demons out through her mouth.

She struggled, hissed, cried out and foamed at the mouth, and this was hailed as the defeat of the demons. Unfortunately, two were still left inside her. Efforts were renewed to expel them, as a result of which Joan died of internal injuries.

Later, a pathologist found that Joan's death was due to cardiac arrest, probably caused by compression of her neck. Her exorcists commanded her in the name of God to return to life, but she remained obstinately dead. Two days later, when the body was badly decomposed, the police were informed. Her husband announced that at her funeral Joan would return to life, but she did not do so—and can we blame her? The exorcists were acquitted of manslaughter charges, but blamed for contributing to Joan's death.

For millions of religious fundamentalists, the Devil is an abiding reality.

RITUAL MAGIC

One of man's oldest beliefs is that by performing appropriate rituals, he can summon spirits of the dead from the grave and command demons to obey him. The myth of the magus—the skilled practitioner of the magic arts—is astonishingly durable, considering that there is no convincing evidence that in either of these operations—summoning the dead or commanding evil spirits—anyone has ever been successful, despite more than 2000 years of trying.

For centuries, individuals have claimed to have obtained esoteric secrets by chance, accident or design. We have already come across several instances of purveyors of esoteric truths who claim to have acquired their knowledge from Tibetan monasteries, Indian temples and the like. James Churchward, the champion of the lost continent of Mu, was one. Madame Blavatsky, Georgei Ivanovitch Gurdjieff, George Adamski and George Hunt Williamson are just some of the self-anointed mystics who claimed to have studied in secret places where occult learning is passed on only to initiates who show themselves worthy to receive it.

This has led to a belief in secret societies—the Rosicrucians, the Elders of Sion, the Synarchie and many more—who are the repositories of ancient esoteric knowledge. It does not seem to have done them much good. Bill Gates has acquired far more wealth by being clever with computers than any magician did by exploiting access to supernatural powers.

Some forms of magic are relatively easy to understand. There is a kind of primitive logic in thinking that if a farmer and his wife make love in their fields at seed time, this will encourage their crops to grow. Other kinds of magic, notably cursing and healing, seem to work thanks to the power of suggestion.

But there is also a kind of magic which does not operate directly on nature, as in fertility rites, but on the forces behind natural happenings. Religious belief systems act on the assumption that someone, somewhere, is responsible, directly or indirectly, for everything that happens. In Judeo-Christian religion, God is regarded as omnipotent and omniscient.

Consequently, by controlling those responsible, you can control literally everything. Judeo-Christians believe that God will listen to prayer and modify his behavior accordingly. In Chapter One, we saw how He took the advice of Moses, and on other occasions, He has been persuaded to make the sun stand still (for Joshua and for Charlemagne), raise the dead (for Francisco Javier and many other saints), and turn back the enemy (for the emperor Constantine in 312, and for the British Army in 1914).

This belief was gradually transformed into a belief in magic. When Evans-Prichard lived among the Azande of the Sudan, he came to understand that for them, there were no such things as accidents. Everything that happened —a house burning down, a crop failure, a woman falling sick—did so because someone or something wished it to happen. That "someone" might be either a demon acting on its own, or one that had been invoked by a magician, using magic skills on behalf of a client. So procedures were worked out whereby the spirit or demon responsible could be identified, and means found to influence or control it.

There is an enormous literature of magic, most of it obscure to the point of gibberish. The earliest magical texts known to us relate to practices and procedures of this kind. They come from Assyria, and probably date from 1800 B.C. or earlier. The practices themselves

Magicians believed that demons were all-powerful but that, armed with the right spells, they themselves could command the demons.

This Seventeenth Century painting depicts the celebration of the witches' Sabbath and the fear that such a union of magical and supernatural power caused in ordinary people.

arranged actions in elaborate ceremonies which are supposed to bring about the desired result.

Awesome invocations, relying heavily on the weight of words, were intended to compel the demon to respond to the summons. Here is a brief extract—the whole thing goes on for pages—from a typical invocation, taken by Aleister Crowley from the Goetia attributed to King Solomon, the Tenth Century B.C. King of Israel:

> I do invocate, conjure, and command thee, O thou Spirit … to appear and to show thyself visibly unto me before this Circle in fair and comely shape, without any deformity or tortuosity … by the name ZABAOTH, which Moses named and all the rivers were turned into blood … by the name ALPHA and OMEGA, which Daniel named, and destroyed Bel, and slew the Dragon … by these and by all the other names of the LIVING and TRUE GOD, I do exorcize and command thee, O Spirit, by the Sea of Glass … by the four beasts … by the holy angels of Heaven … I do potently exorcize thee, that thou appearest here, to fulfil my will in all things which shall seem good to me …

Why would a powerful demon quit Hell and come to Earth prepared to do any task, however menial, for a mere mortal? Because it is constrained by the magic formulas. But these formulas are only words, man-made things, so why should these superhuman powers be subject to human commands? The simple fact that they are has been believed throughout the ages, and the belief clearly refers to physical, material entities who are expected to appear in person. An Egyptian invocation provides instructions as to how the magician should behave in the presence of the invoked being, who—although he has come at the magician's bidding like a servant—is nonetheless a divinity and should be treated with respect!

Magic can be worked in a variety of ways. Here, for example, is one recommended procedure:

> The method proposed by Abramelin for calling forth the Four Princes of the Evil of the World is by means of magical squares containing, in certain formations, various letters and names. These squares,

Magic is full of symbolism: In this decoration created by Fuller for Aleister Crowley's Temple, every element has a hidden meaning beneath its surface.

of course were doubtless far older than the texts, which are very practical documents, as functional as a modern pharmacopoeia. The spirits responsible for sickness and other evils are named, and the appropriate ritual actions specified.

This has been the pattern of magic ever since. Different individuals, or schools of occultism, have sought to formalize the procedures whereby man could control his universe by controlling the beings responsible. Little by little, each one elaborating on his predecessors, magicians have put words together in powerful formulas and when charged and energized by the magical will, set up a magnetic or electrical strain in the Astral Light to which certain beings consonant to that strain respond in the performance of acts ordered by the Magician.

How did magicians discover that by manipulating magic squares they could control the universe? The knowledge can have been obtained only in one of two ways. Either a divine power told the first magician the secret formula, and he passed it on to his spiritual heir, and so on, or the magicians themselves discovered it, trying each magic number, square and so forth in turn until they hit on the right one and—Whoops! —the demon appeared.

Just to make things more difficult still, there are all kinds of variables the magician must take into account. The invocation must take place on appropriate days, seasons, hours of the day, and the location may be crucial. The magician must abstain from sex, alcohol, even food, for a given period. If plants and animals are involved, they must be collected by moonlight, or on St. John's Day, or at the solstice. The magician must wear the correct clothing, avoiding certain colors; if even a single one of these elements is neglected, the entire operation is liable to fail.

That being so, it is not surprising that, so far as I know, there has never been a successful raising of a spirit of the dead or invocation of a demon. Many stories claim that it has been achieved, of course, but no account comes accompanied by sufficient evidence for us to take it on trust. Participants tell of seeing a "misty form" or some such, but the impression is subjective and identification dubious.

One of the most detailed accounts of the magical invocation of a spirit is that of the demon Choronzon, also known as The Dweller in the Abyss. In 1909, the occultist Aleister Crowley, who had a high opinion of himself as a magician, went with one of his disciples, Victor Neuberg, into the desert near Algiers. After sacrificing three pigeons, Neuberg placed himself in a magic circle, and Crowley placed himself in a triangle where he proposed to allow himself to be possessed by the demon. The invocation rituals were performed—all went well, and Choronzon arrived. At

first he was invisible, and his voice was that of Crowley, whom he had possessed.

What Neuberg then saw at this stage was not Crowley, but a beautiful courtesan he once loved in Paris. Sensibly, he recognized this as a trick on the demon's part, and he resisted the lady's attempts to lure him out of his protective circle. So Choronzon appeared and admitted it was a trick; pretending to recognize Neuberg's obvious superiority, he offered to come inside the circle and serve him as his slave. Again, Neuberg was not deceived. Choronzon tried changing his shape a few more times, even impersonating Crowley himself, who appeared to crawl out of his triangle and beg a drink of water. Neuberg had the will to refuse him, and once again Choronzon admitted the deception.

Neuberg, who amid all this excitement was coolly taking down every word in shorthand, recorded that Choronzon— who was obviously partial to "ye olde English" parlance—explained:

When I made myself like unto a beautiful woman, if thou hadst come to me, I would have rotted thy body with the pox and thy liver with the cancer. And if I had seduced thy pride, and thou hadst bidden me to come into the circle, I would have trampled thee under foot, and for a thousand years shouldst thou have been but one of the tapeworms that is in me. And if I had seduced thy pity, and thou hadst poured one drop of water outside the circle, then would I have blasted thee with flame. But I was not able to prevail against thee.

But though this fine speech gave the impression that Choronzon was a good loser, it was yet another trick, for throughout, he was throwing sand onto the outer ring of Neuberg's protective circle, thus creating a breach in the defences. Having brought his speech to a neat close, he suddenly leapt through the gap and threw Neuberg to the ground. Luckily, Neuberg had the good sense to bring a magical dagger with him, and with this he forced the demon to retire.

Was Neuberg hallucinating? Was Crowley tricking Neuberg, playing the part of Choronzon himself? Or was the experience what it seemed to be, the genuine invocation of occult powers, summoned from the Abyss by the potent

words prepared by Crowley? Since we have only Neuberg's own word for it— Crowley himself occupied in being possessed by the demon—there is really no knowing. If genuine, it is one of the very few invocations of a demon ever recounted, and perhaps the only successful one. The point of it all, though, remains obscure, since the two magicians do not seem to have employed Choronzon to bring them gold, sexual partners or, indeed, anything useful at all.

In Shakespeare's *Henry IV*, the self-important Welsh rebel Owen Glendower boasts to young Harry Hotspur:

I can call spirits from the vasty deep.

To this, the unimpressed Hotspur replies:

Why, so can I, or so can any man. But will they come when you do call for them?

The invocation of otherworldly beings is one of the most durable myths in man's relations with the Cosmos. Though many attribute it to a wish to believe that we are not so powerless as we seem to be, for others it is evidence that we inhabit a demon-haunted world.

Aleister Crowley—writer, mountaineer, drug addict, occultist—was known to his mother as "the Great Beast," an image he tried to live up to.

Observers and Operators

✦

For tens of thousands of American citizens, the future is already present. The science fiction that was a dream for their grandfathers has become a real-life nightmare. The alien invaders Wells warned them about are currently visiting Earth's air space. Tonight and every night, they will enter victims' bedrooms, carry them up to their spacecraft on beams of light, and perform sinister surgical operations on them before returning them to their beds. Whether they know it or not, whether they like it or not, whether they believe it or not, the victims can do nothing to stop it.

David Jacobs, Associate Professor of History at Temple University, Philadelphia, takes a pessimistic, not to say alarmist, view of the proliferation of abduction claims:

> The evidence clearly indicates that the aliens are conducting a widespread, systematic program of physiological exploitation of human beings ... Everything the aliens do is logical, rational, and goal-oriented ... They are engaging in the systematic and clandestine physiological exploitation, and perhaps alteration, of human beings for the purposes of passing on their genetic capabilities to progeny who will integrate into the human society and, without doubt, control it. Their agenda is self-centered.

Not everyone takes so negative a view of alien abductions. Pessimists and optimists alike agree, however, that abductions are the indication that there is a massive, planned operation in progress, which will profoundly affect the future of the human race. This could be the most important thing to ever happen to humanity, but the authorities seem oblivious to the implications.

Something is certainly happening.

This image conveys the crazed fear that afflicts the abducted as they are forced into alien surroundings and confronted with the unknown.

Twenty years ago, scarcely anyone was claiming to have made personal contact with extraterrestrials. Today, if we can believe those who have made a study of such things, abductees are numbered in tens of thousands. The leading investigator into abductions, American artist Budd Hopkins, claims to have investigated 1500 cases—and he made that claim in 1993. He is far from being the only investigator with a substantial case file, to say nothing of the countless cases that haven't surfaced because the witnesses chose not to report them, or were not even aware that they ever took place. One of the characteristics of abductions is that often they do not come to light until long after the event, when some other circumstance reveals them by chance.

In 1992, a poll was carried out which seemed to show that millions of Americans may have been abducted by aliens from other worlds. If we can believe the findings of the Roper Poll, the probable total for the United States alone is 3.7 million. This suggests that—unless the U.S. is being specifically targeted—anywhere between 16 and 200 million (depending on how you interpret the figures) have been abducted world-wide. Even if we take the lowest estimate, 16 million is a lot of people. Moreover, that figure does not include the millions of "Star People" we met in Chapter Two, who are already living among us.

Furthermore, it is rare for an abductee to have just the one experience. Barney and Betty Hill were unusual in this respect. Most of those whom Jacobs has questioned claim repeated abductions. Gloria Kane was abducted 54 times during the 8 months between July 1988 and February 1989; in November and December of 1993, Kay Summers was abducted 14 times, and 38-year-old Charles Petrie has consciously remembered more than 200 abductions—and counting.

Such figures should certainly justify the claims that a mighty change is taking place in humankind's interaction with the Cosmos. Yet, paradoxically, there is no convincing evidence that any of these events are taking place at all, and there are many reasons to question whether

Though Earth scientists monitor nearby space around the clock, they have never detected an extraterrestrial intruder.

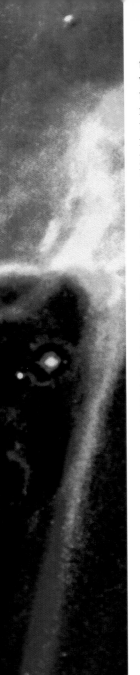

there is any otherworldly involvement whatsoever. Each and every one of those abductions was, ostensibly, a material and therefore observable event taking place in our Earthly air space, yet none has been reliably witnessed by passers-by, police patrols, aircraft or whoever.

The absence of physical evidence and of confirmatory testimony is often explained away on the grounds that abductions occur on some other level of reality than the here-and-now level of what we term "reality." But as we saw in Chapter Five, the "abductions are real" agenda of Hopkins, Jacobs and fellow abductionists requires that there are physical explanations for such phenomena as humans passing through walls, being impregnated and so on. If abductions really happen, they happen within the same kind of reality as that in which you and I go out of our homes or go about our lives.

THE IMAGINARY ABDUCTEE EXPERIMENTS

In 1977, Professor Alvin Lawson and Dr. W. C. McCall carried out a unique experiment in a hospital in Anaheim, California. Having investigated a number of alleged abduction cases, Lawson was puzzled by various ambiguous indications, and suspected that some of his witnesses, though

"Real" abductee Judy Kendall draws her abduction for Alvin Lawson and Dr. McCall. Her experience matched that of the "imaginary abductees."

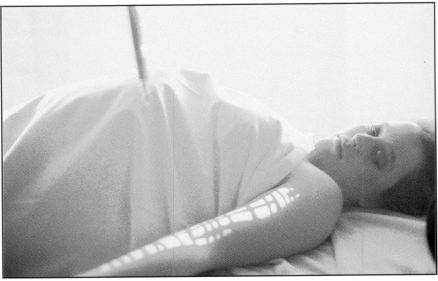

If the abductees are right, physical examinations like this one – a scene from the X-Files *television series – are taking place every night in our skies.*

plausible and seemingly sincere, had not actually experienced the abduction they claimed. He wondered how their stories would compare with those concocted by people who were definitely known not to have had any such experience.

Sixteen volunteers, "who knew little of and cared less about UFOs," were enlisted. Each "witness" was hypnotised and given the suggestion that they had been involved in a UFO abduction situation. The subject was taken, step by step, through a stereotype abduction sequence, with only the bare bones of each phase being supplied:

1. Subject perceives a UFO.
2. Subject is taken aboard.
3. Subject perceives the interior of the UFO.
4. Subject perceives occupants.
5. Subject is "examined" by them.
6. Subject is given a "message."
7. Subject is returned.
8. Aftermath, involving possible behavioral effects

At each stage, the subject was asked to describe what he or she perceived. What the investigators expected was:

that we would get garbage from the imaginary subjects – an amalgam of TV, film, sci/fi and UFO lore from media and myth. We presumed we would thus have a means of determining "real" accounts from phony ones. No wonder we were

stunned when both our first two subjects (and most of the rest) just had verbal eruptions all over that hospital room. Because that means that there was no difference between real and imaginary close encounters, and thus no real abductions. Ultimately, it was all in the mind.

To get the full impact, the accounts have to be studied in detail. These sample extracts tell how subjects, during the second phase, perceived being taken aboard the alien spacecraft:

- "A long tube came out of it, and it was about 2 ft. above me … and this long cylinder-like tube came down. It was grey and … was like all colored lights inside of it … I seemed to be floating for a second, and then I was inside."
- "…gentle suction … it just sort of drew me up into it, sort of through the bottom … like some sort of tunnel of air and light, drawing me up inside of it … I'm inside of a tube when I first come in …"
- "I was pulled in … a particle of dust into a vacuum cleaner. I mean, I'm just suddenly there …"

These quotations are from the fantasies of the *imaginary* abductees, yet they match closely accounts given time and again by "real" abductees. The experience almost invariably starts with very bright lights, often pulsating. The witness experiences a sense of "floating" when being taken from one location to another, often passing through solid walls or floors, and has a feeling of "paralysis" at various moments. The witness is taken into a big, brightly lit room and sees "TV screens" aboard the spacecraft on which scenes are presented by the abductors. The UFO becomes larger and smaller...and so on. Yet these complex stories have been replicated in the minds of people with minimal interest in the subject, and with no conscious awareness of having read abduction accounts – certainly not with sufficient attention to have noted such detail.

Informal experiments by independent researcher Dennis Stillings confirm the Lawson/McCall findings. The original

combines the stimulus with data from the imagination, memory, or knowledge about UFOs to create an encounter experience so intense that it is perceived as physically real.

However, though their "stories" are similar, there is a marked difference in the way the "real" and the "imaginary" abductees respond emotionally to their experience. This is not surprising. Lawson's subjects were volunteers, and even under hypnosis would be subconsciously aware of that fact. They were not subject to the stress and other psychological factors that affect the "real" abductees. Consequently, we would not expect them to suffer the

...but their creations have no firmer basis in reality than the science-fiction scenarios of H. G. Wells or the "pulp" writers of the 1920s and 1930s ...

Movie and television producers have no difficulty creating scenes which echo the abductees' stories ...

small-scale study would need to be more solidly grounded, however, and the protocol modified to take in other parameters, before any conclusive inferences could be justified.

Nevertheless the central finding is unequivocal—such similarities cannot be explained away as coincidence or cryptomnesia (thoughts that are really memories). It is simply unrealistic to suppose that each and every one of the volunteers was drawing on hidden memories of abduction stories they had forgotten they'd read, or even experienced themselves!

Lawson and McCall suggest that what may be happening in a "real" abduction experience is that the witness, triggered by some external stimulus such as a bright pulsating light,

psychological after-effects experienced by the "real" abductees—amnesia, dreams, nightmares or psychic experiences, and a variety of physical effects ranging from nausea and migraine to scars and scratches.

The abductionists often point to these behavioral features and physical marks as evidence for the reality of the abduction experience. But while they certainly show that an experience of *some kind* has occurred, they do not prove that the individual was abducted by aliens. All they demonstrate is that the "real" abductee is in a truly emotional state— but it is at least as likely that a witness has an abduction experience because he is in an emotional state as that his emotional state is the consequence of an abduction experience.

... and ultimately they tell us more about the inner world of our hopes and fears than about anything occurring in the outer world.

THE BIRTH TRAUMA HYPOTHESIS

The imaginary abductee experiments, like so many advances in knowledge, raise more questions than they satisfy. In particular, they present the puzzle of how it is that so many people, whether they are describing experiences that are real to them or simply fantasizing, come up with such strikingly similar accounts?

To Lawson, it was because both sets of narrators were drawing on one and the same source, presumably elements in our shared cultural heritage. Studying the accounts, he found parallels with many different kinds of experience— hallucinations, near-death experiences, mystical experiences, shamanistic trances, migraine attacks, folklore beliefs and birth-trauma "memories."

The parallels with this last experience seemed particularly close. The entities described fall into a number of categories, ranging from human-like via robot to monster, but by far the largest category is that of the short humanoid with the over-large head. Such entities are described by Andreasson, the Hills, Strieber, Kathie Davis—indeed, by a majority of witnesses.

Lawson was struck by the many points of similarity between these entities and the human fetus—not only the disproportionately large head and prominent eyes contrasting with underdeveloped ears, but also the lack of sex differentiation, less-developed

The imaginary abductees perceived aliens in just the same way as the "real" abductees – and fantasy film-makers.

hands, hairlessness and so on. Even the points of difference are, significantly, close to those that might be invented by someone who was seeking to combine the fetus concept with the spaceman concept—for instance, the seamless clothing which is frequently reported. Whereas humans wear clothing which is unmistakably separate from our bodies, witnesses are frequently unable to say whether their aliens are wearing clothing or not, for if they are, it is skin-tight and seamless, with no sign of buttons, zips, patterns, insignia and so on.

Lawson saw that the abduction experience matches, in a remarkably high number of aspects, the birth experience. For instance, witnesses describe traveling through a tunnel and emerging into a strikingly brightly illuminated "room." Striking support for the hypothesis came when he compared reports by his imaginary abduction witnesses who had normal births with those who had Caesarean births. Of eight in the Caesarean category, seven made no reference to tubes or tunnels in their abduction stories. Moreover, the eighth actually strengthened the case, for it turned out that the baby had been treated as a normal birth until his mother had a hemmorrhage and a Caesarean operation became necessary!

That submerged memories of the birth experience remain in the subconscious and emerge at critical times has been persuasively alleged by psychologists such as Arthur Janov and Stanislas Grof. Grof notes their occurrence under the influence of LSD, when subjects will refer to their experiences quite explicitly as reliving their birth trauma.

This would explain why abduction stories tend to follow the same basic pattern—birth is something we have all experienced. And just as every birth experience has its individual features, so no two abduction stories are absolutely alike.

Lawson is careful not to claim too much for his hypothesis. If a witness embodies his birth trauma in his experience, it does not thereby invalidate the experience as such. But even if we accept that a real-life UFO encounter is involved, we have to account for the fact that it triggers

imagery which so closely resembles the birth experience.

Lawson's suggestion has been met with almost universal derision by researchers in his own country, though outside the United States it has been more favorably received. Paradoxically, the virulent opposition to the hypothesis can be seen as a demonstration of its validity. If the suggestion that the abduction experience exposes our deeply hidden memories alarms so many people, it may be because they, too, fear that their own buried feelings may be revealed.

This brings us back to a feature we have observed throughout this study— the "change of life" brought about by the ostensibly otherworldly encounter. Many UFO witnesses, Star People, contactees and abductees resemble religious visionaries, in that their experience marks a turning point in their lives, a fresh start, a new direction. Such a spiritual rebirth could hardly be more vividly expressed than by an imagined experience which echoed the process of birth!

THE SEARCH FOR THE TRUE EXPERIENCER

If Lawson's theories are not widely accepted, it is partly because abductees are not easily tested. The person who claims to have an otherworldly encounter is typically a solitary individual in an isolated situation whose movements cannot be checked, who can produce no convincing objective evidence that anything happened, and whose account is unsupported by independent testimony from others.

All there is to give us is the story. So everything stands or falls on one question: can we believe the story the witness tells us? Since the experience usually strikes out of the blue, there is little record of earlier life beyond what the researcher is told. Consequently, we cannot compare the after-the-event witness with the before-the-event witness. Moreover, witnesses are not generally keen to take part in scientific research—why should someone waste time testing the reality of an experience which he or she knows without doubt to be real? Even if they are willing, it is not clear what kind of scientific testing would be appropriate for this category of experience, whose most striking features are its subjective character and its value for the individual.

THE WITNESS ACCORDING TO SPRINKLE

The American psychologist Leo Sprinkle, who in the course of his counseling work has probably met more encounter witnesses than any other researcher, has been asking himself the question of what kind of person has this kind of experience since 1962.

In his opening address to his first (1980) Rocky Mountain Conference, he listed the characteristics he personally had noted in witnesses, based on a study of 225 subjects over a 17-year period:

- They seem to be average, normal people in their social and psychological functioning.
- They seem to be highly susceptible to hypnotic suggestion.
- They seem to experience many psychic phenomena and/or possess some psychic abilities.
- They exhibit loving concern for all mankind.
- They often report a feeling of being monitored or experiencing continued contact with UFO entities.
- They sometimes report a feeling of having been "chosen" or selected as an UFO contactee.
- They act as if they have an important mission or task in life.
- They sometimes express anxiety about the "state of humankind" and they may warn others of the possibility of future catastrophes.
- They often express the feeling that they are not only Planetary Persons but also Cosmic Citizens.
- They sometimes feel as if their real "home" is beyond Earth.

This profile, you will notice, overlaps strikingly with that of the "Star People" we met in Chapter Two. Since then, Sprinkle has revealed that he himself is an abductee, though, given his beliefs, he would certainly describe his experience as an overwhelmingly positive one. Many of us would feel that anyone exhibiting a profile such as the one above must be more than a little eccentric, to put it kindly. Sprinkle, however, insists that his findings do not support the "psychosis hypothesis"—experiencers do not exhibit neurotic or psychotic reactions in any way.

THE WITNESS ACCORDING TO PARNELL

Dr. June Parnell, who works with Sprinkle at the University of Wyoming, has adopted a more formal statistical approach. By questionnaire, she established the degree of UFO involvement experienced by a sample of 225 subjects (a third male, two-thirds female), then looked at their psychological make-up.

Parnell found that participants in the study who claimed experiences involving communication with UFO occupants or space beings were not pathological in any clinical sense. At the same time, they had a significantly greater tendency to:

- endorse unusual feelings, thoughts, and attitudes.
- be suspicious or distrustful.
- be creative, imaginative or possibly have schizoid tendencies.

Again, the value of this finding is limited by our not knowing the individual's psychological make-up previous to the experience. Parnell's findings are a useful and important indication of the kind of people who have had the experience. However, they do not offer much help in answering the more interesting question of what sort of people do these things happen to?

THE WITNESS ACCORDING TO FUFOR

That encounter witnesses are neither neurotic nor psychotic was confirmed by the 1981–1985 survey conducted by the Fund for UFO Research. This set out to answer the question, "What is the mental state of people who report UFO abductions?" Nine persons (five men and four women), who had made credible claims to have been abducted, submitted to tests administered by a psychologist, Dr. Elizabeth Slater. Dr. Slater was not informed until the tests were over of their purpose, nor of the kind of experience the subjects claimed to have had. She found that:

> The first and most critical question is whether our subjects' reported experiences could be accounted for strictly on the basis of psychopathology, i.e. mental disorder. The answer is a firm no ... There is no apparent psychological explanation for the reports.

On the other hand, she described the subjects as a distinctive and interesting group who were not typical of the population as a whole. When she was told that the group all claimed abduction experiences, she was not surprised:

> The nine subjects ... did share several characteristics. Those characteristics may relate to other aspects of the subjects' lives and have no connection whatsoever to UFO abduction. There is really no way of knowing. However, at least one may say that these features are not inconsistent with what one might anticipate as the psychological consequences of such a startling, disturbing event as UFO abduction.

The report concludes that "the test results neither support the 'psychological explanation' of UFO abductions, nor in any way contradict the disturbing hypothesis that these nine people are recalling actual experiences."

To both these statements, however, objections may reasonably be made.

Psychologists look beneath "surface reality". Many conclude that an abduction experience may be the mask for some inner conflict within the individual.

First, to speak of *the* psychological explanation, as though there were one way and one way only in which psychology could explain the phenomenon, is patently ridiculous. Second, while the findings do not contradict the hypothesis that the witness is recalling an actual experience, the possibility remains that, while "actual," it may have been something quite other than what was reported. For example, an abduction fantasy might be a psychological disguise for an incestuous rape which the individual could not bear to face up to. Moreover, once again, while the tests give us the psychological profile of the witnesses after the experience, they cannot tell us what they were like *before* it. So when we hear that the nine subjects share "a degree of identity disturbance, some deficits in the interpersonal sphere, and generally mild paranoia phenomena (hypersensitivity, wariness etc.)," we cannot be sure that they acquired these characteristics along with—and as a result of—their experience, or whether they were that way before. In the latter case, their personality profile could have facilitated their experience, or even actually caused it to happen.

THE WITNESS ACCORDING TO ABDUCTIONISTS

Aileen and Dan Edwards operate the UFO Contact Center, an institution designed to help encounter witnesses come to terms with their experience. Their findings, based on hands-on experience rather than formal scientific testing, are that specific clues indicate close approaches or possibly direct contact:

- loss of time
- disturbing dreams of an alien encounter
- skin eruptions suddenly appearing on the body
- pain in shoulder and/or lower back and/or the dip of the knee
- implants in the body
- light-sensitive eyes
- unexplained lumps, lesions or scars
- hearing voices and seeing visions
- bed shaking
- loss of breath
- feeling alone on earth
- feeling adopted even though one is not

The Edwards' list, like the Steigers' check list for "Star People," sets out a set of criteria by which you and I can evaluate whether or not we are experiencers. Sprinkle's informal list is equally broad. The scientist, on the other hand, sees only minimal measurable differences. Who understands the abductee better—the behavioral scientist to whom he is a subject for study, or the hands-on therapist for whom the patient is an individual who has gone through a traumatic experience?

Many of those who accept the abductees' stories at face value want to have it both ways. On the one hand, they welcome the scientists' finding that experiencers are not pathologically inclined, that clinically speaking abductees are "just plain folk." But at the same time, they are concerned to show that experiencers are "different," that they are chosen people, marked out for their cosmic role.

To abductionists like the Edwards, the Steigers and Sprinkle, the possession of these symptoms is an indication of otherworldly contact. But you don't have to be a professional psychologist to recognize that most of them could be outward signs of inner conflict totally unrelated to extraterrestrial visitors. The fact that the abductionists interpret them as they do shows how much they, like their subjects, have been caught up in the "authorized myth" of alien visitation.

THE "FANTASY-PRONE" WITNESS

In 1981, two American psychologists, Wilson and Barber, proposed the label "fantasy-prone" for a category of people who seem to live on the borders of the real and the imaginary. They, too, were able to list distinctive characteristics. Fantasy-prone people

- are easily hypnotized
- as children, play in a fantasy world, often have invisible playmates
- spend a significant amount of time fantasizing
- often believe they have psychic abilities
- often have out-of-the-body experiences
- have very vivid dreams
- receive messages from unknown sources

Such people live much of their time in a make-believe world, and fantasize for as much as half of their adult lives, continually playing games with themselves or with others.

For instance, while riding on a bus just the day before the interview, one of our subjects introduced herself as an Eskimo to the person sitting next to her and then proceeded to tell the intrigued stranger all about her (imagined) life in Alaska.

Two other psychologists, American Robert Bartholomew and Australian Keith Basterfield, proposed that the

An "out-of-body" experience is not a near-death experience and is often remembered as a dream.

likely to report such experiences—and that it is the same for near-death experiences and those who have UFO encounters.

That is to say, the abduction experience and the near-death experience may come about because of elements in the witness' psychological make-up.

This book is about otherworldly visitors to our planet: Does it matter what kind of people make up the reception committee? Yes, it matters very much. If we find that some people are more likely than others to meet them, we must conclude that what happens to them occurs because they are special people, distinguished by their personality traits and psychological profiles.

This in itself doesn't prove that their experiences are real or otherwise, because it could after all be that they receive their psychological profile as a gift from God, or the Cosmic Guardians, or whoever runs the universe. If the "Star People" really are who they claim they are, or if, as contactees like Adamski, Menger and King claim, they are actually chosen by the Space People as peculiarly gifted for the purposes of contact, it is understandable that they would be exceptional people.

At the same time, an alternative interpretation would be that what is happening is some kind of psychological process, specific to the individual.

"fantasy-prone" findings could apply to the abductees. Examining the encounter claims of 152 subjects, they found that 132 of them displayed some fantasy-prone characteristics. American psychologist Robert Baker, who shares this view, cites Whitley Strieber, who we met in Chapter Five, as a "classic example of the genre," and skeptic Joe Nickell found fantasy-prone traits in every one of the alleged abductees described by Harvard professor John Mack in his 1994 book, *Abduction*. In my own study of altered states of consciousness, I have shown how some people are by nature more easily triggered into fantasy experiences by external factors such as diet, excitement, climatic conditions, even a full moon!

A New England psychologist, Dr. Kenneth Ring of Connecticut University, wondered if tendencies to fantasy were relevant to his own studies of people who report extraordinary experiences. Starting with those who had had undergone the "Near-Death Experience," he subsequently extended his field to include those who had had UFO or alien-related experiences.

A 1990 study of 264 subjects gave no indication that witnesses were fantasy-prone according to the Wilson/Barber profile, but provided good reason to describe them as "encounter-prone."

What my study shows quite unmistakably is that there is a distinctive psychological profile for the person who is especially

His studies have convinced Dr. Kenneth Ring that a percentage of the population, without being mentally ill, are "encounter-prone."

VISIONS OF THE VIRGIN MARY

The issues are probably seen at their clearest in one of the most striking forms of visitation by otherworldly beings—encounters with Mary, the mother of Jesus of Nazareth, who is supposed by many to return to Earth in her own physical likeness.

The Roman Catholic Church believes that Mary was a specially privileged person, who though she may have started her adult life as a Palestinian housewife, ended it in some transcended form due to having been chosen to carry and bring into the world the "son of God"—that is to say, God made flesh. Catholic teaching says that when Mary died she was "taken to Heaven," and exists now on some superhuman level. However, she still retains many of her human attributes, in particular a concern for suffering humanity. For this reason, she makes periodic visits to Earth.

Several thousand claims to have encountered her during these visits have been recorded, most of them either by Catholic believers or by persons wavering over whether to believe. Not all of these have received the approval of the Church authorities, though a good many have. But many questions impose themselves.

What is seen when the Virgin is seen? Surely it is not her physical body, the one she had when she lived on Earth, miraculously preserved? Apart from anything else, almost everyone who sees her describes her differently.

Since it doesn't make sense that she would herself vary her appearance for each visit, we must suppose that it is the visionary herself who is responsible for the variations. Does this mean that visions of Mary are nothing but hallucinations, possessing no objective basis? Not necessarily: Some kind of interaction between Mary and the mind of the visionaries must be involved. Perhaps they see her as they expect to see her, consciously or unconsciously.

I have been privileged to personally know a girl who says she met the Virgin Mary on many occasions. In October, 1981, Blandine Piegay of La Talaudière, near Lyon in southwest France, was told by an angel as she walked to school that she would shortly meet the Virgin Mary. A few days later, she did so—the first of more than thirty meetings during which she talked with Mary in the kitchen of the family home. The Virgin gave Blandine advice about her own life, urged her father not to drink so much, told Blandine she should not eat so many sweets … and passed on the customary warnings for mankind, that we should mend our wicked ways.

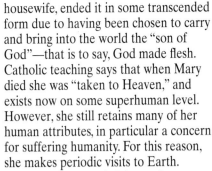

The Virgin Mary with the Baby Jesus in her arms appears before the adoring crowds.

No one else saw Mary. There is no material evidence of the visits. Though thousands came by car and coach to visit the humble house which the Queen of Heaven had deigned to visit, the local curé was skeptical and advised people to stay away. The Catholic Church has never recognized Blandine's experiences as genuine. Yet she herself continues to insist that the meetings really took place.

About a hundred years earlier, another French teenager had eleven visions of the Virgin Mary. But few of the millions of pilgrims who flock to Lourdes every year are aware that Bernadette Soubirous was by no means the first person in the district to report a meeting with the Virgin Mary, nor that she was only one of dozens of people—mostly adolescents like herself—who had visionary experiences at Lourdes about the same time. Confronted with this disconcerting situation, even that perceptive researcher, the Jesuit Herbert Thurston, has to temporize. Thurston accepts Bernadette's visions as genuine and the rest as spurious, but the criteria by which he makes the distinction are not precise.

Should we believe that 14-year old Blandine had an otherworldly visitation? That *something* happened to her seems certain. But that the mother of Jesus—even if she is surviving in some form elsewhere in the Cosmos—is revisiting Earth in order to talk with a French teenager is so implausible that it seems sensible to look for alternative explanations.

GLENDA AND THE SPACEWOMAN

In the 1980s, I was involved in the investigation of a case involving an English girl who had experienced a number of strange happenings. One day when she was 12, Glenda came home from school and went upstairs to her room in the house where she lived with her parents and sister. A little while later, she realized she was not alone in her room. With her was a stranger, female, whom she would later describe as a "spacewoman." Humanoid, but extravagantly dressed, Glenda described her as something you might see on television.

This being manifested intermittently in Glenda's life over the next five years—sometimes visibly, but generally as an unseen "presence," sensed but not seen. Sometimes she would figure in Glenda's dreams. She was neither malevolent, nor particularly benevolent, but she seemed clearly concerned for Glenda's well-being, giving her advice about her private affairs.

If she was an alien, she made no attempt to abduct Glenda onto her spaceship. If she was a demon, she made no attempt to seduce Glenda into any form of evil. If there is any being we have come across in these pages to which it is possible to compare her, it is the Guardian Angel. Of all those we have met, this type—so long as we forget the stereotype angel and picture some benevolent, caring, protective being—seems the most positive and purposeful.

But the Guardian Angel shares, with other entities, an elusive, subjective quality—it is almost invariably seen by one person and one alone. No other member of Glenda's family ever saw her "spacewoman," just as no other member of Blandine's family ever saw the Virgin Mary.

WHO BENEFITS FROM THE ENCOUNTER?

The case of Glenda is very important. She benefited greatly from the experience, finding someone to share her problems with. Both Glenda and Blandine benefited personally from their experiences. Blandine was given a boost in her self-esteem, while Glenda found someone to share her problems with.

The psychological well-being of two adolescent girls on planet Earth doesn't seem as though it would be a matter of concern for those who control the Universe, despite sentimental perceptions of gods who care even about the fall of a sparrow. It seems scarcely enough to justify a cosmic journey by an ascended divinity or a spaceperson. But the visits mattered very much to Glenda and Blandine. So it is reasonable to ask whether they had these experiences because *they needed to have them?*

Looking back through this book, we realize that we could ask the same question concerning many, perhaps most of the cases reported. The benefits of the visitation to the visitors are generally far from evident. We have seen how the extraterrestrials take no interest in our achievements or sights, they don't rob us of our minerals or anything else, and their medical research (if that's what it is) is a farce. In his thoughtful and seductive 1998 book *The Threat,* Professor Jacobs outlines an alien agenda which seems purposeful and beneficial, to them if not to us. There is no objective source for this agenda, however; he has pieced it together, item by item, from hints derived from the stories told by the abductees themselves. He asserts that "the evidence suggests that all the alien procedures serve a reproductive agenda," but that "evidence" could as well be an artifact of the mind-set of the abductees as an indication of alien intention.

On the other hand, time after time, the encounter seems to do a great job for the individual experiencer. Could it be that this is the *primary* purpose of the event, not merely a secondary side effect?

An important clue is one thread which runs through a wide range of these experiences—contactees, abductees, even those who encounter MIB. They are changed by their experience, and frequently, the witness claims after-effects which are distinctly *positive.*

Here is a witness from the Laramie Rocky Mountain conferences:

> Because of my encounter in June 1977, I became more sensitive to the true meaning and the realistic value of life itself! On a spiritual level, it awakened a dormant knowledge ... My "Cosmic Companions" have given me the

opportunity to grow spiritually and spiral upwards.

Speaking of the Men in Black, folklorist Peter Rojcewicz says that the lives of witnesses are frequently changed by their experience. "Some become more successful in their jobs and marriages and report a joy of life." Scores of abductees have testified to what amounts to a "born again" experience as a result of their encounter with extraterrestrials, yet all that ostensibly happened to them was they received a cold, dispassionate medical inspection from unfeeling aliens who didn't give a damn about their human guinea pigs and seemingly had no other object than to acquire biological information about the human species.

It is hard to make sense of this seeming contradiction other than by supposing that the ostensible abduction

Fantasy writers have perceived aliens as conducting heartless experiments on humankind. Do abduction stories also originate in the imagination?

and examination constitutes only an objective cover-story masking a subjective experience. We may go further. We may suppose that the inner, subjective story may actually be more important than the outer, objective one. In fact, we may even go further still— we may consider the possibility that the outer, ostensible, objective story has no importance or reality at all, but is simply a device, an elaborately constructed decor to provide a stage for what is *really* important, the subjective experience which the individual undergoes.

NEGATIVE CONSEQUENCES OF BELIEF

It can be argued that, since these experiences are beneficial, it doesn't much matter whether they are "real" or not. Whether beings visit us from a physical other world, from other levels of reality, or from the depths of the subconscious mind, is unimportant —it is the effects that are significant.

That point of view might be acceptable if the effects were *always* beneficial. Unfortunately that isn't the case. Beliefs can lead to actions whose consequences are disastrous. We saw in Chapter Six how the followers of Applewhite and Nettles, convinced that they were going to be transported to a great extraterrestrial spaceship traveling in the wake of the Hale-Bopp comet, killed themselves. It is not an isolated example.

Gloria Lee Byrd was an American contactee, author of two books detailing her connections with the extraterrestrials, and founder of the "Cosmon Research Foundation," which had 2000 members. In the autumn of 1962—at which time she was 37— together with a follower, Hedy Hood, she went to Washington with plans for a spaceship channeled from her Space Contact, "J.W.," from the planet Jupiter. They had intended to stay only two days, but when government officials refused to look at the plans, they booked into a Washington hotel,

where she announced that "J.W. has ordered me to go on a fast for peace until he sends a 'light elevator' to take me to Jupiter." Gloria began her fast on September 23. Her husband learned that she was ill and sent an ambulance to the hotel on November 28, but four days later, she died in the hospital. Her companion was indignant with the police for taking Gloria away, accusing them of "ruining a scientific experiment for peace."

"Woman dies after 4-week wait for UFO" was the headline of the Duluth *News-Tribune & Herald* on November 18, 1982. The report told how a motorist found 38-year-old Gerald Flach semiconscious on a remote trail. He said his friend needed medical attention, but when the rescue squad found his companion—48-year-old Laverne Landis—in their car, she was dead of hypothermia, dehydration and starvation. The car was parked in a side road, snowed in and out of fuel.

At the bidding of "messages" received by Laverne, the couple had driven to Loon Lake, at the end of Gunflint Trail, close to Lake Superior near the Canadian border. There— living on the front seat of their compact car, drinking water from the lake and scarcely eating—they had waited for more than four weeks in the expectation of meeting extraterrestrials who never came.

In March, 1993, at Wellington, New Zealand, 25-year-old Wallace Waru Iopata and 45-year-old Huia Tawhai, two followers of the Indian guru Sai Baba, felt called on to spiritually "cleanse" the latter's husband, 79-year-old Erueti Tawhai. They mutilated him with a butcher's knife, and he died as a result. They dismembered his body and tried to burn it, but the house caught fire. Firemen who came to the scene found the two survivors standing naked outside the house—they explained that a UFO was coming to take them to Australia.

In June, 1986, police at Harlesden in northwestern London received a phone call from a woman who said that she and her grand daughters had been attacked by burglars. She met them at the door in a blood-stained nightgown and showed them the lifeless bodies of the children, but police quickly realized her story was false.

As a result of her UFO beliefs, 57-year-old Gloria Stephens was sure that she was visited regularly by aliens who beamed her aboard their spaceship. She kept plastic bags full of clothing and belongings against the day when they took her away for good. Among many bizarre beliefs, she came to think that her grandchildren, 10-year-old Tasha and 7-year-old Andrea, were in danger from the aliens. A machine like a giant vacuum cleaner would suck them to another planet. To save them from the spacemen, she decided to kill them. When they came on a holiday visit, she knifed them and herself, taking an overdose of drugs for good measure, expecting to be reunited with her granddaughters in Paradise. When she did not die, she called the police. Found guilty of manslaughter, she was placed in a psychiatric hospital.

Events such as these show that it *is* important to know what is really happening when an individual claims to be in contact with beings from other worlds. It is not a question of asking whether we should or shouldn't believe Jeanne d'Arc when she tells us she has spoken with angels and they have instructed her to take up arms against the English or Travis Walton when he tells us he was abducted by extraterrestrials. They, like Blandine and Glenda, may well be telling the truth as they see it. It is even possible they are telling the truth as the rest of us would see it.

So it is not a question of *denying* the experience, or necessarily of questioning its value. But we need to *understand* their encounters before we can know what response to make. That involves deciding whether or not these encounters involve beings from other worlds.

OPERATORS AND THINGS

Of all the claims of encounters with beings from other worlds, there is probably none which better helps us to understand the nature of the experience than Barbara O'Brien's 1958 account of her experiences with otherworldly "operators."

What happened was that, following personal troubles involving a lifestyle conflict, O'Brien had an encounter with some otherworldly entities who she called "operators." They persuaded her to pack her bags and leave home, family, job, everything. For months they kept her wandering around the United States, taking casual jobs and living as best she could. All this time, she was living on two worlds—that of the real world, work and the rest, and that of her "operators." Apart from occasional breakdowns, she managed the balancing act pretty well, though she was not helped when she consulted a psychiatrist, who decided the best place for her was a mental clinic.

Finally, the day came when she said to herself that enough was enough, confronted her situation, and confronted the beings, telling them to get out of her life. Only then did she realize that had been the purpose of the experience, to get her to take charge of her own destiny.

What makes her account so valuable is that she is an intelligent, thoughtful and perceptive person who is able to examine her own situation lucidly and objectively. She realizes that what happened to her was that her subconscious mind created a "psychodrama" for her, enabling her to act out her own situation as though it were a stage play:

> There is an amazing lack of accurate knowledge among laymen concerning the effects of schizophrenia. The most prevalent notion is that the individual becomes two people, two distinct personalities, or even multiple personalities … In most cases, however, the unconscious appears to prefer not the techniques of the actor, but those of the director. It does not create a new personality, but, instead, stages a play. The major difference is that the conscious mind is permitted to remain, an audience of one, watching a drama on which it cannot walk out … As you sit watching your Martian, it is your unconscious mind which is flashing the picture before your eyes, sounding the man's voice in your ears. More than this, it is blowing a fog of hypnosis over your conscious mind so that

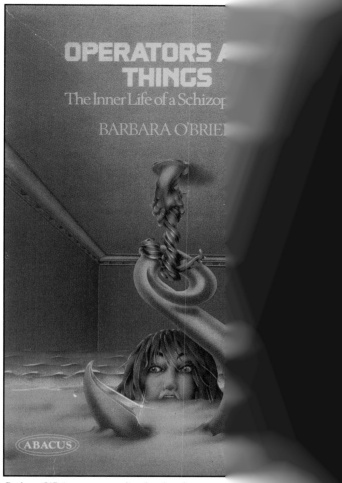

Barbara O'Brien came to realize that the otherworldly "operators" who had taken control of her life were creations of her own subconscious mind.

consciously you see and hear, and the delusions that accompany the hallucinations are real.

THE ULTIMATE QUESTION

If our Earth is receiving otherworldly visitors, why don't more of us get to meet them? With that question comes another, too: Are the people who do meet them lucky, unlucky, special —or simply deluded?

In every case cited in this book, there were people—sometimes only the witness, sometimes many others—who believed that an actual encounter took place with visitors from other worlds. It is equally true to say that, regarding each and every case, there were people who listened to the same story and

either rejected it out of hand, or found some alternative explanation for it which did not involve otherworldly beings.

Though these visitors have been reported as coming to our planet throughout more than 2000 years of history—and possibly for long before that—there is not a scrap of totally convincing evidence that they have actually done so. Subjective human testimony abounds, most of it from sincere people who deserve to be listened to with respect, but it is not supported by any objective evidence.

On the other hand, those who offer explanations which do not involve otherworldly beings—such as psychological experiences of some

kind—are also unable to provide evidence for their version of the matter. Apart from the general difficulty of proving a negative, we have seen that there are some cases in which, if they really happened as narrated, we must invoke either otherworldly beings or paranormal powers of some nature. For example, consider those cases in which information is provided which the witness would not normally have had access to—as when 5-year old Starlitt climbed her cliff, or when Edith Folz-Stearns was saved from crashing her airplane.

What should our attitude be towards the storytellers we have met in this book, or towards someone who comes

Unexplained magic and power: An extraterrestrial spacecraft hovers over the ancient, stone worship sites of the druids and witches.

to us with his or her own story of otherworldly visitors?

Certainly, we must not look for a single all-or-nothing explanation. Probably no one believes in the physical reality of every single one of the otherworldly visitations we have looked at. But if we cannot accept them all, which of them, if any, should we accept and which reject? In the end, each of us must judge each instance on its own merits, and come to a personal decision.

I deliberately saved Barbara O'Brien's experience with beings from other worlds until last, because I believe it is her case more than any other which shows us how to see through the outer facade to the inner reality of the otherworldly encounter. Her final evaluation of what happened to her is that the experience—traumatic and frequently frightening though it may have been—was not a breakdown, a negative experience, but a necessary, purposeful and ultimately beneficial process, a process which restored order and balance to her life.

The same may be true of many, perhaps most, ostensible otherworldly encounters. Glenda's spacewoman and Andreasson's aliens may both be the equivalent of guardian angels whose function is to set the individual on a surer, better course of life. Seen in this light, even seemingly horrific encounters —alien attacks, demonic possession, and so on—can be seen as ultimately beneficial, a kind of spiritual surgery.

Sometimes, the experience turns out badly, just as surgery sometimes fails. Gloria Lee Byrd, Laverne Landis, and Andrea, Tasha and even Gloria Stephens were victims, due to lack of understanding. But with rare exceptions, throughout all the myths, legends, claimed experiences and case histories we have looked at in this book, there runs one constant and very revealing thread. The ones who benefit most from these visitations are not the visiting aliens, but we on Earth who receive their visits. They don't need us—it is we who need these visitors from other worlds.

Science has put man on the Moon and given us this view of Earth's surface. However, the extent of outer space and who or what inhabits it is still unknown to mankind.

Index

★

Further Reading

Almost every topic touched on in this book has been treated at length elsewhere – sometimes, as is the case in the visits with Mary, Mother of Jesus, in many thousands of books. This list offers only a sampling. Nor are these necessarily the "best" books. The finest book on Lourdes is doubtless René Laurentin's 13-volume history, but it is more than most people want to read on the subject. Moreover, it is important to also read some of the "worst" books: the personal narratives of the contactees, for example, give a feel for the contactee experience that no commentary, however perceptive, can offer.

It is important, too, to read books on both sides of the questions – Von Däniken championing the Ancient Astronauts as well as Ronald Story pointing out the weakness of each case. Even if you believe that alien abductions are "all in the mind," it is enlightening to listen to what an experiencer like Debbie Jordan has to say, then hear how a "believer" like David Jacobs perceives her experience, then ponder what a doubter like John Rimmer has to suggest as an alternative interpretation.

Every fact or citation in this book has been taken from original accounts or commentaries. To provide references for each and every one would occupy many pages. If you wish to follow up on a specific point you may contact the author by fax on +44 (0) 181 297 9819, by email at hevans@satven.co.uk, or by mail at 59 Tranquil Vale, London, SE3 OBS, England.

GENERAL SOURCES
William R Corliss (compiler) *The Sourcebook Project*, Glen Arm 1982: sixteen volumes of this unique encyclopedia of scientific anomalies have been published and more are promised. They provide an eye-opening view of what extraordinary things can and do happen in our universe.

Fate Magazine, St Paul, Minnesota, published monthly, is an indispensable source of personal experiences and ideas.

The partwork *The Unexplained* was a uniquely comprehensive survey of mysteries and anomalies: it has been republished in more conveniently arranged format as a 26-volume series entitled *Mysteries of Mind, Space and Time*, Stuttman, Westport, Connecticut.

OTHERWORLDLY VISITATION IN GENERAL
Hilary Evans, *Visions, Apparitions, Alien Visitors* and *Gods, Spirits and Cosmic Guardians*, Aquarian, Wellingborough, 1984, 1987: a comprehensive overview of the encounter enigma.
There is good documentation in Lucian Bola, *L'Exploration Imaginaire de L'Espace*, La Decouverte, Paris, 1987 Marjorie Nicholson, *Voyages to the Moon*, Macmillan, New York, 1948 is excellent on the earliest accounts of space travel.

GODS
Two excellent references are Elizabeth Hallam (editor), *Gods and Goddesses*, Blandford, London 1997; and Arthur Cotterell, *The Illustrated Encyclopedia of Myths and Legends*, Marshall Editions, London, 1999

SCIENCE FICTION
There are three fine encyclopedias of science fiction in English: Brian Ash, *The Visual Encyclopedia of Science Fiction*, Tribune, London, 1978; Peter Nicholls, *The Encyclopedia of Science Fiction*, Granada, London, 1979; and John Clute, *Science Fiction: The Illustrated Encyclopedia*, Dorling Kindersley, London, 1995. All give fair mention to Gernsback and the pre-1939 pulps although none really gives the "feel" of these unique publications, which have to be seen to be appreciated.

Pierre Versins', *Encyclopédie de l'Utopie et de la Science Fiction L'Age d'Homme*, Lausanne, 1972 is broader and more philosophical. Peter Nicholls excellent, *The Science in Science Fiction*, Crescent Books, London, 1982, covers in greater depth many of the topics I have had space only to touch on.

The landmark classic of space travel is, of course, Jules Verne's *De la Terre a la Lune* and its sequel *Autor de la Lune*, Paris, 1865, 1870 (*From the Earth to the Moon*; *Round the Moon*): but the anonymous "Letters from the Planets", published in *Cassell's Family Magazine*, starting in February 1887, gives a unique idea of how the Victorians thought about adventuring into space.

ANCIENT ASTRONAUTS
The Tunguska event has been reported in depth by John Baxter and Thomas Atkins in *The Fire Came By*, Doubleday, New York, 1976. TR LeMaire's excellent *Stones from the Stars*, Prentice-Hall, Englewood Cliffs, 1980, sets it in a wider perspective which raises troublesome questions.

There is a substantial and exhilarating literature seeking to document the various "ancient astronaut" scenarios, Paul Misraki (writing as "Paul Thomas") was one of the first, with *Les Extraterrestres*, Pion, Paris 1962, translated as *Flying Saucers Through the Ages*, Spearman, London, 1965. Of his followers, the best known is Eric Von Däniken whose *Chariots of the Gods?*, Souvenir, London, 1968, was one of many. Other representative books are Robert Charroux, *L'Inconnu Mysterieux*, Leffont, Paris, 1972, translated as the *Mysterious Unknown*, Spearman, London, 1972; Maurice Chatelain, *Nos Ancêtres Venus du Cosmos*, Laffont, Paris, 1975, translated as *Our Ancestors Came From Outer Space*, Doubleday, New York, 1977; Perter Kolosimo, *Astronavi Sulla Preistoria*, Sugarco, Milano, 1971, translated as *Spaceships in Prehistory*, University Books, Seacaucus, 1975; each of these authors wrote other similar books. An interesting collective work is Jacques Bergier (editor) *Extraterrestrial Intervention: The Evidence*, Regenery, Chicago, 1974. James Churchward first launched his Mu ideas in *The Lost Continent of Mu*, Rider, 1931, and followed it up with several other volumes.

Many writers have questioned the ancient astronaut scenario: two good debunkings are Ronald Story, *Guardians of the Universe*, New English Library, London, 1980; and Peter White, *The Past is Human*, Angus and Robertson, Sydney, 1974.

STAR PEOPLE
Brad and Francie Steiger, *The Star People*, Berkeley, New York, 1981 is one of a series of books on the subject; more recently, Scott Mandelker, *From Elsewhere: Being ET in America*, Dell, New York, 1995 has given it a more "scientific" status.

SPACEMEN IN HISTORY
W Raymond Drake, *God and Spacemen Throughout History*, Spearman, London, 1975 is one of many collections he has made of possible precursors of today's UFOs. Two Belgian researchers have made thoughtful selections of plausible cases: Christiane Piens, *Les OVNIs du Passé*, Marabout, Paris 1977 and Michel Bougard, *La Chronique des OVNIs*, Editions Universitaires, Paris 1977.

THE MARTIAN TERROR
Camille Flammarion promoted space exploration in book after book: *Les Mondes Imaginaires*, Paris, 1866, is the one of most directly related to the theme of this book. For more on Mrs Cleaveland, read James H Hyslop, *Psychical Research and the Resurrection*, Fisher Unwin, London, 1908 Catherine Muller: Theodore Flournoy, *Des Indes à la Planète Mars*, Geneva, 1899, translated as *From India to the Planet Mars* Helene Prieswerk: Carl Gustav Jung, On the Psychology and "Pathology of So-Called Occult Phenomena", Leipzig, 1902, in *Psychiatric Studies*, Vol.1 of this collected works published by Routeldge and Kegan Paul, London, 1957 Mirelle: Albert des Roches, *Les Vies Successives*, Chacornac, Paris, 1911 Cedric Allingham, *Flying Saucer From Mars*, British Book Centre, New York, 1955, describes a curious incident purporting to be a Martian's visit to Britain.

The Orson Welles broadcast is analyzed in Hadley Cantril, *The Invasion From Mars*, Princeton, 1940; and recounted in Howard Koch, *The Panic Broadcast*, Avon, 1970, which includes text of the broadcast. The original book is HG Wells, *War of the Worlds*, London, 1898, arguably the finest science fiction novel ever written.

EXTRATERRESTRIAL TYPES
Two valuable comparative guides to the varieties of entity species are Patrick Huyghe, *The Field Guide to Extraterrestrials*, Avon, New York, 1996; Eric Zurcher, *Les Apparitions d'Humanoïdes*, Lefeuvre, Paris, 1979 Selenites: HG Wells, *The First Men on the Moon*, London, 1901

AERIAL LIFE-FORMS
John Philip Bessor, "UFOs, Animal of Mineral?", Fate, November 1967 Trevor James [Constable], *They Live in the Sky*, New Age Publishing, Los Angeles, 1958; Conan Doyle's story, "The Horror of Heights", appeared in *The Strand,* November 1913 Star Jelly: Hilary Belcher and Erica Swale, "Catch a Falling Star", Folklore, vol.95:ii, 1984 Fred Hoyle and Chandra Wickramasinge presented their challenging theory in *Space Travellers*, University College Cardiff Press, 1981 and in other related books.

BALLS OF LIGHT
A brief general overview of the BOL phenomenon is in Hilary Evans (editor), *Frontiers of Reality*, Thorsons, 1989. For specific aspects: Richard Haines, *Advanced Aerial Devices Reported During the Korean War,* LDA Press, Los Altos, 1990. The Yakima Sightings are chronicled in Greg Long, Examining the Earthlight Theory: theYakima UFO Microcosm, CUFOS, Chicago, 1990: Harley D Rutledge recounts his investigation into the Piedmont lights in *Project Identification*, Prentice Hall, 1981: a report on the Norwegian lights was made by project leader Erling Strand in *Project Hessdalen, 1984: The Final Technical Report*, UFO Norge, 1985

UFOs IN GENERAL
The best general introduction I know to the UFO phenomenon is Peter Brookesmith, *UFO: The Complete Sightings Catalogue*, Blandford, London, 1995; the most comprehensive resource is Jerome Clark's magnificent unwieldy 3-volume *The UFO Encyclopedia, Omnigraphics*, Detroit 1990–1996. Hilary Evans and John Spencer (editors), *UFOs 1947–1987*, John Brown Publishing, London, 1987 and Hilary Evans and Dennis Stacey (editors), *UFOs 1947–1997*, John Brown Publishing, London, 1997, both offer a many-faceted choice of perspectives on the entire phenomenon.

Carl Gustav Jung, *Flying Saucers: A Modern Myth of Things Seen in the Skies*, Harcourt, Brace, New York, 1959, is a brilliantly perceptive psycho-social view. Michel Carrouges, *Les Apparitions de Martiens*, 1963, was an early book to recognize the sophistication of the UFO phenomenon: Allan Hendry, *The UFO Handbook*, Doubleday, New York, 1979, showed that the key to the UFO problem is often the UFO witnesses. Douglas Curran's wonderful, *In Advance of the Landing*, Abbeville Press, New York, 1985, is a unique look at UFOs from the popular perspective. The alleged UFO crash at Roswell has generated a prolific literature: I found Kal K Korff, *The Roswell UFO Crash*, Prometheus Amherst, 1997 the most convincing.

SPECIFIC ASPECTS OF UFOS
Aliens as healers: Preston Dennett, *UFO Healings*, Wild Flower Press, 1996.
Men In Black: chapter in Evans, *Visions, Apparitions, Alien Visitors* (listed previously).

Manmade UFOs: Renato Vesco, *Intercettateli Senza Sparare*, Mursia, Milano, 1968, translated as *Intercept But Don't Shoot*, Grove Press, New York, 1971 is impressively researched.

CONTACTEES
During the 1950s many contactees were guests on Long John Nebel's late-night radio show, and his *The Way Out World*, Prentice Hall, Englewood Cliffs, 1961, includes several revealing interviews. Frank Spearman, *The Janos People*, Spearman, 1980.

CONTACTEES OWN STORIES
The book that started it all was Desmond Leslie and George Adamski, *Flying Saucers Have Landed*, Werner Laurie, London, 1953. Following Adamski, virtually every contactee wrote an account of his/her adventure. Three representative books are Howard and Connie Menger, *The High Bridge Incident*, published by the authors, 1991 (an update of their earlier account); Orfeo Angelucci, *The Secret of the Saucers*, Amherst Press, 1955; Stefan Denaerde, *UFO Contact From Planet Iarga*, UFO Photo Archives, Tucson, 1982 (the English translation of his 1967 book). But all the contactee books are worth reading for the light they throw on the individuals and their experiences.

ABDUCTEE CASES
The case of Betty and Barney Hill was told, with little critical analysis, by John G Fukker in *The Interrupted Journey*, Dial Press, New York, 1966: Betty Hill's own book, *A Common Sense Approach to UFOs*, published by the author in 1995, lives up to its title and throws valuable light on the abduction experience as a whole. The leading abduction investigator, Budd Hopkins, has set out his best cases in three impressive books: *Missing Time*, Marek, New York, 1981; *Intruders*, Random House, New York, 1987; *Witnessed*, Pocket Books, New York, 1996. Debbie Jordan, the protagonist of *Intruders*, tells her own story in *Abducted!*, Caroll and Graf, New York, 1994. Betty Andreasson's experiences have been analyzed in greater depth than any other, thanks to the devoted work of Raymond Fowler, starting in *The Andreasson Affair*, Prentice Hall, Englewood Cliffs, 1997; and continued in three subsequent books. The Pascagoula incident is well documented in Charles Hickson and William Mendez, *UFO Contact at Pascagoula*, Wendelle C Stevens, Tucson, 1983. Travis Walton writes eloquently of his own experiences in *Fire in the Sky*, updated editions Marlowe, New York, 1996. A skeptical view is given by Philip J Klass in *UFOs: The Public Deceived*, Prometheus, Buffalo, 1983. Whitley Streiber explores his state of mind in *Communion*, Beech Tree Books, New York, 1987, and seemingly endless sequels.

GHOSTS
Though there are countless books on ghosts, only a minority concern themselves specifically with revenants. Hornell Hart, *The Enigma of Survival*, Rider, London, 1959 and Raymond Bayless, *Apparitions and Survival of Death*, University

Books, Seacaucus, 1973 are two of the best: also recommended is Celia Green and Charles McCreery, *Apparitions*, Hamish Hamilton, London, 1975.

SPIRITUALISM
Conan Doyle's *The History of Spiritualism*, Cassell, London, 1926 is an informative insider's view. Ronald Pearsall's *The Table Rappers*, Michael Joseph, London, 1972 is a more objective account.

Spirit photography is well documented in Fred Gettings, *Ghosts in Photographs*, Harmony Books, New York, 1978: he accepts some photographs as authentic.
William Marriott's brilliant skeptical articles appeared in *Pearson's Magazine*, commencing March 1910.

CHANELING
Jon Klimo's *Chaneling*, Tarcher, Los Angeles, 1987, is a massive overview: Ramtha's *I Am Ramtha*, Beyond Words, Portland 1986 gives the feeling of the channelled messages. Festinger et al *When Prophecy Fails*, University of Minnesota, 1956, a sociological account of a collective disappointment is essential reading.

ANGELS
Joy Snell, *The Ministry of Angels*, The Greater World Association, London, 1918 is a valuable witness account: Malcom Godwin gives and informative overview in *Angels: An Endangered Species*, New Leaf, London, 1990: Gustav Davidson, *A Dictionary of Angels*, The Free Press, New York, 1967 is a fine reference.

DEMONS
Berbuguier gave a full account of his experience with demons in his *Les Farfadets*, Paris, 1821: Eric Dingwall summarizes and comments on it in *Some Human Oddities*, Home and Van Thal, London, 1947. Padre Pio: Ennemond Boniface, *Padre Pio le Crucifé*, Nouvelles Editions, Paris, 1971, and Paul Lesourd and JM Benjamin, *Les Mystères du Padre Pio*, France-Empire, Paris 1970. Demons in present-day society are featured in many books: some, such as Hiley H Ward, *The Far Out Saints of the Jesus Communes*, Association Press, New York, 1972, aim at balanced reportage. Others, emanating from Christian Fundamentalists, take a more extreme view: it would be invidious to pick out any for special mention. Cynthia Pettiward, *The Case for Possession*, Colin Smythe, Gerrards Cross, 1975, argues intelligently for the reality of possession, as does Felicitas D Goodman, *How About Demons?*, Indiana University Press, 1988. TK Oseterreich's classic, *Possession, Demonical and Other*, Kegan Paul, London, 1939, presents the psychological alternative. Two related books are Gray Barker, *The Knew Too Much About Flying-Saucers*, University Books, New York, 1956 and Jerome Clark and Loren Coleman, *Creatures of the Outer Edge*, Warner Books, New York, 1978.

MAGIC
Richard Cavendish, *The Black Arts*, Routledge, London, 1967 gives an excellent overview. EM Butler's *Ritual Magic*, Cambridge University Press, 1949 and other books by the same writer approach the subject from a more academic perspective with fascinating references. Richard Kieckhefer's *Forbidden Rights*, Sutton, Stroud, 1997, takes us inside a fifteenth-century manual to see how the inner motivations express themselves in action.

Crowley's magic working is narrated in Jean Overton Fuller, *The Magical Dilemma of Victor Neuberg*, WH Allen, London 1965.

VISIONS OF THE VIRGIN MARY
Thousands of books have been published on apparitions of the Virgin Mary. Joachim Bouflet,

writing from a Roman Catholic viewpoint but with critical perception has written a fine popular introduction, *Les Apparitions de la Vierge*, Calmann-Lévy, Paris, 1996 and with Phillipe Boutry, the more scholarly *Un Signe dans le Ciel*, Grasset, Paris 1997, Kevin McClure, *The Evidence For Visions of the Virgin Mary*, Aquarian, Wellingborough, 1983, though sympathetic, is critical.

THE ENCOUNTER WITNESS
The Roper Organization's Unusual Personal Experiences, Bigelow Holding Corporation, Las Vegas, 1992, shows that millions of Americans may have been abducted by aliens. Final Report on the Psychological Testing of UFO "Abductees" published by the fund for UFO Research, Mount Ranier, 1985, encourages the view that abductions happen to normal people.

The Lawson and McCall "imaginary abductee" experiment is reported in *Journal of UFO Studies*, no.1, circa 1983. The birth trauma hypothesis is presented in the journal, *Magnolia*, October 1982. Fantasy Proneness, SC Wilson and TX Barber, "Vivid Fantasy and Hallucinatory Abilities in the Life Histories of Excellent Hypnotic Subjects" in E Klinger (ed.) *Imagery: Concepts, Results and Applications*, Plenum, New York, 1981. The Encounter-Prone hypothesis is proposed in Kenneth Ring, *The Omega Project*, Morrow, New York, 1992. For an experiencer's perspective, Barbara O'Brien, *Operators and Things*, AS Barnes, South Bruswick and New York, 1958, offers remarkable insights.

Picture Credits